DATE DUE

ILL 12-2015	

D1603406

PRINTED IN U.S.A.

GUIDES FOR THE PERPLEXED

Guides for the Perplexed are clear, concise, and accessible introductions to thinkers, writers, and subjects that students and readers can find especially challenging—or indeed downright bewildering. Concentrating specifically on what it is that makes the subject difficult to grasp, these books explain and explore key themes and ideas, guiding the reader toward a thorough understanding of demanding material.

A GUIDE FOR THE PERPLEXED

Daoism

LOUIS KOMJATHY

BLOOMSBURY

LONDON • NEW DELHI • NEW YORK • SYDNEY

Bloomsbury Academic

An imprint of Bloomsbury Publishing Plc

50 Bedford Square
London
WC1B 3DP
UK

1385 Broadway
New York
NY 10018
USA

www.bloomsbury.com

Bloomsbury is a registered trade mark of Bloomsbury Publishing Plc

First published 2014

© Louis Komjathy, 2014

Image permissions © Cover: Louis Komjathy; Fig. 6.2: Livia Kohn;
Fig. 6.3: Michael Saso; Fig. 8.1: Louis Komjathy and Kate Townsend;
Fig. 9.1: British Taoist Association.

British Library Cataloguing-in-Publication Data
A catalogue record for this book is available from the British Library.

ISBN: HB: 978-1-44115-795-9
PB: 978-1-44114-815-5
ePDF: 978-1-44113-921-4
ePub: 978-1-44113-468-4

Library of Congress Cataloging-in-Publication Data
A catalog record for this book is available from the Library of Congress.

Typeset by Newgen Knowledge Works (P) Ltd., Chennai, India
Printed and bound in India

知不知上，不知知病。夫唯病病，是以不病。

To know that one does not know is best; not to know that one is knowing is sickness. It is only by being sick of sickness that one ceases being sick.

Laozi 老子, *ch. 71*

可不謂有大揚榷乎？闔不亦問是已，奚惑然為？以不惑解惑，復於不惑，是尚大不惑。

We may say that there is a great aspiration, may we not? Why not inquire about it? Why act in such perplexity? If we use unperplexity to dispel perplexity and return to non-perplexity, this will be the greatest non-perplexity.

Zhuangzi 莊子, *ch. 24*

CONTENTS

CONVENTIONS

The present book utilizes traditional Chinese characters; modern Mandarin pronunciations; Pinyin Romanization, with occasional reference to Wade-Giles; historical periodization based on Chinese dynasties; and standardized numbering systems for Daoist textual collections based on my *Title Index to Daoist Collections* (Three Pines Press, 2002).

Chinese history is divided into the following dynasties and periods.

Shang (ca. 1600–1045 BCE)
Zhou (1045–256 BCE)
    Western/Early (1045–771 BCE)
    Eastern/Later (771–256 BCE)
       Spring and Autumn (770–480 BCE)
       Warring States (480–222 BCE)
Qin (221–206 BCE)
Han (202 BCE–220 CE)
    Western/Early (202 BCE–9 CE)
    Eastern/Later (25–220)
Six Dynasties/Period of Disunion (220–589)[1]
Sui (581–618)
Tang (618–907)
Five Dynasties and Ten Kingdoms (907–979)
Song (960–1279)
    Northern (960–1127)
    Southern (1127–1279)
Yuan (1260–1368)
Ming (1368–1644)
Qing (1644–1911)
Republic of China (1911–49; 1949–)
People's Republic of China (1949–)

The following abbreviations are used for important Daoist textual collections.

DH Dunhuang manuscripts
DZ *Zhengtong daozang* and *Xu daozang*
JH *Daozang jinghua*
JHL *Daozang jinghua lu*
JY *Daozang jiyao*
XB *Daozang xubian*
ZH *Zhonghua daozang*
ZW *Zangwai daoshu*

In order to avoid unnecessary complexity, I have not referenced extant translations, unless my translation is based on them. Interested readers may review my "Daoist Texts in Translation" (2003), which provides a comprehensive, annotated catalogue of Daoist texts translated to date and its forthcoming supplement. Unless otherwise indicated, all translations are my own.

The book also uses the following abbreviations:

abbr.   abbreviated
b.   born
BCE   Before the Common Era
c.   century
ca.   circa
CE   Common Era
cf.   compare
d.   died
dat.   dated
d.u.   dates unknown
est.   established
j.   juan (scroll)
per. comm. personal communication
r.   ruled
trad.   traditional
trl.   translated

Generally speaking, when "ch." appears without additional information, it indicates chapters in the present book.

Note

1   As the names suggest, the so-called Period of Disunion as well as the Five Dynasties and Ten Kingdoms are extremely complex and consist of many different dynasties. This also is true of the Song dynasty, which actually existed concurrently with three other "non-Chinese" dynasties: Khitan Liao, Tangut Xixia, and Jurchen Jin.

LIST OF FIGURES

Introduction: On guidance and perplexity

Daoism, written "Taoism" in the older Wade-Giles Romanization system but still pronounced with a "d" sound, is an indigenous Chinese religion deeply rooted in traditional Chinese culture. "Daoism" may be understood as the "tradition of the Dao," with the Dao (Tao; Way) referring to the sacred or ultimate concern of Daoists. "Daoism" is a placeholder for Daoist adherents, communities, and their religious expressions. Daoists (Taoists) are adherents of Daoism, although there are diverse modes of adherence and expressions of affiliation. In the modern world, Daoism has become a global religious tradition characterized by cultural, ethnic, linguistic, and national diversity. While rooted in "Chinese Daoism" as source-tradition, global Daoism is a religion with worldwide distribution and international adherence.

The study of Daoism can be perplexing. This is especially the case with respect to initial attempts to gain "religious literacy" and to navigate various influences. The latter often include outdated and inaccurate interpretations, specifically ones rooted in particular intellectual legacies and popular constructions with little actual engagement with or understanding of Daoism. There are various sources of confusion that produce obstacles to authentic learning and understanding. However, one may become determined to overcome perplexity by seeking guidance. One may seek out reliable sources and informed perspectives. One may find an orientation and approach that provides access and deeper familiarity. One may, in turn, begin inquiry into Daoism by addressing perplexity, finding guidance, and initiating considerate approach.

Perplexity

Perplexity may be both beneficial and detrimental. As we saw in the epigraphs at the beginning of this book, Daoists value "non-knowing" (*wuzhi*), but also endeavor to resolve "perplexity" (*huo*), especially in the form of confusion, distortion, and delusion. Perplexity may involve receptivity and exploration; it may also be characterized by bewilderment and incomprehension.

Daoists have traditionally described the Dao (Tao; Way), the sacred, or ultimate concern of Daoists, as formless, mysterious, nameless, numinous, and unknowable. From a Daoist perspective, that which is referred to as "Dao" is beyond language and conception. The Dao has been described as "dark" (*xuan*), "indistinct" (*hu*), "obscure" (*huang*), "silent" (*mo*), and so forth. While ultimately unknowable, the Dao may be experienced. This is because the Dao pervades the world and being; from a Daoist perspective, it is oneself. "Knowing" may, in turn, inhibit true learning and understanding. As a cognitive state, "knowing" is often characterized by attachment, division, hierarchy, and rigidity. It is often calcified understanding and experience. It stands in contrast to open inquiry, exploration, and discovery. Thus many Daoists have embraced mysteriousness and delighted in obscurity, including paradox and apparent absurdity. Such a way of being, and of practice and expression, reasonably leads to perplexity among individuals unfamiliar with the tradition. Such perplexity may lead to deeper inquiry, including a commitment to intellectual humility and the search for deeper understanding. However, such perplexity may inhibit learning, as confusion may become an obstacle. The study of Daoism often subverts easy explanations and totalizing interpretations. This is partially due to the diversity and relative inclusivity of the tradition. For every apparently authoritative statement, one can often find a counter-example. The same is true for various essentializations and generalizations. It is a near truism that Daoism is one of the most misunderstood religious traditions. Perplexity surrounding Daoism is not simply a matter of a scarcity of reliable information; it is also related to systematic misrepresentation, including deep attachment to various misconceptions. There is a "conspiracy of ignorance," including intentional exclusion of informed views, reliable sources, as well as adherent and academic perspectives. The study of Daoism is thus as much about the context of reception and ingrained opinions, as about Daoism as such. Some perplexity related to Daoism is connected to received views and conventional interpretive frameworks. Historically speaking, these derive from and are rooted in traditional Confucian and Chinese literati prejudices, Christian missionary sensibilities, European colonialist constructions, and Orientalist fantasies. Unfortunately, much of what goes by the name of "Daoism" in the modern world is fabrication, fiction, and fantasy. This is Daoism engaged as museum piece, taxidermy trophy, and mining site. There are interpretive legacies in the Western engagement with Daoism.

Here we should familiarize ourselves with some of the most influential received views of Daoism in order to avoid unreliable sources and untenable interpretations, in order not to increase perplexity by relying on the perplexed and perplexing. Drawing upon classical Daoist sources, we may begin by unlearning, and then move into a state of "non-perplexity." The latter relates to clarity and stillness (*qingjing*), a state of insight and non-agitation.

One of the most enduring and reproduced misconceptions about Daoism is that there are "two Daoisms," namely, so-called "philosophical Daoism" and so-called "religious Daoism." This view is epidemic among non-specialists. It diverges from both Daoist adherent and informed academic views, that is, interpretations rooted in a deep understanding of the tradition. This "bifurcated view" of Daoism claims that there was a pure and original philosophical expression of Daoism that was lost by the later Daoist religion. So-called "philosophical Daoism" is claimed to relate to the *Daode jing* (*Tao-te-ching*; Scripture on the Dao and Inner Power) and *Zhuangzi* (*Chuang-tzu*; Book of Master Zhuang). Its supposed founder was Laozi (Lao-tzu; Master Lao) and his alleged follower Zhuangzi (Chuang-tzu; Master Zhuang). So-called "religious Daoism" is claimed to refer to everything else, especially to Daoism as institutional religion. So-called "philosophical Daoism" is identified as a "system of thought" (disembodied ideas) that existed during the Warring States period, while so-called "religious Daoism" is identified as a religion that emerged during the Later Han dynasty. Equally problematic, so-called "religious Daoism" encompasses almost 2,000 years of Daoist history. Some individuals have also attempted to equate so-called "philosophical Daoism" with the indigenous Chinese term *daojia* (*tao-chia*) and so-called "religious Daoism" with *daojiao* (*tao-chiao*).

This received interpretative framework is untenable on multiple grounds. In terms of the indigenous terms, *daojia* literally means "Family of the Dao," while *daojiao* literally means "Teachings of the Dao." Both highlight the central importance of the Dao as a Daoist cosmological and theological concept. Neither involves a "philosophical/religious" distinction. The association of *daojia* with "thought" (*sixiang*) and of *daojiao* with "religion" (*zongjiao*) is a modern Chinese construction largely rooted in earlier Chinese literati, European colonialist, and Protestant missionary interpretations. Historically speaking, the term *daojia* first emerged as a bibliographical and taxonomic category during the Early Han dynasty. It was primarily a way of categorizing texts. Daoists eventually used the term in the early and early medieval period as a designation for the Daoist community, especially ordained Daoist priests (*daoshi*) and Daoist movements. *Daojiao* was originally used by Daoists in the early medieval period in order to distinguish their tradition from Buddhism (*fojiao*) (Kirkland 1997a; Kobayashi 1995). This *daojiao* included so-called *daojia*. That is, there was a unified religious tradition characterized by diversity. The bifurcated view of Daoism, especially its claims about "philosophy," is also challenged by a sophisticated understanding of the period and texts in question. The texts of the earliest period of Daoism, the classical period, reveal a religious community composed of master–disciple lineages. These lineages emphasized the practice of apophatic (emptiness- and stillness-based) meditation aimed at mystical union with the Dao (see, Roth 1999a). That is, Daoism was a religious tradition from the beginning, and perplexity will remain unresolved as long as individuals cling to a bifurcated view of Daoism. Any use of the terms "philosophical Daoism" and "religious Daoism" should be taken *ipso facto* as indicative of misunderstanding and inaccuracy with respect to Daoism.

In response to the bifurcated view, some individuals, especially earlier scholars and those familiar with their work, have suggested that Daoism as a religion only begins with the Tianshi (Celestial Masters) movement (see, Bokenkamp 1997; Kleeman 1998; Strickmann 1977, 1979). As discussed in detail in the chapters that follow, the Celestial Masters began with a revelation from Laojun (Lord Lao), the deified Laozi, to Zhang Daoling around 142 CE. Individuals who advocate this "truncated view" of Daoism claim that anything that pre-dates the Celestial Masters is not part of the Daoist tradition. Rather, Daoism technically only refers to the Celestial Masters movement and its derivatives. In place of Laozi as the supposed founder of Daoism, this approach nominates Zhang Daoling.

This earlier revisionist framework is also untenable. It presupposes the philosophical/religious distinction. It privileges the latter by elevating the Celestial Masters to the position of the "first Daoist movement," to the beginning of Daoism as religion. Such an interpretation fails to recognize the religious dimensions of classical Daoism, the connections between classical Daoism and organized Daoism, as well as the diversity of early Daoism itself. Moreover, it overemphasizes, largely due to the influence of modern Taiwanese Zhengyi (Orthodox Unity) Daoists, the relative importance of the Celestial Masters movement. This movement was only one of a number of early Daoist movements (see, Hendrischke 2000, 2007), albeit the most influential one. As problematically, although the Celestial Masters played a seminal role in the emergence of organized Daoism, many Daoists and Daoists communities were not connected to the Celestial Masters and did not recognize Zhang Daoling as "founder." As discussed in more detail in the following chapters, diverse lineages, movements, revelations, and textual corpuses comprise the Daoist tradition. Perplexity will remain unresolved as long as individuals cling to a truncated view of Daoism.

Beyond such interpretive debates, there are various popular misconceptions that inhibit understanding of the religious tradition which is Daoism. Some of the most common and widely perpetuated are the following:

- Dao (Tao) is a trans-religious, universal name for the sacred.
- Daoism (Taoism) is not a religion. It is a philosophy, spirituality, and "way of life."
- Daoism is non-theistic.
- Daoism is about "going with the flow."
- Daoism is whatever self-identified Daoists (Taoists) say it is.
- Laozi (Lao-tzu) is the "founder" of Daoism.
- The *Daode jing* (*Tao-te ching*) is the "Daoist bible," "spiritual classic," or "wisdom literature."
- Daoists (Taoists) are those who believe in the Dao.
- All Daoists are "nature-lovers."
- Popular versions and adaptations of Daoist texts are the texts themselves.
- Fengshui, Qigong (Ch'i-kung; Qi Exercises), Taiji quan (T'ai-chi ch'üan; Great Ultimate Boxing), or Traditional Chinese Medicine (TCM) are Daoist.
- So-called "Daoist yoga," including so-called "Daoist sexual yoga," is a Daoist practice. (Komjathy 2011b)

These are just a sampling of the common misconceptions that surround and contribute to perplexity concerning Daoism in the modern world. Many of these views will be addressed throughout the present book. Here one might simply pause and reflect on some questions regarding the modern engagement with and reception of Daoism, including our own intellectual genealogies. Why is Daoism being constructed in certain ways? Why is Daoism considered in such radically different terms than other prominent religions? What are the sources of these representations? In approaching such questions, we might consider the Daoist principle of "returning to the Source" (*guigen*) in concert with the practice of translation. Actual translation involves a "carrying over," a movement from a source-language to a target-language. An actual source-text is involved, and the "task of the translator" centers of engagement, fidelity, and transmission. Interpretations of Daoism may, in turn, be compared to translation. To what extent do the interpretations accurately re-present the source-tradition? Are they informed by actual Daoist views and sources? We may consider various sources, including the origin of our opinions and interpretations. In the case of inquiry into Daoism, we may consider the degree to which our sources are Daoist or informed by Daoist ones.

We may begin the resolution of perplexity by recognizing Daoism as an indigenous Chinese religion deeply rooted in traditional Chinese culture. We may begin by recognizing Daoists as adherents of Daoism, as individuals with some connection to the religious tradition. This tradition is characterized by diversity. Such diversity includes various important figures, communities, movements, places, and texts. It includes many models of practice and attainment. This is Daoism as a lived and living tradition comprised of dedicated adherents and place-specific communities. It is Daoism as consisting of specific people living in specific places at specific times. For such Daoists, Daoism itself may be the portal into the Dao, the tradition that preserves and transmits the Dao in the world.

Guidance

Daoism was a religious tradition from the beginning, here dated to the Warring States period and Early Han dynasty. Such a statement of course begs the question about what we mean by "religion." This requires deep inquiry and critical reflection. While many conflate the category of "religion" with religious institutions, institution is simply one expression of the "communal" or "social dimension" of religion, to use Ninian Smart's framework. From my perspective, although often synonymous with "culture," one distinguishing feature of "religion" involves belief in a sacred or "ultimate concern" (Paul Tillich). Whatever one's own assumptions, opinions, and commitments, if one does not recognize the theological and soteriological dimension of religious adherence, one will miss an essential characteristic. Something is considered sacred, and the "ultimate purpose" of human existence is understood in relation to "it." While one need not privilege the theological dimension, one must consider it. From these initial insights, and again drawing upon Ninian Smart, we may consider the cultural, doctrinal, ethical, material, narrative, philosophical, practical, psychological, and social aspects of religion. In addition, we may attempt to understand the distinctive culture, "symbol system" (Clifford Geertz) and informing "worldview" of particular religious traditions. We may attempt to understand "reality" from multiple perspectives, including ones that may be mutually exclusive and equally convincing. The "philosophical" dimension is relevant here, but we must recognize that so-called "Daoist philosophy" is almost always located in a more encompassing soteriology and theology. If there is such a thing as Daoist philosophy, it tends to be embodied, practical, and experiential.

What is the basis for viewing Daoism as a religion, and specifically as a unified religious tradition characterized by complexity and diversity? Briefly stated, the earliest form of Daoism, the "inner cultivation lineages" (Harold Roth) of classical Daoism, consisted of master–disciple communities. These individuals oriented themselves toward the Dao as sacred. In this context, the Chinese character 道, pronounced *dao* in modern Mandarin dialect, became used as a Daoist cosmological and theological concept. Generally speaking, these early Daoists emphasized the practice of apophatic meditation aimed at mystical union with the Dao (see, Roth 1999a). Thus, classical Daoism, referred to as so-called "philosophical Daoism" in outdated and inaccurate accounts, had communal, doctrinal, practical, psychological, soteriological, and theological dimensions. Although yet to receive detailed studies, these early Daoist lineages mingled with Fangshi ("formula master") communities, lineages, and practices, which in turn became absorbed into the earliest organized Daoist movements in the early period. The careful student of Daoism must be attentive to continuities and departures, divergences and convergences. Such is the nature of "tradition" not as a monolithic entity and homogenous monoculture, but as a living and transforming expression of individuals and communities. This is Daoism engaged as intact culture, old growth forest, and sacred site.

Two revisionist frameworks will assist us in our inquiry into Daoism and provide orientation throughout the present book. These are historical periodization and models of practice and attainment. Developing the work of Russell Kirkland (1997a, 2002), I would propose the historical periodization of Daoism based on seven major periods and four basic divisions (Komjathy 2011a). The seven periods would roughly correspond to major watersheds for Daoism in Chinese dynastic and post-dynastic history: (1) Warring States (480–222 BCE), Qin (221–206 BCE), and Early Han (202 BCE–9 CE); (2) Later Han (25–220 CE); (3) Period of Disunion (220–589) and Sui (581–618); (4) Tang (618–907), Song (Northern: 960–1127; Southern: 1127–1279), and Yuan (1260–1368); (5) Ming (1368–1644) and Qing (1644–1911); and (6) Republican (1912–49; 1949–) and early Communist (1949–78). I would, in turn, divide the modern period into "early modern Daoism" (1912–78) and "late modern Daoism" (1978–present), with the latter including contemporary expressions and developments (Figure 0.1).

In terms of Chinese history, 1978 is used as the key date because that was when Deng Xiaoping (1904–97) initiated the so-called Four Modernizations, socio-economic reforms that also led to an increase in religious freedom and eventually to the "revitalization" of Daoism. In concert with the Chinese Communist revolution (1949) and the subsequent flight of the Nationalists/Republicans to Taiwan, this was also a decisive factor in the globalization of Daoism. Period seven, in turn, encompasses more contemporary developments in mainland China, Hong Kong, and Taiwan. It also includes the transmission and transformation of Daoism in other Asian, European, and North American contexts, as well as the

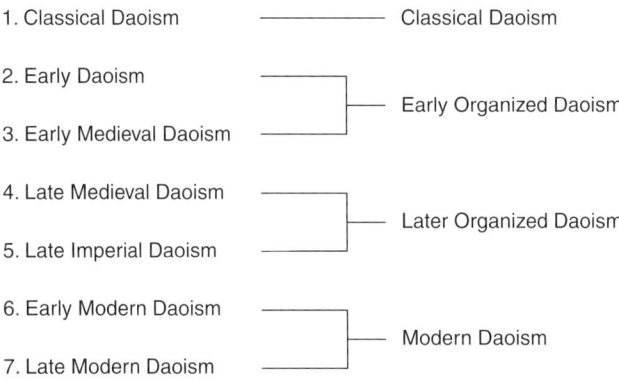

FIGURE 0.1 *Seven Periods and Four Divisions of Daoist History.*

establishment of the field of Daoist Studies throughout the world. While helpful, such periods should not lull one into believing that they encompass the dramatic changes that occurred between, for instance, the Tang and Song dynasties.

As discussed in the next chapter, each of these periods saw the emergence of specific communities and movements. Briefly stated, classical Daoism encompasses the diverse communities and "schools" of the inner cultivation lineages as well as Huang-Lao dao (Way of the Yellow Emperor and Laozi). Major movements associated with early Daoism include Taiping (Great Peace) and Tianshi (Celestial Masters). Early medieval Daoism consisted of such important movements as Taiqing (Great Clarity), Shangqing (Highest Clarity), and Lingbao (Numinous Treasure). Late medieval Daoism included a variety of internal alchemy lineages, including Quanzhen (Complete Perfection) and so-called Nanzong (Southern School), as well as new deity cults and ritual movements. Late imperial and modern Daoism was dominated by Zhengyi (Orthodox Unity; a.k.a. Tianshi) and Complete Perfection, though it also saw the emergence of major lineages of the latter as well as new lineages of internal alchemy. The constituents of global Daoism are a highly complex topic, which will be partially addressed in the final chapter of this book. Briefly stated, from a tradition-based and institutional perspective, global Daoism remains primarily an Orthodox Unity-Complete Perfection tradition. However, there are also dynamic (and problematic) recent developments, including mediumistic cult influences, obscure family lineages, and diverse organizations. The student of Daoism is, in turn, faced with many perplexities and challenges when studying the contemporary landscape of things identified as "Daoist."

For simplicity's sake, we might further speak of four basic divisions of Daoism: (1) classical Daoism; (2) early organized Daoism; (3) later organized Daoism; (4) modern Daoism. The rationale for this grouping is to distinguish historical developments, types of community, and distinctive models of practice. It draws our attention to the ways in which the inner cultivation lineages of classical Daoism differ from the householder, ascetic, and eremitic communities of early organized Daoism, as the Later Han dynasty witnessed the emergence of Daoism as an organized religious tradition with enduring institutions. Early organized Daoism may be distinguished from later organized Daoism based on the ascendance of a monastic model in the latter and the emergence of new models of practice, especially internal alchemy. Modern Daoism corresponds to the end of dynastic rule in China and the increasing influence of Western values and political ideologies. In its more contemporary form, it directs our attention toward Daoism as a global religious tradition with worldwide distribution and international adherence.

Our second interpretative framework involves "models of practice and attainment" (Komjathy 2008b). While it may seem self-evident that "realization of the Dao" or "attunement with the Way" is both the origin and culmination of a Daoist training regimen, one cannot deny that Daoists have developed and advocated different and perhaps competing models for such realization or attunement. Some traditional models of Daoist praxis include the following:

1 Alchemical: Transformation of self through ingestion of various substances (external) and/or through complex physiological practices (internal).

2 Ascetic: Renunciation, perhaps even body-negation. May involve psychological purification (internal) or practices such as fasting, sleep deprivation, voluntary poverty, etc. (external).

3 Cosmological: Emphasis on cosmological integration and seasonal attunement.

4 Dietetic: Attentiveness to consumption patterns and influences.

5 Ethical: Emphasis on morality and ethics, including precept study and application.

6 Hermeneutical: Emphasis on scripture study and interpretation, often resulting in the production of commentaries.

7 Meditative: Meditation as central, with the recognition of diverse types of meditation.

8 Quietistic: "Non-action" (*wuwei*), involving non-interference, non-intervention, and effortless activity, as central.

9 Ritualistic: Ritual as central, with the recognition of diverse types of ritual expression and activity.

As touched upon in the next chapter and throughout this introduction, these models emerge in specific contexts and may be associated with particular Daoist movements, but most Daoists employed and recommended a combination.

Taken together, an interpretative framework based on historical periodization and models of practice and attainment may help to resolve perplexity and provide guidance for approaching the complexity and diversity of Daoism. The seven periods and four divisions offer a relatively simple and nuanced framework for discussing Daoism from a historical perspective, including attentiveness to larger cultural and social developments. In the following chapter I provide a concise overview of Daoist history based on this periodization model. It will also be utilized as one of the primary interpretive frameworks throughout the subsequent chapters. Similarly, an approach based on models helps one to understand the diverse expressions of Daoist religiosity and "paths to the Dao." This interpretative framework will, in turn, be used throughout the present book. In concert with insights derived from and applicable to Religious Studies, it supplies at least one of the organizational structures of our inquiry, specifically attentiveness to view, practice, and experience.

Approach

The present book provides a concise and foundational introduction to Daoism as an indigenous Chinese and now global religious tradition. It presents Daoism as a living and lived religion characterized by diversity and complexity. Such diversity includes various key figures, communities, movements, places, and texts. This introduction is, in turn, informed by Daoist Studies, the academic field dedicated to study, education and publication on Daoism, and Religious Studies, the academic field dedicated to study, education and publication on "religion." In their fullest expressions, both of these fields are interdisciplinary and multi-perspectival. This book includes insights gleaned from viewing Daoism in terms of ethnography, history, literary studies, translation, and so forth. It includes a post-colonial, post-modern, and participant-observation dimension. Such an approach is informed by sustained academic engagement over 20 years and direct experience with living Daoists and Daoist communities, both in mainland China and throughout the modern world. It is post-colonial because it engages the perspectives of actual Daoists, and because it overcomes Orientalism by neither excluding nor privileging Chinese Daoists. From this perspective, one may endeavor to take Daoism seriously on its own terms. One may consider both adherent and academic perspectives. One may learn to "think through Daoism." Alternating between sympathetic and critical interpretive strategies, one may understand how Daoists view the world, and perhaps gain insights into the nature of "reality" in the process. Along the way, one may investigate one's own assumptions and ingrained opinions as well as clarify one's own commitments.

The book is organized into nine primary chapters: (1) Tradition; (2) Community; (3) Identity; (4) View; (5) Personhood; (6) Practice; (7) Experience; (8) Place; and (9) Modernity. The first chapter provides an overview of the Daoist tradition with particular attention to key figures, movements, and texts. Chapter two discusses different types and models of community, specifically hermits, householders, and monastics. The third chapter examines religious adherence and affiliation through the lens of lineage, revelation, and ordination. Chapter four discusses foundational Daoist worldviews with particular attention to views related to human existence, the universe, and the sacred. The fifth chapter covers personhood, or Daoist views of self; distinctive Daoist views related to embodiment, psychology, and self-transformation are addressed. Chapter six discusses the complex topic of Daoist practice; it provides information on Daoist dietetics, ethics, health and longevity techniques, meditation, ritual, and scripture study. The seventh chapter addresses the diverse forms of "Daoist experience," including attunement, encounter, and pervasion. Chapter eight discusses the central importance of place and place-specific community in Daoism; it includes information on important geographical schema, key sacred sites, as well as architecture and spatial arrangement. The final chapter examines Daoism in the modern world and as a global religious tradition, including as practiced (and constructed) in the West. Throughout these chapters, one encounters Daoism as an engaging, multidimensional, and profound religious tradition.

Readers of my *The Daoist Tradition: An Introduction* (Bloomsbury Academic, 2013) will note some overlap in content.

This is unavoidable. The former title is intended to be a more comprehensive introduction to Daoism. The present book is intended to be a concise introduction, especially for individuals engaging in initial inquiries and seeking foundational understanding. Although there is some repetition of content, especially in chapters 2, 3, and 8 of the present work, the organization and much of the content is new, or at least presented in a different manner. I have also kept references to a minimum, unless I am relying on them. As indicated in the "further reading" sections and the bibliography, I am deeply indebted to the work of members of the Daoist Studies community, that is, individuals who have dedicated their lives to study, education, and publication on Daoism.

The landscape of Daoism is vast and multifaceted. There are mountains to climb; rivers to ford; scenery to appreciate; abodes to visit; and inhabitants to meet. One may encounter the landscape of Daoism as inhabitant, as pilgrim, or as tourist. Depending on one's orientation and approach, the resulting experiences will be different. The present book is intended to provide a map for exploring that landscape. However, we must remember that the map is not the territory. The landscape exists beyond orientation-points and contour-lines. The Daoist tradition exists beyond the pages of this book, beyond encompassing walls, whether physical or cognitive. It exists in the lives and communities of Daoists, of members of the religious tradition which is Daoism.

Further reading

Kirkland, Russell. 2004, *Taoism: The Enduring Tradition*. London and New York: Routledge.

Kohn, Livia, ed. 2000, *Daoism Handbook*. Leiden: Brill.

Komjathy, Louis. 2013, *The Daoist Tradition: An Introduction*. London and New York: Bloomsbury Academic.

Pregadio, Fabrizio, ed. 2008, *The Encyclopedia of Taoism*. 2 vols. London and New York: Routledge.

CHAPTER ONE

Tradition

Daoism, the tradition of the Dao, is an indigenous Chinese religion deeply rooted in traditional Chinese culture and characterized by complexity and diversity. The Daoist tradition is at once singular and plural, varied and unified. It is a religious tradition comprised of various *traditions*. These include the adherents, communities, movements, lineages, and places that inhabit the contours of Daoist history. Such traditions encompass various views, practices, experiences, goals, and ideals. They also include a wide variety of religious expressions, with scriptures being especially important. In this respect, it is important to recognize the varied dimensions of Daoist "material religion," including aesthetics, architecture, art, calligraphy, literature, and so forth.

Chinese Daoists have tended to speak of their tradition in terms of a "family" (*jia*) and "teachings" (*jiao*), with the assumption of teachers and scriptures as major sources of those teachings. The traditions of the Dao, the specific communities, movements, and lineages that comprise Daoism, also receive other designations. "Movements" tend to be referred to as *dao* ("ways") or as *liu* ("streams"). "Lineages," usually sub-divisions of larger movements, tend to be referred to as *pai* ("tributaries"). That is, movements are paths or ways to the Dao, to the Way. These are the major expressions of the Daoist tradition; some important movements include Tianshi dao (Way of the Celestial Masters), Shangqing dao (Way of Highest Clarity), Quanzhen dao (Way of Complete Perfection), and so forth. These are usually associated with particular "founders," revelations, scriptures, and often places. Such movements are streams flowing into and out of the larger tradition, with the latter comparable to a river flowing toward the ocean of the Dao. Lineages are the tributaries that flow into and out of the streams of the Daoist movements. These are usually associated with major teachers or systems of practice. Viewed from a more comprehensive, Daoists also have tended to view "tradition" through the lens of the external Three Treasures, namely, the Dao (Way), scriptures (*jing*), and teachers (*shi*), with the latter often indicating the Daoist religious community as a whole. We may, in turn, approach the Daoist tradition in terms of key personages, movements, and scriptures.

Personages

There is no founder of Daoism as such. Rather, there are founders of specific movements, patriarchs of various lineages, key representatives and personages, including immortals, and so forth.

In terms of the inner cultivation lineages of classical Daoism, the two key personages are Lao Dan, also known as Laozi, and Zhuang Zhou, also known as Zhuangzi. Although often elevated to the position of "founders" of Daoism, these individuals are better understood as elders of the inner cultivation lineages (Roth 1999a). We may also think of them as placeholders for classical Daoism more generally.

Lao Dan (Lao Tan; 6th c. BCE?) is mentioned throughout the *Zhuangzi* (Book of Master Zhuang) as a central figure and sage (*shengren*) of the earliest Daoist religious community. Some of his teachings may also be contained in the *Laozi*, conventionally translated as the *Book of Master Lao*. Little is known about Lao Dan, and he may not have existed at all. He was eventually combined as one element of a composite and pseudo-historical figure known as Laozi (Lao-tzu; Master Lao), whose name may mean "Old Child" and/or "Old Master." Laozi is also known as Li Er and Li Boyang. According to his standard "biography," Laozi was born in Quren village in the Lai district of Hu province in the state of Chu. He is said to have been an archivist of the Zhou dynasty as well as a senior contemporary and perhaps teacher of Kongzi (Master Kong; "Confucius;" 551–479 BCE). In addition, Laozi is identified as the author of "a book in two parts, discussing the Dao and inner power in 5,000 words," that is, the *Daode jing*. Although revisionist scholarship has conclusively demonstrated that Laozi was a pseudo-historical figure (Graham 1998), he became elevated as one of the most important personages in the Daoist tradition and in Chinese culture more generally. In organized Daoism, he also became associated with the god Laojun (Lord Lao) and various revelations were attributed to him (Kohn 1998a).

Zhuang Zhou (Chuang Chou; ca. 370–290 BCE) is generally considered to be an actual historical figure, but even less is known about him. He is honorifically referred to as Zhuangzi (Chuang Tzu; Master Zhuang). The earliest Chinese sources simply tell us that he was from Meng, the actual location of which is lost to the annals of history. Zhuang Zhou is generally regarded as the author of or individual whose teachings are contained in the so-called Inner Chapters (chs 1–7) of the *Zhuangzi*. As a classical Daoist elder, Zhuang Zhou gained a following. Some members of his lineage, the so-called Zhuangists, revered him as a model of Daoist self-cultivation and composed writings that attempted to emulate the master. Their writings appear in chapters 17 through 22 of the received *Zhuangzi*. Zhuangzi also is sometimes misidentified as a "disciple of Laozi," but he is better understood as a fellow elder of classical Daoism. In organized Daoism, Zhuangzi is less emphasized than Laozi, but he was, nonetheless, venerated as a central figure of the tradition, and the text associated with him continued to exert some influence.

Moving into early organized Daoism, the most important figure associated with the Tianshi (Celestial Masters) movement is Zhang Daoling (Chang Tao-ling; fl. 140s CE). Although sometimes misidentified as the "founder of Daoism," Zhang Daoling is better understood as the founder of the Celestial Masters and a central figure in the formation of Daoism as an organized religious tradition. Like Laozi and Zhuangzi, there is scant reliable information about Zhang's life. He was supposedly born in Feng in the kingdom of Pei (Jiangsu). At some point he moved to the state of Shu (Sichuan). According to tradition, in 142 CE, Zhang Daoling received a revelation from Lord Lao, the deified Laozi, on Heming shan (Crane Cry Mountain; Dayi, Sichuan). During this revelation, Zhang was appointed as the Celestial Master, Lord Lao's empowered terrestrial representative (Figure 1.1).

FIGURE 1.1 *Late Imperial Depiction of Zhang Daoling.*
Source: *Xianfo qizong* (Marvelous Traces of Immortals and Buddhas).

With the help of his son Zhang Heng (d. 179) and grandson Zhang Lu (d. 215), the second and third Celestial Master, respectively, Zhang established a semi-independent Daoist society in Sichuan. Although Zhang Daoling and the position of the Celestial Master, a patrilineal line in the Zhang family, remained central throughout Daoist history, including into the modern world, the Celestial Masters, also known as Zhengyi (Orthodox Unity), eventually came to center more on various family lineages and local communities.

Other central personages in early organized Daoism include Ge Hong in the Taiqing (Great Clarity) movement; Yang Xi, the Xu family, and Tao Hongjing in the Shangqing (Highest Clarity) movement; and Ge Chaofu and Lu Xiujing in the Lingbao (Numinous Treasure) movement.

Ge Hong (Ko Hung; 283–343), whose Daoist name was Baopu (Embracing Simplicity), was born and raised in Jurong (near Nanjing, Jiangsu). His family was famous in the area for providing scholar-officials to the imperial bureaucracy. Ge was the grandnephew of Ge Xuan (Ko Hsuan; 164–244), a renowned Fangshi (magico-religious practitioner) and disciple of Zuo Ci (ca. 220–ca. 260 CE). At the age of fourteen, Ge Hong became a disciple of Zheng Yin (ca. 215–ca. 300), who traced his lineage to Ge Xuan. After Zheng Yin's retirement in 302, Ge Hong spent most of his life in pursuit of the elixir of immortality. He eventually became a recluse in the Luofu mountains (Boluo, Guangdong). Ge Hong is remembered in Daoist history as the systematizer of Great Clarity and as the author of the *Baopuzi neipian* (Inner Chapters of Master Embracing Simplicity; DZ 1185) and *Shenxian zhuan* (Biographies of Spirit Immortals; JY 89; JH 54).

Yang Xi (Yang Hsi; 330–86?) was a spirit-medium in Jurong known for his visions and calligraphy. Very little additional information on Yang is available. He emerges in Daoist history as the principal agent of the Highest Clarity revelations. He was hired by the aristocratic Xu (Hsu) family of Jurong, specifically by Xu Mi (303–76) and his third son Xu Hui (341–ca. 370), in order to establish contact with Tao Kedou (d. 362), Xu Mi's deceased wife. Between 364 and 370, Yang Xi received a variety of revelations that became the basis of the Highest Clarity movement. One of the principal agents of these revelations was Wei Huacun (251–334), a deceased female Celestial Master libationer who would later become associated with Hengshan (Mount Heng; Southern

Marchmount; near Hengyang, Hunan) and highly venerated among female Daoists. In terms of the Xu family, they were related to the Ge and Tao families. Little else is known about the biographical specifics of Xu Mi and Xu Hui except that they eventually retired to Maoshan (Mount Mao; near Nanjing, Jiangsu) following Yang Xi's revelations. Another central figure in early Highest Clarity was Tao Hongjing (T'ao Hung-ching; 456–536), whose Daoist name was Tongming (Pervading Illumination). Tao was born to a southern aristocratic family in Danyang (near Nanjing, Jiangsu). During his youth, Tao studied Daoist literature, pharmacology, and health and longevity practices. Around 486, he became a disciple of Sun Youyue (399–489), a member of the Numinous Treasure movement. After seeing one of the original Highest Clarity manuscripts, the calligraphy of which appeared infused with numinosity, Tao decided to collect the original manuscripts, which had been disseminated earlier by a member of Xu family. After collecting the manuscripts, and in the process of developing a method to distinguish authentic from spurious, Tao retired to Mount Mao. There he completed his editorial work, which resulted in the *Zhen'gao* (Declarations of the Perfected; DZ 1016). He also completed a reconstructed version of the *Shennong bencao jing* (Divine Farmer's Classic of Herbology; partially lost), one of the most important works of Chinese medicine. With respect to Daoist history, Yang Xi and the Xu family are primarily remembered as the recipients and transmitters of the Highest Clarity revelations. Tao Hongjing is venerated as the preserver of the manuscripts and the systematizer of Highest Clarity.

Ge Chaofu (fl. 390s) was also born in Jurong. He was a grandnephew of Ge Hong. Little is known about Ge Chaofu's early life, but he eventually claimed to have received esoteric manuscripts that originated in a set of revelations to Ge Xuan. This lineage became the foundation for the emergence of the Numinous Treasure movement. Ge Chaofu also is sometimes identified as the author of the *Wupian zhenwen* (Perfect Writings in Five Sections; DZ 22), the first scripture in the Lingbao Catalogue. While Ge Chaofu is generally regarded as the "founder" of Numinous Treasure, the movement was systematized by Lu Xiujing (406–77), whose Daoist names were Yuande (Original Virtue) and Jianji (Unadorned Silence). Lu was born in Dongqian in present-day Zhejiang. He was a descendent of prominent scholar-officials. There is scant information on his early life, but Lu eventually established a Daoist hermitage on Lushan (Mount Lu; Jiujiang, Jiangxi). He lived and trained disciples there from 453–67. Lu gained patronage from various members of the Chinese cultural elite, and the emperor eventually endowed him with the Chongxu guan (Temple for Venerating Emptiness) near the capital. During his lifetime, Lu Xiujing was pivotal in the establishment of the Daoist tradition as such, including a systematized canon, ritual protocol, and ordination procedures (Kirkland 1997a, 2004; Kobayashi 1995). He edited and codified the Numinous Treasure scriptures into the Lingbao Catalogue; compiled the first comprehensive catalogue of Daoist texts, the *Sandong jingshu mulu* (Catalogue of Scriptures and Writings of the Three Caverns; dat. 471); and wrote a revised version of Celestial Master conduct guidelines titled the *Daomen keliie* (Abridged Codes for the Daoist Community; DZ 1127). After his death in the capital in 477, Lu's body was interred on Mount Lu. In the Daoist tradition, Ge Chaofu is remembered as the founder of the Numinous Treasure, while Lu Xiujing is recognized as its systematizer. In addition, along with Tao Hongjing and Du Guangting (850–933), Lu Xiujing was one of the most important intellectuals and scholastics in Daoist history.

Moving into later organized Daoism, while there are many key figures in a variety of movements and lineages, viewed retrospectively one individual stands out as most important. This is Wang Zhe (1113–70), whose Daoist name was Chongyang (Redoubled Yang). Wang Zhe is the founder of the Quanzhen (Complete Perfection) movement. Much more is known about Wang Zhe and his disciples than his early medieval counterparts, but here a brief sketch must suffice. Wang was born into a wealthy land-owning family near Xianyang (near Xi'an, Shaanxi). With a formal elite education, Wang eventually pursued a career in officialdom, and then in the military. He also married and had one or more children. Then, beginning in 1159, Wang had a series of mystical encounters with Daoist immortals. These events changed his life. He became a renunciant, abandoning his ancestral ties and family responsibilities. He first lived in a hermitage called Huo siren mu (Tomb for Reviving the Dead) from 1160 to 1163, and then in the eremitic community of Liujiang (present-day Huxian, Shaanxi). In 1167, he burned down his hermitage and began a westward journey. He eventually arrived in the eastern peninsula of Shandong, where he met Ma Yu. Having recognized Wang as an extraordinary individual, Ma allowed Wang to build a hermitage on his Shandong estate. This was the Quanzhen an (Hermitage of Complete Perfection; Ninghai [Muping], Shandong), which is the source of the movement's name. After training a number of disciples and establishing a variety of local Daoist associations, Wang died in Bianliang (Kaifeng, Henan), on his way back to Shaanxi. His body was later interred in Liujiang, where Chongyang gong (Palace of Chongyang) was eventually established. While in Shandong, Wang gathered seven senior disciples, later known as the Seven Perfected: (1) Hao Datong (1140–1212), born in Ninghai, whose Daoist names were Taigu (Grand Antiquity) and Guangning (Expansive Serenity); (2) Liu Chuxuan (1147–1203), born in Donglai, whose Daoist name was Changsheng (Perpetual Life); (3) Ma Yu (1123–84), born in Ninghai, whose Daoist name was Danyang (Elixir Yang); (4) Qiu Chuji (1148–1227), born in Qixia, whose Daoist name was Changchun (Perpetual Spring); (5) Sun Buer (1119–82), born in Ninghai, the ex-wife of Ma whose Daoist name was Qingjing (Clear Stillness); (6) Tan Chuduan (1123–85), born in Ninghai, whose Daoist name was Changzhen (Perpetual Perfection); and (7) Wang Chuyi, born in Ninghai, whose Daoist name was Yuyang (Jade Yang). For present purposes, Ma, Qiu, and Sun are most important. In the larger parameters of Daoist history, Wang Zhe is remembered as the founder of Complete Perfection; Ma Yu as Wang's senior disciple and the second Patriarch; Qiu Chuji as the third Patriarch and individual most responsible for the formation of a monastic order; and Sun Buer as the only senior female disciple and later a matriarch of female alchemy.

Another key figure in later organized Daoism, specifically in the late imperial period, is Wang Changyue (1622?–80), whose Daoist name was Kunyang (Paradisiacal Yang). Wang Changyue is the founder of the official, "orthodox" Longmen (Dragon Gate) lineage of Complete Perfection Daoism. He was born into a Daoist family in Lu'an, Shanxi. At a young age, he began travelling to famous mountains in search of a teacher. In 1628, tradition tells us that he met and became a disciple of Zhao Fuyang (fl. 1600–40), who is identified retrospectively as a sixth Longmen Patriarch. Wang trained under and was ordained by Zhao on Wangwu shan (Mount Wangwu; Henan). Wang Changyue eventually became the abbot of Baiyun guan (White Cloud Monastery; Beijing) in 1655.

There he established the official Dragon Gate lineage. Specifically, he created a three-tiered ordination system based on three corresponding texts that he compiled. These include the *Chuzhen jie, Zhongji jie,* and *Tianxian jie.* Wang also authored another guide to Complete Perfection monastic life titled the *Longmen xinfa* (Central Teachings of Dragon Gate; ZW 201), which also appears in a slightly divergent version titled the *Biyuan tanjing* (Platform Sutra of the Jade Garden; ZW 330). With respect to Daoist history, although the Dragon Gate lineage is conventionally associated with Qiu Chuji, Wang Changyue was the founder of the official, "orthodox" lineage. Wang also was a key figure in the revitalization of Complete Perfection monastic life during the late imperial period.

A more complete account of the Daoist tradition would have to mention many other individuals. In addition to various historically identifiable ones, there are also mythological and pseudo-historical personages. These include gods, immortals, and Perfected. Some of the more famous immortals include Zhongli Quan (fl. 2nd c. CE?) and his supposed student Lü Dongbin (b. 798?), whose Daoist names are Zhengyang (Aligned Yang) and Chunyang (Pure Yang), respectively. These immortals are associated with the Zhong-Lü lineage of internal alchemy. While they are often identified as the founding Patriarchs of internal alchemy more generally, Zhongli Quan and Lü Dongbin became especially venerated in Complete Perfection as two of its Five Patriarchs. Some Complete Perfection accounts claim that these were the immortals who transmitted secret teachings to Wang Zhe. Zhongli and Lü were eventually incorporated into a famous group of immortals known as the Eight Immortals, who are a more popular and "trans-Daoist" (pan-Chinese) group. The most famous and popular list includes Cao Guojiu, Han Xiangzi, Han Zhongli (Zhongli Quan), He Xiangu, Lan Caihe, Li Tieguai, Lü Dongbin, and Zhang Guolao. There are many popular stories about these characters, both within Daoism and in late medieval and late imperial Chinese fiction and theatre.

Movements

Here a movement refers to a self-conscious community with an identifiable and enduring social organization. There was no "movement" in the classical period. Nonetheless, we may profitably think of the inner cultivation lineages of classical Daoism as the beginning of the Daoist tradition (Roth 1999a). The classical inner cultivation lineages were a series of loose-affiliated master–disciple communities. The earliest evidence for their existence comes from the Warring States period, and they continued to flourish into the Early Han dynasty. The most famous representatives of these communities are Lao Dan and Zhuang Zhou, although many other teachers and adherents are mentioned throughout the texts of classical Daoism, especially in the *Book of Master Zhuang*. Members of the inner cultivation lineages had a shared worldview and set of practices. The former included foundational values and religious commitments as well as a distinctive psychology, cosmology, and theology. The foundational worldview emphasized the Dao as sacred, and the universe and each individual being as a manifestation of the Dao. Classical Daoist adherents emphasized the practice of apophatic meditation aimed at mystical union with the Dao. This is a type of meditation that is contentless, non-conceptual, and non-dualistic. Members of the inner cultivation lineages also had different ways of being-in-the-world. This resulted in different applications of Daoist practice and views concerning social engagement. Some of these individuals became hermits and attempted to avoid the socio-political turmoil of the time. Others endeavored to establish a harmonious society, specifically by advancing a vision of an ideal sage-king. Members of the inner cultivation lineages were pivotal in Daoist history for the compilation, preservation, and transmission of classical Daoist texts. They also eventually became involved in cultural centers like the Jixia (Chi-hsia) Academy in the state of Qi (Shandong) and in later movements such as Huang-Lao (Way of the Yellow Emperor and Laozi). The latter was a syncretic movement that combined elements of Daoism and Legalism, and for a short period it was the state ideology of the Early Han dynasty. Some of the inner cultivation lineages may also have flowed into Fangshi (magico-religious practitioners) communities. The latter played a central role in the emergence of organized Daoism.

Moving into early organized Daoism, the most important movements were Tianshi, Taiqing, Shangqing, and Lingbao. The Tianshi movement, which is frequently elevated to the position of the "first organized Daoist movement," began in the Later Han dynasty, while the other three movements emerged during the Period of Disunion.

The Tianshi (T'ien-shih; Celestial Masters) movement began in the state of Shu (present-day Sichuan) (Bokenkamp 1997; Kleeman 1998). The name refers to the highest leadership position in the movement. According to traditional accounts, in 142 CE Zhang Daoling received a revelation from Lord Lao, the "deified" form of Laozi and personification of the Dao, on Crane Cry Mountain. The Celestial Masters movement is sometimes referred to as Zhengyi (Cheng-i; Orthodox Unity), because of a description of its founding revelation as the "covenant of orthodox unity" (*zhengyi mengwei*), or as Wudoumi dao (Way of Five Pecks of Rice), because of its supposed requirement of an annual donation of "five pecks of rice" for religious membership. The latter practice was more likely a food distribution network. A more esoteric reading suggests that these five handfuls of rice were used to demarcate ritual space, specifically the five cardinal directions. During Lord Lao's revelation, Zhang was appointed as terrestrial representative, the "Celestial Master," and given healing powers as a sign of his empowerment. The movement in turn became patrilineal, passing from Zhang Daoling to his son Zhang Heng and then to the latter's son Zhang Lu. The Celestial Masters established 24 "parishes" or "dioceses" with hierarchically ranked followers, wherein the so-called libationers were the highest (Kleeman 2012; Verellen 2003). The intent was to establish "seed people" who would populate an earth made ritually and morally pure. If a moral transgression occurred, a purification rite was performed. This consisted of an officiating priest utilizing his or her "registers," which gave him or her power over specific spirits, and submitting "petitions" to the so-called Three Bureaus of heaven, earth, and water. This was done through burning, burial, and submersion. In addition, the individual was secluded in "pure rooms" or "chambers of quiescence," where they were supposed to reflect upon their actions and repent. The Celestial Masters were eventually forced to migrate to various parts of China, and in southern China they began collaborating and competing with other southern traditions. This also led to a split in the Celestial Masters movement, which is sometimes referred to as the so-called Northern and Southern Celestial Masters (Kohn 2000b; Nickerson 2000). The former is associated with Kou Qianzhi (365–448), whose Daoist name was Fuzhen (Supporting

Perfection), and the Daoist theocracy of the Toba-Wei dynasty, while the latter is more diffused. During the Period of Disunion and Tang dynasty, the Celestial Masters also became incorporated into an emerging, integrated Daoist tradition, including into the formative canon and ordination system. It appears that the patrilineal Zhang family lineage of the Celestial Master was disrupted and then reconstructed during the Tang dynasty, and Orthodox Unity came to center more on various family lineages than the Celestial Master himself. The fate of the movement oscillated in subsequent periods, but Orthodox Unity remains one of the two primary forms of institutional Daoism to survive into the modern world, with Mount Mao and Longhu shan (Dragon-Tiger Mountain; Yingtan, Jiangxi) being its most important sacred sites in mainland China. Tradition records 65 Celestial Masters (Kleeman 2008), with Zhang Jiyu (b. 1962) generally recognized as the current one. Orthodox Unity largely consists of ordained, married priests and a larger, supporting lay community. The former tend to perform ritual for communal benefit, while the latter tend to focus on popular morality and devotionalism. The Celestial Masters movement is centrally important in Daoist history for establishing an enduring social organization, including hierarchically ranked adherents with various commitments and responsibilities; an ordained clergy of householder priests; as well as ethics and ritual as primary components of Daoist religiosity.

The next major early Daoist movement was Taiqing (T'ai-ch'ing; Great Clarity), which began in Jurong (near Nanjing, Jiangsu) (Campany 2002; Pregadio 2006a). With roots in Han dynasty magico-religious and immortality-seeker movements, Great Clarity was a tradition of external alchemy (*waidan*; lit., "outer cinnabar"), also referred to as "laboratory" or "operational alchemy" (Needham et al. 1976). The tradition claimed that the original revelations were received by the Fangshi Zuo Ci, who was Ge Xuan's teacher. The name of the movement refers to the alchemically transformed ontological condition that could be attained through the Great Clarity system of external alchemy and to the heaven with which the alchemical methods were associated. Great Clarity is known to us principally due to the efforts of Ge Hong, its most well-known member. Great Clarity emphasized levels of attainment and involved the concoction of a mineral elixir (*dan*), which consisted of highly toxic elements such as cinnabar, lead, mercury, and realgar. The process of elixir formation also involved complex purificatory practices, cosmological considerations, and ritual procedures. The post-medieval fate of Great Clarity is currently unclear, but external alchemy remained a central element of the Daoist tradition into the late medieval and even into the modern period. In terms of Daoist history, Great Clarity helped to transmit many earlier beliefs and practices as well as establish a fully systematized form of Daoist external alchemy.

The Shangqing (Shang-ch'ing; Highest Clarity) movement emerged out of a cross-pollination of the Celestial Masters, Great Clarity and earlier unidentified southern movements (Miller 2008; Robinet 1993, 2000). The movement started in Jurong. The name refers to the heaven from which its revelations derived. Highest Clarity began in the 360s when the aristocratic Xu family hired the spirit-medium Yang Xi. Through a series of revelations, Yang described the organization and population of the subtle realms of the cosmos, particularly the heaven of Shangqing (Highest Clarity). This heaven was located among the Three Heavens of Yuqing (Jade Clarity; highest), Highest Clarity (middle), and Taiqing (Great Clarity; lowest). The various celestial communications included methods for spirit travel, visualizations, and alchemical concoctions. The revelations were, in turn, written down by Yang Xi and the Xu family in a calligraphic style that seemed divine. After the revelations ended in 370, members of the Xu family and other Highest Clarity adherents established a Daoist community on Mount Mao (Strickmann 1977, 1979). In subsequent generations, the original Highest Clarity manuscripts were disseminated to various Daoist families, but they were eventually collected by Tao Hongjing. Tao also established a religious center on Mount Mao. In the following centuries, Highest Clarity Daoism became infused with Buddhism, especially Buddhist meditation methods, and integrated into the Tang dynasty monastic system. Specifically, Highest Clarity was the highest ordination rank in that system (Kohn 2003, 2004b). It appears that Highest Clarity Daoism continued to flourish as a semi-independent movement into the Song dynasty. Tradition records 45 Highest Clarity Patriarchs, with Liu Dabin (fl. 1317–28) being the last one (Robinet 2008). Within the larger contours of the Daoist tradition, Highest Clarity contributed new visions of personhood, including body-gods; systematized new meditation methods such as visualization; and preserved and transmitted a new set of revelations and associated manuscripts. Highest Clarity also included various elements that became part of Daoist internal alchemy (*neidan*); this is so much the case that the movement could be characterized as proto-*neidan*.

The final major movement of early organized Daoism was Lingbao (Ling-pao; Numinous Treasure), which also began in Jurong (Bokenkamp 1983, 1997; Yamada 2000). Numinous Treasure developed partially in response to the Highest Clarity revelations in combination with the more pervasive influence of Mahāyāna (Greater Vehicle) Buddhism, including its bodhisattva ideal and vision of universal salvation. The movement's name refers to a medium or sacred object (*bao*; "treasure") infused with numinosity (*ling*), especially the sacred talismans that Numinous Treasure believed to have created and maintained the cosmos. A more esoteric interpretation understands *ling* as the celestial half of a talisman and *bao* as the terrestrial half. For our purposes, Numinous Treasure refers to the tradition established by Ge Chaofu, apparently a Highest Clarity affiliate and grandnephew of Ge Hong. Lingbao may, in turn, be seen to have connections with each of the three earlier major Daoist movements, namely, the Celestial Masters, Great Clarity, and Highest Clarity. Ge Chaofu, who inherited the library of Ge Hong, claimed that the original Numinous Treasure revelation went back to Ge Xuan and was thus older (= more authoritative) than the Highest Clarity revelations. Early Numinous Treasure Daoism centered on a cosmocrat (cosmic ruler) and magical manipulation of the cosmos. This cosmocrat, who resembles Mahāvairocana (Cosmic Sun Buddha) of the Buddhist Tantric tradition, was Yuanshi tianzun (Celestial Worthy of Original Beginning). Early Numinous Treasure emphasized levels of celestial realms, celestial administrators, and a host of divine beings, in combination with Han-dynasty correlative cosmology, Fangshi ideas and practices, and Celestial Masters ritual. A representative work documenting the magical dimension of Numinous Treasure is the *Lingbao wufu xu* (Explanations of the Five Numinous Treasure Talismans; DZ 388). These "five talismans," corresponding to the five cardinal directions (east, south, center, west, north) were the foundation for harmony and control, whether personal, communal, socio-political, or cosmological. The movement also maintained soteriological aims, namely, the salvation of humanity as a whole. Following Mahāyāna Buddhism, this is referred to as "universal salvation" (*pudu*). The Numinous Treasure scriptures became codified by the Daoist ritualist and bibliographer Lu Xiujing in the so-called "Lingbao Catalogue." The post-medieval fate of Numinous Treasure is currently unclear. However, the movement's codification of Daoist ritual, in combination with elements of Celestial Masters ritual, became the foundation for standardized Daoist ritual more generally. In addition, during the Song dynasty, Lingbao dafa (Great Rites of Numinous Treasure), a syncretic ritual tradition that modified and revitalized Numinous Treasure to some extent, emerged (Boltz 1987; Skar 2000). In terms of the larger Daoist tradition, Numinous Treasure was the first Daoist movement to incorporate major elements from Buddhism. It also helped to standardize Daoist ritual, including a radically new soteriological goal.

Moving into later organized Daoism, the most important movement was Quanzhen (Ch'uan-chen; Complete Perfection) (Eskildsen 2004; Komjathy 2007a, 2013a), the name of which is also translated as "Complete Reality" and "Completion of Authenticity." The name of the movement refers to the alchemically transformed ontological condition that could be attained through the Complete Perfection system of internal alchemy. Complete Perfection began in seminal form in Liujiang (Huxian, Shaanxi), but became an identifiable Daoist movement in Ninghai (Muping, Shandong). This occurred in the late 1160s. Complete Perfection was founded by Wang Zhe with his senior disciples, conventionally referred to as the Seven Perfected. The early eremitic community eventually became a regional Shandong movement, with five associations or meeting-houses located throughout Shandong's eastern peninsula. These associations consisted of a small spiritual elite as well as a larger lay community. The former adhered to foundational Complete Perfection principles and practices, including asceticism, inner alchemical practice, and mystical experiencing. The latter practiced basic meditation, popular morality, and devotionalism. They also supported the movement's various eremitic communities. Through Wang's disciples, especially Ma Yu and Qiu Chuji, Complete Perfection eventually became a more widespread movement and then a monastic order with nationwide distribution and temple networks. The fate of the movement oscillated in subsequent periods, but Complete Perfection remains one of the two primary forms of institutional Daoism to survive into the modern world, with Complete Perfection monastics inhabiting most of the sacred sites and temples in mainland China. Historically speaking, some of its most important sacred sites include Chongyang gong (Palace of Chongyang; Huxian, Shaanxi), where Wang Zhe engaged in intensive training and where his tomb is located; the Kunyu mountains (near Weihai and Yantai, Shandong), where Wang Zhe trained some of his early disciples; Longmen dong (Dragon Gate Grotto; Longxian, Shaanxi), where Qiu Chuji engaged in intensive training; and Baiyun guan (White Cloud Monastery; Beijing), where Qiu Chuji, Wang Changyue, and others served as abbots and which is the current headquarters of the monastic order. In modern mainland China, Complete Perfection largely consists of monastics who observe celibacy (no sex), sobriety (no intoxicants), and vegetarianism (no meat), as well as a larger, supporting lay community. Complete Perfection Daoists also practice various forms of lineage-based internal alchemy and daily recite the movement's liturgy in the morning and evening. Although Daoist monasticism was established as early as the fifth century under Buddhist influence, and although monasticism became a major form of Daoist social organization from at least the Tang dynasty forward, the Complete Perfection movement is centrally important in Daoist history for establishing an enduring monastic order. Complete Perfection also developed a viable Daoist training program rooted in asceticism and inner alchemical transformation.

Within modern Complete Perfection, the Longmen (Lung-men; Dragon Gate) lineage is the largest and most powerful (Esposito 2000, 2001, 2004). The name of this lineage derives from Dragon Gate Grotto, the place where Qiu Chuji engaged in intensive training. Although conventionally associated with Qiu, the official, "orthodox" lineage was established by Wang Changyue while he was abbot of White Cloud Monastery in the late 1600s. More than likely, all of the Complete Perfection lineages, of which there are seven official ones, were formally established during the Qing dynasty. The Dragon Gate lineage, like every Complete Perfection lineage, is primarily a monastic one. According to Wang Changyue's standardization, formal Dragon Gate adherence consists of three ordination levels, namely, Wondrous Perfection/Initial Perfection, Wondrous Virtue/Medium Ultimate, and Wondrous Dao/Celestial Immortality. These correspond to three monastic manuals and precept texts compiled by Wang. In addition, ordinands receive training under a specific master-father (*shifu*), who bestows a Dragon Gate lineage-name upon ordination. The modern situation of Dragon Gate is complicated by globalization. There are self-identified family Dragon Gate lineages in Hong Kong and Taiwan as well as in other parts of the world. There are also a variety of popular Western fictions about the lineage, including fabricated lineage connections and techniques.

Scriptures

Scriptures are sacred and authoritative texts of religious traditions. In the case of Daoism, "scripture" translates *jing*, which may also be translated as "classic" or "canon." From a Daoist perspective, Daoist scriptures are inspired or revealed. They are anonymous and/or attributed to particular divine beings. In some sense, Daoist scriptures represent transcriptions of various revelations, and they are one dimension of Daoist material culture. Every Daoist scripture originally was hand-written in classical Chinese using calligraphy and transmitted in manuscript form. This requires reflection on the relationship between translations and the source-texts. Daoists generally view Daoist scriptures as one of the external Three Treasures of the Dao, the scriptures, and the teachers (*shi*).

Just as there is no single founder or primary community in the Daoist tradition, so too there is no single central scripture. Different Daoist adherents and communities privilege different scriptures (Schipper and Verellen 2004). While the *Daode jing* is probably the most influential and consistently privileged text in Daoist history, it is an oversimplification to think of that text as the central scripture of Daoism. In fact, when speaking about texts in the Daoist tradition, we should first discuss either the movement-specific textual corpuses or the *Daozang*, the primary collection of Daoist texts from the late medieval period forward. Moreover, different scriptures occupy a central position in different Daoist movements and lineages. While some Daoist texts have received almost universal recognition and circulation throughout the Daoist tradition, others were lineage-specific.

In terms of classical Daoism, there were no "scriptures" (*jing*) strictly speaking. This category of Daoist literature first emerged as an honorific title in the Early Han dynasty, but it was not until the Later Han dynasty, in the context of early organized Daoism, that Daoist scriptures, as inspired and revealed, became composed. Nonetheless, two works of classical Daoism eventually became canonized as *jing*. These are the *Laozi* and *Zhuangzi*. The *Laozi* (*Lao-tzu*; Book of Venerable Masters) is traditionally attributed to Laozi, with the title conventionally translated as the *Book of Master Lao*. However, the *Book of Venerable Masters* is actually a multi-vocal anthology consisting of a variety of historical and textual layers; in certain respects, it is a collection of oral teachings of various members of the inner cultivation lineages (LaFargue 1992). This understanding of the text is supported by the discovery of two archaeological manuscripts, including Guodian (Jingmen, Hubei) and Mawangdui (Changsha, Hunan) (Henricks 1989, 2000). Dating to around 300 BCE and discovered in 1993, the Guodian *Laozi* ("Bamboo *Laozi*") consists of 71 bamboo slips. The arrangement of the passages differs significantly from the received version, and there are numerous variant and/or archaic characters. In terms of content, it is noteworthy that many of the polemical and anti-Confucian passages are absent. Dating to around 168 BCE and discovered in 1973, the Mawangdui discoveries include two copies of the *Laozi* written on silk ("Silk *Laozi*"). The text is similar to the received version except that the divisions are reversed: the Mawangdui manuscripts begin with Chapters 38–81 and end with Chapters 1–37. This means that the basic organization and content of the received text was established by at least the second century BCE. One may, in turn, tentatively identify at least five phases in the historical compilation of the received text: (1) oral traditions, including mnemonic aphorisms; (2) collections of sayings; (3) early anthologies; (4) codified, classified, and edited anthologies; and (5) fully integrated and standardized editions (Komjathy 2008a, v. 2). Also known as the Five Thousand Character Classic, the *Laozi* was, in turn, canonized as the *Daode jing* (*Tao-te ching*; Scripture on the Dao and Inner Power) around 150 BCE. The received text, usually the Wang Bi (226–49) redaction, consists of 81 verse chapters, with Chapters 1–37 usually identified as the so-called "Dao section" (*daojing*) and Chapters 38–81 designated as the so-called "inner power section" (*dejing*). The text consists of cryptic principles and instructions on Daoist self-cultivation. In terms of Daoist practice, it emphasizes Daoist apophatic meditation aimed at mystical union with the Dao as the foundation.

The *Zhuangzi* (*Chuang-tzu*; Book of Master Zhuang) is traditionally attributed to Zhuang Zhou ("Master Zhuang"). However, the *Book of Master Zhuang* is actually a multi-vocal anthology consisting of a variety of historical and textual layers; it is a collection of the teachings, writings, and practices of various members of the inner cultivation lineages of classical Daoism. The received edition consists of 33 prose chapters. It was redacted from an earlier 52-chapter version by Guo Xiang (252?–312), who, like Wang Bi, was a member of the Xuanxue (Hsüan-hsüeh; Profound Learning) literati movement. The text is conventionally divided into the so-called Inner Chapters (1–7), Outer Chapters (8–22), and Miscellaneous Chapters (23–33). While the Inner Chapters most likely contain the teachings and writings of Zhuang Zhou, revisionist scholarship identifies a variety of Daoist lineages within the rest of the text. These include the following: (1) Primitivists (Chapters 8–10; parts of 11, 12, and 14); (2) Individualists (Chapters 28–31); (3) Syncretists (Chapters 12–16, 33); (4) Zhuangists (Chapters 17–22); and (5) Anthologists (chs 23–27, 32) (Mair 2000). The *Book of Master Zhuang* eventually became canonized in 742 CE as the *Nanhua zhenjing* (Perfect Scripture of Perfected Nanhua; DZ 670), with Nanhua (Southern Florescence) being an honorific name for Master Zhuang. Taken as a whole, the *Book of Master Zhuang* is characterized by fascinating characters, some of whom were probably elders of the classical Daoist communities, as well as by entertaining, enlightening, and often subversive stories. There also are many passages on foundational Daoist views, principles, and practices, including Daoist apophatic meditation and realized ontological conditions. In terms of later Daoism, and beyond the Profound Learning movement, which has probably exerted the most influence on interpretive traditions and Western reception of the text, the stories of the *Book of Master Zhuang* became a central element of Daoist oral tradition.

Revisionist scholarship would also add other works to the textual corpus of classical Daoism (Roth 1999a). These include at least parts of the *Guanzi* (Book of Master Guan), *Huainanzi* (Book of the Huainan Masters; DZ 1184), and *Lüshi chunqiu* (Spring and Autumn Annals of Mister Lü). The relevant sections clarify classical Daoist views and practices by providing additional glimpses into classical Daoist cosmogony, cosmology, psychology, theology, and so forth. Especially fascinating are the so-called "Xinshu" (Techniques of the Heart-mind) chapters (36–38 & 49) of the *Book of Master Guan*. In particular, the "Neiye" (Inward Training) chapter provides technical specifics on Daoist apophatic meditation, which clarifies important passages in the *Book of Venerable Masters* and *Book of Master Zhuang*.

Moving into early organized Daoism, the early Celestial Masters did not have a founding scripture. Instead, the *Scripture on the Dao and Inner Power* occupied a central place in the early movement (Bokenkamp 1997). This was so much the case that Zhang Lu, the third Celestial Master, appears to have written one of the earliest Daoist commentaries, which is titled the *Laozi xiang'er zhu* (Commentary Thinking Through the *Laozi*; DH 56; S. 6825). The early Celestial Masters community also developed an ethical system based on precepts derived from the *Scripture on the Dao and Inner Power* and the *Xiang'er* commentary. The former includes the so-called Nine Practices, while the latter includes the so-called 27 Xiang'er Precepts. For members of the early Celestial Masters movement, the *Scripture on the Dao and Inner Power* thus provided principles and inspiration for living a Daoist religious life. In the early medieval Southern Celestial Masters community, the *Xiang'er* commentary and the *Santian neijie jing* (Scripture on the Inner Explanations of the Three Heavens; DZ 1205) were especially important. The latter contains a distinctive Daoist worldview, wherein political and social changes are described as the results of an ongoing cosmic revolution in which the correct emanations of the Three Heavens embodied in Laozi alternate with the noxious emanations of the Six Heavens. Each of Laozi's manifestations in the world mark a renewal of the cosmic order based on the Three Teachings (Way of Nonaction, Way of the Buddha, and Way of the Pure Covenant [Tianshi]), which Laozi instituted at different times, in different places, and in response to different needs. Other important later texts include the Southern Celestial Masters *Daomen keliie* (Abridged Codes for the Daoist Community; DZ 1127) by Lu Xiujing and the Northern Celestial Masters *Laojun yinsong jiejing* (Precept Scripture of Lord Lao for Recitation; "New Code"; DZ 785) by Kou Qianzhi, which provide guidelines for conduct and social organization. In modern Orthodox Unity, more emphasis is placed on esoteric family manuscripts, specifically ritual manuals and lists of spirit registers.

According to Ge Hong, there were three scriptures that formed the core of the Great Clarity textual tradition: the *Taiqing jing* (Scripture on Great Clarity), *Jiudan jing* (Scripture on the Nine Elixirs), and *Jinye jing* (Scripture on the Gold Liquid) (Campany 2002; Pregadio 2006a). These texts describe the ingredients and procedures for elixir decoction, including those associated with the Great Clarity elixir itself. Ge Hong also had a large library, part of which was inherited from his granduncle Ge Xuan, and which was eventually transmitted to Ge Hong's grandnephew Ge Chaofu, who is in turn associated with the Numinous Treasure movement. Finally, Ge Hong's own works, the *Baopuzi neipian* (Inner Chapters of Master Embracing Simplicity; DZ 1185) and *Shenxian zhuan* (Biographies of Spirit Immortals; JY 89; JH 54), are pivotal in Daoist history. The former is a *summa* of early medieval Daoist beliefs and practices, while the later is one of the most influential Daoist hagiographies (biographies of saints). The *Biographies of Spirit Immortals* also reveals some of the ways in which "tradition" was understood in this period of Daoist history.

The original Highest Clarity revelations of Yang Xi and the Xu family resulted in 34 manuscripts (Robinet 1993, 2000, 2008). Of these, the *Dadong zhenjing* (Perfect Scripture of the Great Cavern; DZ 5–7; DZ 103) and *Lingshu ziwen* (Purple Texts Inscribed by the Spirits; DZ 179; DZ 255; DZ 442; DZ 639) were especially influential. In addition, it appears that Highest Clarity incorporated earlier scriptures of currently unidentified southern movements. In particular, the *Huangting waijing jing* (Scripture on the Outer View of the Yellow Court; DZ 332) became especially important. This became the basis of the *Huangting neijing jing* (Scripture on the Inner View of the Yellow Court; DZ 331), which may be of actual Highest Clarity provenance. The early Highest Clarity texts describe the hidden structure of the cosmos, consisting of Daoist sacred realms as well as deities and Perfected, and provide technical instructions on Highest Clarity religious practice, including qi ingestion, visualization, and proto-*neidan*. The original manuscripts were later re-collected and compiled by Tao Hongjing in his *Zhen'gao* (Declarations of the Perfected; DZ 1016). In late medieval Highest Clarity, later Buddhist-influenced texts, such as the *Zuowang lun* (Discourse on Sitting-in-Forgetfulness; DZ 1036) by Sima Chengzhen (Szu-ma Ch'eng-chen; Zhenyi [Pure Unity]; 647–735), the twelfth Patriarch of Shangqing Daoism, became highly influential (Kohn 1987). The *Discourse on Sitting-in-Forgetfulness* maps Daoist meditation in terms of seven stages: (1) Respect and Trust; (2) Interception of Karma; (3) Taming the Mind; (4) Detachment from Affairs; (5) Perfect Observation; (6) Intense Concentration; and (7) Realizing the Dao.

In terms of the Numinous Treasure movement, Ge Chaofu claimed that the original scriptures derived from revelations to Ge Xuan, while the actual textual corpus was systematized by Lu Xiujing. Early Numinous Treasure centered on a group of 40 texts known as the "ancient Lingbao corpus," which were defined as such in the so-called Lingbao Catalogue by Lu (Bokenkamp 1983; Yamada 2000). The texts in the corpus can be divided into three kinds: two ancient Numinous Treasure texts that contain the five talismans and the belief in the Five Thearchs of the five directions; scriptures revealed by the Buddhist-inspired deity Yuanshi tianzun (Celestial Worthy of Original Beginning); and texts associated with Great Clarity and the immortal Ge Xuan. Important early Numinous Treasure texts include the *Lingbao wufu xu* (Explanations of the Five Numinous Treasure Talismans; DZ 388) and *Duren jing* (Scripture on Salvation; DZ 1; DZ 87–93). Key characteristics of the Numinous Treasure corpus include magico-religious control of the universe, especially through talismans and ritual activity, as well as an emphasis on universal salvation (*pudu*). As mentioned, Numinous Treasure established the foundations of standardized Daoist ritual (Dean 1993; Lagerwey 1987), and later members of the movement compiled a wide variety of ritual manuals and compendiums.

Moving into later organized Daoism, the Complete Perfection movement is especially noteworthy with respect to the central importance of scripture (Komjathy 2007a, 2013a). Given its enduring prominence within the Daoist tradition and into the modern world, Complete Perfection is all the more significant. While Highest Clarity and Numinous Treasure composed their own scriptures, with the accompanying claim of new revelations, it appears that Complete Perfection did not exhibit a similar pattern. The tradition does indeed claim secret transmissions from immortals, but these did not become the basis of new scriptures.

Instead, they were expressed in oral transmissions, informed Complete Perfection religious practice, and were incorporated into Complete Perfection hagiographies. Thus there are no originary texts that can be labeled "Quanzhen scriptures." Rather than compiling new scriptures, members of early Complete Perfection adopted the *Scripture on the Dao and Inner Power*, the sixth-century *Yinfu jing* (Scripture on the Hidden Talisman; DZ 31), and the eighth-century *Qingjing jing* (Scripture on Clarity and Stillness; DZ 620) as their central texts (Komjathy 2008a). These texts emphasize the central importance of Daoist self-cultivation focusing on the heart-mind, with purity of consciousness and spirit being primary. In addition, none of the writings of the early Complete Perfection adherents became canonical, although some of the poetry and discourse records exerted modest influence. Taken as a whole, the Complete Perfection textual corpus emphasizes asceticism, alchemical transformation, and mystical experiencing. In particular, the early adherents advocate consistent and prolonged practice of stillness-based meditation and internal alchemy. The *Lijiao shiwu lun* (Fifteen Discourses to Establish the Teachings; DZ 1233), attributed to the founder Wang Zhe, has been especially influential. Although conventionally elevated to the status of the central Complete Perfection text, this work is better understood as a manual for aspiring Complete Perfection adepts and as a general introduction to foundational Complete Perfection religious praxis. In the later Complete Perfection monastic order, the *Scripture on the Dao and Inner Power*, *Scripture on the Hidden Talisman*, and *Scripture on Clarity and Stillness* remained centrally important. However, different texts became privileged in different lineages. For example, the Dragon Gate lineage focuses on texts associated with Qiu Chuji. More than these, it emphasizes study and application of the three precept texts compiled by Wang Changyue, namely, the *Chuzhen jie* (Precepts of Initial Perfection; JY 292; ZW 404), *Zhongji jie* (Precepts of Medium Ultimate; JY 293; ZW 405), and *Tianxian jie* (Precepts of Celestial Immortality; JY 291; ZW 403) (Kohn 2004c; Komjathy 2013a). These texts discuss ethical reflection and application as well as dimensions of daily monastic life. Specially, they emphasize the 10 Precepts of Initial Perfection, 300 Precepts of Medium Ultimate, and 10 Virtues of Celestial Immortality and the 27 Virtuous Activities of Celestial Immortality, respectively.

In the larger parameters of the Daoist tradition, specifically from the late medieval period forward, the *Daozang* (Daoist Canon) became the primary Daoist textual collection (Komjathy 2002; Schipper and Verellen 2004). At various periods in Chinese history, prominent Daoist leaders, usually with imperial patronage and/or aristocratic support, compiled collections of Daoist texts. Such collections received the designation of *Daozang*, which literally means "storehouse of the Dao." The compilation of such Daoist collections is indebted to Lu Xiujing, who also compiled the above-mentioned Lingbao Catalogue. Lu created the earliest known catalogue of Daoist texts, which was titled the *Sandong jingshu mulu* (Catalogue of the Scriptures and Writings of the Three Caverns). It was presented to Emperor Ming (r. 465–72) of the Liu-Song dynasty (420–79) in 471.

Various earlier editions preceded the compilation of the "received Daoist Canon," a term that refers to the edition compiled during the Ming dynasty. This edition survives into the modern world and remains the primary textual source for the academic study of Daoism. The received Daoist Canon technically consists of two collections: the *Zhengtong daozang* (Daoist Canon of the Zhengtong Reign) and *Xu daozang* (Supplement to the Daoist Canon). Dated to 1445 and consisting of 5,318 scrolls, the former was compiled under the direction of Zhang Yuchu (1361–1410) and Zhang Yuqing (d. 1426), the forty-third and forty-fourth Celestial Master, respectively, and Ren Ziyuan (fl. 1400–22), the general intendant of Mount Wudang (Hubei), with the imperial patronage of the Yongle Emperor (Chengzu; r. 1403–24). Dating to 1607 and consisting of 240 scrolls, the *Xu daozang* was compiled under the direction of Zhang Guoxiang (d. 1611), the fiftieth Celestial Master, with the imperial patronage of Emperor Shenzong (r. 1572–1619).

The central organizing principle for Daoist textual collections is a tripartite classification system known as the Three Caverns (*sandong*). Dating from at least as early as the fifth century, the designation imitates the Three Vehicles of Buddhism and originally referred to three distinct scriptural or revelatory traditions: (1) Cavern Perfection (*dongzhen*), corresponding to the Highest Clarity movement; (2) Cavern Mystery (*dongxuan*), corresponding to the Numinous Treasure movement; and (3) Cavern Spirit (*dongshen*), corresponding to the Sanhuang (Three Sovereigns) movement.

Each "cavern" is further divided into 12 Sections (*shier bu*). After the first half of the sixth century, when there was an increase in the number and diversity of Daoist texts, four supplementary divisions were developed. These are the so-called Four Supplements (*sifu*). Given the continuous addition of new Daoist texts, these divisions prove relatively unhelpful with respect to the received Daoist Canon, although they do provide some insight into an earlier structure and underlying substrate.

The received, Ming-dynasty Daoist Canon in total consists of 1,487 texts. This Daoist textual collection is usually cited according to one of two numbering systems, namely, the Harvard Yenching Index (1935), compiled by Weng Dujian and abbreviated as "HY," or the *Concordance du Tao Tsang* (1975), compiled Kristofer Schipper and his colleagues and abbreviated "CT" or "DZ." The received Daoist Canon also exists in the modern world in a variety of mechanically reproduced editions, with the two most prominent ones being a 60-volume version published in Taiwan and a 36-volume edition published in mainland China. There are also various "extra-canonical" or "supplemental" Daoist textual collections (Komjathy 2002).

Further reading

Kirkland, Russell. 2004, *Taoism: The Enduring Tradition*. London and New York: Routledge.

Kohn, Livia. 2004 (2001), *Daoism and Chinese Culture*, 2nd rev. edn. Cambridge, MA: Three Pines Press.

Komjathy, Louis. 2013, *The Daoist Tradition: An Introduction*. London and New York: Bloomsbury Academic.

Miller, James. 2003, *Daoism: A Short Introduction*. Oxford: Oneworld.

CHAPTER TWO

Community

Community, especially place-specific community, is a major value and defining characteristic of the Daoist tradition. This is so much the case that Daoists frequently understand the entire religious community and tradition as the "Daoist body." Daoist community and social organization include hermits, householders, and monastics. Viewed from a more encompassing perspective, the Daoist community includes ascetics, recluses, families, villages, urban associations, as well as networks of temples and monasteries. Within different Daoist movements and lineages, one finds diverse ideals of social participation: from renunciants living in mountain seclusion through married householder priests ministering to local communities to monks and nuns inhabiting hermitages and monasteries. There are thus various Daoist models of participation, and Daoism is one of the more inclusive religious traditions in terms of diverse forms of inter-subjective being. Of these, following traditional Chinese values, a family-centered model of community has been the primary one throughout Daoist history, but Daoists have also viewed "family" along more spiritual and lineal lines.

Thus, one name for the Daoist tradition is the "Family of the Dao" (*daojia*).

Daoists have also had diverse views with respect to social engagement and political involvement. Some Daoists have rejected conventional social values, including concern for society in general, and have instead chosen to retreat from the mundane world. Others have been committed to various forms of social engagement and participation. On the most complex structural level, Daoists have envisioned a Daoist-inspired society overseen by a Daoist sage-king, characterized by Great Peace, and even culminating in a Daoist theocracy. That is, some Daoists have had utopian visions and imagined a government aligned with the Dao, informed by Daoist values, and overseen by Daoists. Court Daoists have also worked throughout Chinese history to secure aristocratic and imperial patronage, both for themselves, larger temple networks, and the tradition as a whole. On a more personal and grassroots level, Daoists have emphasized "teachers" as primary, and such individuals have been recognized as one the external Three Treasures. Such teachers include community elders who provide spiritual direction and training and who serve as embodiments of the Dao and the Daoist tradition. These individuals are exemplars for the Daoist community. From a Daoist perspective, such teachers and elders may also include immortals and Perfected. Just as traditional Chinese views of ancestors emphasize the "dead" as part of the community of the living, Daoists have recognized disembodied spirit-beings as possible sources of teachings and transmissions. In addition, Daoists have often emphasized the importance of spiritual friendship, of the beneficial influence of relationships rooted in affinity, care, and support. Daoists frequently speak of such friends as "Companions of the Way" (*daoyou*). These various expressions of Daoist community and models of social participation are embodied in hermits, householders, and monastics.

Hermits

Hermits are individuals who choose to live a solitary life in seclusion from the larger society. Hermits have been part of the Daoist tradition from its beginnings in the inner cultivation lineages of classical Daoism. An eremitic model of affiliation and participation, in turn, became central throughout Daoist history (Berkowitz 2000; Vervoorn 1990a). Although hermits tend to be viewed outside of the parameters of community and tradition, there are ways in which, as religious adherents, they are clearly located *within* community and tradition. Hermits frequently have understood themselves as part of a lineage of seclusion, as participating in a specific set of commitments. In addition, Daoist hermits often have lived in areas, whether urban or wild, inhabited by other hermits. While living alone, they have maintained relationships with other hermits and often with temple and monastic communities as well as lay supporters and disciples. Finally, within the larger parameters of the Daoist tradition, various hermits have been recognized as models of a particular Daoist way of life and as inspiration for deeper commitment and practice.

The earliest Daoist eremitic communities existed during the time of classical Daoism. These are the classical inner cultivation lineages already discussed in the previous chapter. Within the *Book of Master Zhuang*, we find evidence to support the existence of hermits and eremitic communities (Komjathy 2013b). Some passages indicate temporary seclusion, while others point toward a more permanent way of life. For example, in Chapter 7 of the Inner Chapters, Huzi (Gourd Master) manifests the formless state of "being-not-yet-emerged-from-the-ancestral" to the shaman Ji Xian, who subsequently flees in terror. Liezi (Master Lie), one of Huzi's disciples who had been momentarily enamored by Ji Xian's apparent power and prognostication skills, decides that he had never really learned anything.

Master Lie enters seclusion

He went home and for three years did not go out. He replaced his wife at the stove, fed the pigs as though he were feeding people, and showed no preferences in the things he did. He got rid of carving and polishing and returned to simplicity (*su*). He let himself stand alone like an uncarved block (*pu*). In the midst of entanglement he remained sealed, and in this Oneness he ended his life. (*Zhuangzi*, Chapter 7; cf. *Daode jing*, Chapter 19)

This passage parallels others wherein three years is identified as the ideal period of temporary seclusion for intensive training: Cook Ding (Chapter 3), Gengsang Chu (Chapter 23), as well as adept Huan and Zhuping Man (Chapter 32). As three years is the traditional Chinese mourning period, one might read these descriptions both literally and metaphorically. One goes into physical seclusion, which also involves the death of one's former self and mundane social concerns. For Master Lie, seclusion establishes a situation conducive for intensive Daoist cultivation. It results in mystical union with the Dao, which may or may not include physical death. Here one also notes that the classical Daoist eremitic ideal did not involve abandoning one's family and property. Such a renunciant model contradicts traditional Chinese values and appears later under the influence of Buddhism.

Seclusion is further emphasized in Chapters 23 and 28 of the *Book of Master Zhuang*, which contain the earliest Daoist occurrences of the phrase *huandu* (lit., "four *du* squared"). This is significant because in later organized Daoism, specifically during the late medieval period, *huandu* took on a technical meaning of "enclosed and shut-off" and "meditation enclosure" (Komjathy 2007a). In the relevant passages we find the expression of classical Daoist eremitic commitments, including architectural requirements: the passage in Chapter 28 states that the recluse lives in a hut constructed from natural, found, and discarded materials, including a thatched roof, woven-bramble door, mulberry-branch doorposts, and broken-jar windows. Such a life is informed by classical Daoist values of simplicity and disengagement from wealth, reputation, and social status. Many of the stories are also framed as critiques of political power and social position, with various rulers and officials visiting Daoist adepts only to be rebuffed. The *Book of Master Zhuang* also documents Daoist recluses associated with particular physical places such as Chu (present-day Hubei, Hunan, Henan, etc.; Chapter 4), the Hao and Pu rivers (Jiangsu; Chapter 17), the Liao river (Liaoning; Chapter 7), Lu (present-day Shandong; Chapters 20 and 28), Mount Gushe (Chapter 1), Mount Kongtong (possibly in Pingliang, Gansu; Chapter 11), Mount Kunlun (Chapters 6, 12, and 18), Mount Tai (Tai'an, Shandong; Chapter 29), Mount Weilei (Chapter 23), Mount Zhong (Chapter 28), and the Ying river (Chapter 28), a tributary of the Huai river (Henan, Anhui, Jiangsu). Interestingly, the *Book of Master Zhuang* utilizes physical places and non-physical places as symbolic of Daoist commitments and spiritual states. Some passages of the text also highlight the eremitic qualities of certain humans and animals, including fishermen (Chapters 17 and 31), firewood-gatherers and wood-cutters (Chapters 20, 26, and 29), warblers and moles (Chapter 1), as well as turtles (Chapters 17 and 26).

An eremitic model of Daoist community also was central in the early Complete Perfection movement (Eskildsen 2004; Komjathy 2007a, 2013a). At the age of 48, Wang Zhe, the founder, completely embraced the life of a Daoist renunciant and moved to Nanshi village, near present-day Huxian, Shaanxi. There he dug himself a "grave" that he named "Tomb for Reviving the Dead," often translated as "Tomb of the Living Dead." This was a mound of dirt several feet high, with a ten-foot high ceiling dug under it. Near the entrance to this underground enclosure Wang placed a plaque that read "Wang Haifeng" (Lunatic Wang). Wang spent three years in this enclosure, most likely engaging in ascetic practices, practicing internal alchemy, and exchanging poetry with those who came to visit him. In the autumn of 1163, Wang Zhe filled in his meditation enclosure and moved to the village of Liujiang (present-day Huxian), located in the Zhongnan mountains. There Wang trained with two hermits, He Dejin (Yuchan [Jade Toad]; d. 1170) and Li Lingyang (Lingyang [Numinous Yang]; d. 1189). It seems that the three renunciants lived on a small piece of land near a stream, where each had a separate grass hut. Wang engaged in solitary practice, focusing on asceticism and internal alchemy. After four years Wang Zhe burned down his hut, dancing while he watched it burn to the ground. This occurred in the summer of 1167, when Wang was 54 years old. Wang then traveled east, eventually arriving in Ninghai (present-day Muping, Shandong). There he built the Quanzhen an (Hermitage of Complete Perfection) on Ma Yu's property. He also trained a number of his senior disciples at Yanxia dong (Cavern of Misty Vapors) in the Kunyu mountains (near Weihai and Yantai, Shandong). The importance of seclusion for Daoist self-cultivation is emphasized in Discourse 1, "Living in Hermitages," of the *Lijiao shiwu lun* (Fifteen Discourses to Establish the Teachings), which is attributed to Wang Zhe.

Seclusion as religious requirement

All renunciants must first retreat to a hermitage. A hermitage is an enclosure, a place where the body may be attuned and entrusted. When the body is attuned and entrusted, the heart-mind gradually realizes serenity. Qi and spirit become harmonious and expansive. Then you may enter the perfect Dao. (*Lijiao shiwu lun*, DZ 1233, 1a)

Following Wang's death and interment in Liujiang in 1170, all of his senior disciples engaged in alchemical, ascetic, and eremitic training, both individual and communal. Each senior first-generation adherent also lived for some period of time as a solitary recluse. All of the first-generation Complete Perfection adherents engaged in solitary ascetic training, most often in mountain locales and hermitages. Hao Datong lived as a mendicant in Wozhou and practiced under the famous Zhaozhou Bridge (Zhaoxian, Hebei) for six years (1175–81). Liu Chuxuan lived as a wandering ascetic in the Luoyang environs (1171–75). Ma Yu practiced meditation enclosure throughout his life, and in his final two years he spent time in seclusion in the Jinyu an (Hermitage of Gold and Jade; in Huangxian, Shandong). Qiu Chuji did solitary practice first at Panxi (1173–81) and then in the mountainous gorges of Longmen dong (Dragon Gate Grotto; near present-day Xinjichuan and Longxian, Shaanxi), training at various times for possibly the next ten years. Sun Buer moved to Luoyang in 1179, where she trained with a female Daoist recluse from Henan named Feng Xiangu (Immortal Maiden Feng; fl. 1145–79). According to one Daoist hagiography, Feng lived in an upper cave and had Sun live in the lower one. Sun practiced and taught there until her death in 1182. After the three-year mourning period for Wang Zhe, Tan Chuduan lived as an urban recluse in Luoyang, Henan, spending time in both Chaoyuan gong (Palace for Attending to the Origin) and the more remote Yunxi an (Hermitage of Cloudy Ravines). Finally, Wang Chuyi engaged in intensive ascetic practice for nine years (1168–77) in Yunguang dong (Cavern of Cloud-like Radiance) of Mount Tiecha (Wendeng, Shandong). Extant Complete Perfection hagiographies contain various stories and miraculous deeds related to the early adepts during these times and in these places. It also should be mentioned that these bio-geographical (geo-biographical) moments included spiritual direction of disciples as well as the composition of voluminous amounts of poetry.

The Complete Perfection case is instructive on multiple levels. It reveals some of the specifics of ascetic training, including the importance of place, seclusion, spiritual direction, spiritual friendship, and intensive training. In addition, Complete Perfection began as a small eremitic community emphasizing ascetic and alchemical praxis. It then became a regional community in Shandong and Shaanxi, which included both fully committed renunciants and lay members. The next phase involved a transition from a regional religious movement to national monastic order. It is especially noteworthy that late medieval Complete Perfection monasteries not only institutionalized asceticism and eremiticism, but also retained those early commitments, forms of practice, and communal dimensions. Many early Complete Perfection monasteries incorporated rows of meditation enclosures into their architecture designs, and these meditation rooms were used for solitary and intensive meditation during *huandu* retreats. Such winter retreats usually occurred from the winter solstice to the end of the lunar New Year period and lasted for 100 days.

Householders

The eremitic model is only one of many forms of Daoist community and social organization. In fact, the dominant form of Daoist community is probably that of the householder living among other householders. Although the category of householder ("laity") is often contrasted with renunciant and monastic, here it simply designates individuals who marry and have families. It is a family-centered form of social organization and parallels dominant Chinese values rooted in Confucianism. It is also congruent with Mahāyāna Buddhist ideals, such as those expressed by the enlightened lay Buddhist in the *Vimalakīrti Sūtra*. In the case of Daoism, many householder communities include ordained, married priests as well as individuals and families living a committed religious life. Such patterns of adherence frequently revolve around specific values and ethical commitments.

In the early Celestial Masters movement, the Daoist community centered on a hierarchically organized theocracy, a semi-independent state (Shu) oriented toward the Dao, organized according to Daoist commitments, and informed by Daoist religious views. Early Celestial Masters Daoism benefited from a variety of political circumstances, including the decline of centralized Han power and the movement's relative geographical remoteness. The same was true of the early Complete Perfection community's location in Shandong during the decline of the Jurchen-Jin dynasty.

The Celestial Masters movement began with a revelation from Lord Lao, the deified Laozi and personification of the Dao, to Zhang Daoling in 142 CE. During Lord Lao's revelation, Zhang was appointed as terrestrial representative, the "Celestial Master," and given healing powers as a sign of his empowerment. The position in turn became patrilineal, passing from Zhang Daoling to his son Zhang Heng and then to his grandson Zhang Lu. The Celestial Masters established 24 "parishes" or "dioceses" with hierarchically ranked followers, wherein the so-called libationers were the highest (Kleeman 2012; Verellen 2003) (Figure 2.1). The intent was to establish "people of the Dao" and "seed people" who would populate an earth made ritually and morally pure.

In the early Celestial Masters, the Celestial Master was the highest socio-political and religious position filled by a single male of the Zhang family. It was patrilineal and hereditary: it passed

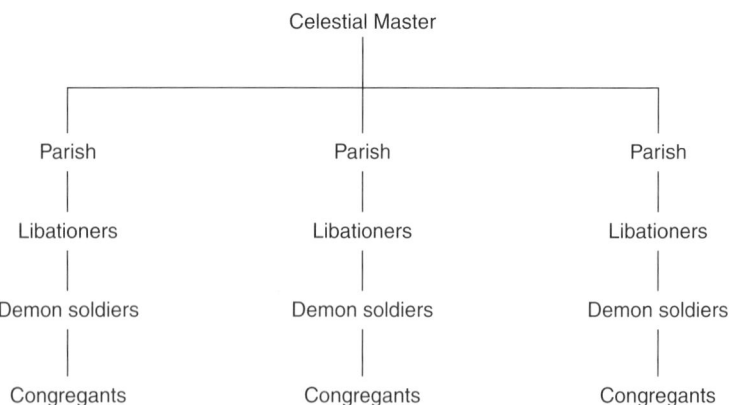

FIGURE 2.1 *Early Celestial Masters Community Organization.*

from the senior male leader (father or elder brother) to next senior male heir (eldest son or brother) in the Zhang family. This remained the case into later and modern Daoist history, though the lineage was disrupted and then reconstructed during the Tang dynasty (Kirkland 2004; Kohn and Kirkland 2000). The libationers were the highest-ranking community members below the Celestial Master and the Zhang family, and they reported directly to the Celestial Master. The libationers were the equivalent of ordained community priests, and they served as leaders of 24 parishes. Their rank was based on the degree of adherence, ordination level with accompanying registers, and ritual attainments. The registers were lists of spirit generals that Celestial Master leaders could use for healing, protection, and exorcism. At the next level of the social organization, demon soldiers were meritorious leaders of households who represented smaller units in the Celestial Masters community. With the exception of the Celestial Master himself, all leadership positions could be filled by men or women, Han Chinese or ethnic minorities (Kleeman 1998). In fact, some evidence suggests that the ideal model for priests was a married couple performing ritual together, thus expressing an embodied balance between yin and yang. At the bottom of the hierarchically ordered organization were congregants or ordinary adherents, who were again organized and counted according to households. Each of these had to contribute rice or its equivalent in silk, paper, brushes, ceramics, or handicrafts. Each Celestial Masters member, from childhood to adulthood, also underwent formal initiations at regular intervals and received the above-mentioned registers, including 75 for unmarried people and 150 for married couples.

Early Celestial Masters Daoism is noteworthy for its influence on later Daoist models of participation and social organization. First, it appears that the position of Celestial Master was modeled on (or designed to replace?) the Chinese emperor as Son of Heaven who held the Mandate of Heaven. This position was viewed through a Daoist lens wherein the political leader should be a high-level Daoist practitioner (sage-king) as described in the *Scripture on the Dao and Inner Power*. There was thus a reciprocal and symbiotic relationship between the Celestial Master as community leader and the community. Expressing a vision of communal welfare, each was responsible for the well-being of the other and for the community as a whole. Rather than viewing early Celestial Masters grain collection as a "tax" or "membership fee," it is probably more accurate to understand it as a "food distribution system." It was a form of charity that supported the community as a whole. It was used to help other members in need and to ensure social harmony. Here we find a specific example of Daoist utopianism, which also appears on a smaller scale in classical Daoism, especially among its Primitivist strain. Second, the early Celestial Masters movement attempted to create a community oriented toward the Dao. According to its own founding account, the inspiration for the movement came from Lord Lao as a personal manifestation of the Dao. Under a generous reading, the early community accepted the direction of that divine communication through Zhang Daoling and his successors. These Daoist religious leaders in turn attempted to guide a community to maintain and propagate Daoist religious commitments, values, and ideals. Finally, and perhaps most importantly, the Celestial Masters movement established a hierarchically organized community, wherein deeper levels of religious commitment and degrees of adherence led to higher positions in the community. That is, as is the case in most traditional Daoist communities and forms of social organization, early Celestial Masters Daoism was an elder-centered system. Here "elder" is not solely a matter of age seniority; it is also based on level of commitment, training, and expertise.

The early, Shu-based Celestial Masters community under the leadership of Zhang Lu, the third Celestial Master, was eventually conquered by General Cao Cao (155–220) in 215 CE. Cao Cao, who was instrumental in laying the foundations for the Cao Wei dynasty (220–65), then forced members of the Tianshi community to migrate to different parts of China. This geographical diffusion was pivotal for the emergence of subsequent Daoist movements, and for the development of a more diverse, integrated, and large-scale Daoist tradition.

In terms of Daoist social organization, Celestial Masters dissemination eventually led to a division within the community between the so-called Northern and Southern Celestial Masters (Kohn 2000b; Nickerson 2000), so named because of their respective locations in northern and southern China. A descendant of a Northern Celestial Masters family in Chang'an, Shaanxi, Kou Qianzhi, was a pivotal figure in the formation of the first formal Daoist theocracy (government ruled through the divine), which occurred through an alliance with the Toba (Northern) Wei dynasty

(Mather 1979). After going into seclusion on Songshan (Mount Song; Dengfeng, Henan), Kou supposedly received a revelation from Lord Lao. In 415, he received a divinely transmitted text titled *Yunzhong yinsong xinke jiejing* (Precept Scripture of the New Code, Recited in the Clouds; abbr. "New Code"; partially lost; DZ 785), which contained a set of precepts for a newly envisioned Daoist community. According to this revelation, Kou was to replace the Zhang family as the Celestial Master, abolish some of their received practices, and establish a community based on 36 rules. In 424, Kou obtained a court audience with Emperor Taiwu (408–52; r. 424–52) and gained support from the Prime Minister Cui Hao (381–450). Kou and Cui convinced the ruler to put the "New Code" into practice and thus established the Daoist theocracy of the Northern Wei. Kou became the official leader with the title of Celestial Master, while his disciples were invited to the capital to perform regular rituals. Within the early Toba Wei theocracy, Kou lived in a converted-palace monastery, the Chongxu si (Monastery for Venerating Emptiness), in the capital with some 120 disciples and administrators. In 431, Daoist institutions, including temples, ordained clergy, moral rules, and rituals, were also established in the provinces, thus extending the reach of Daoist and state control farther into the countryside. The pinnacle of the theocracy occurred in 440, when the emperor underwent Daoist investiture rites and changed the reign title to Taiping zhenjun (Perfect Lord of Great Peace). Following Kou's death in 448, Daoism eventually fell out of favor, and the Daoist theocratic experiment came to an end, with Buddhism taking its place.

The Northern Wei Daoist theocracy provides another glimpse into forms of Daoist community and social organization. Here we find an example of state-sponsored Daoism, specifically through the systematic integration of Daoist religious institutions, clergy, and values into the larger society and political system. One key issue, yet to be adequately explored, is the actual political policies, the larger societal institutions and practices, which were inspired by Daoism. What actually occurred on the ground, and how did it affect the daily lives of the average person? To what degree and in what ways was it "Daoist"? Historically, many court Daoists sought imperial patronage, both for themselves and the larger tradition, while many Chinese rulers and governments sought support and legitimation through Daoism. Such an expression of

Daoist community, still rooted in a certain utopian vision, reveals a political dimension. In this respect, Daoists competed with the dominant Confucian political project and with the increasingly powerful Buddhist monasteries.

The search for imperial patronage had diverse motivations and dimensions. Sometimes it involved an integrated vision for Chinese society and the Daoist tradition, but at other times, it involved intra-Daoist and inter-religious competition, especially with Buddhists. Some prominent examples include the alliance of the Southern Celestial Masters with the Liu-Song dynasty (Bokenkamp 1997), partially as a result of Celestial Masters competition with the Great Clarity and Highest Clarity Daoist movements; the Tang dynasty elevation of Daoism to state religion, partially as a result of the imperial Li family tracing their ancestral line back to Li Er (Laozi) (Kohn and Kirkland 2000); Yuan dynasty support of the Complete Perfection monastic order, which was eventually lost through a series of Buddho-Daoist debates and subsequent anti-Daoist edicts (Komjathy 2007a); and Qing dynasty support of the Dragon Gate lineage of Complete Perfection (Komjathy 2008c).

In early medieval China, Buddhism gained a stronger role in Chinese culture and society. Han people, the indigenous ethnic majority of traditional China, found Buddhism increasingly attractive, primarily due to its alternative soteriological model and promise of relief from everyday suffering, and large numbers began converting to Buddhism. In addition, Buddhism provided a new model of community and social organization, namely, monasticism. Here we should remember that the model of eremitic communities already had a long and revered history in China, but, in keeping with traditional Chinese values, rejection of family and social reproduction (celibacy) was largely unheard of. Under Buddhist influence, Daoists began adopting and experimenting with quasi-monastic and monastic communities. Tao Hongjing's Highest Clarity community at Maoshan (Mount Mao; Jurong, Jiangsu) is one representative expression of Daoist quasi- or proto-monasticism (Strickmann 1977, 1979). Tao Hongjing was a descendent of Tao Kedou, who was allied through marriage with the Xu family of the original Highest Clarity revelations. Tao Hongjing ranks as one of the most famous Daoists in Chinese history because of his collection and identification of the original Highest Clarity manuscripts, his development of a critical pharmacology, and his commitment to alchemical experimentation, especially through the search for external elixirs. While mourning the death of his father (484–86), Tao received Daoist training under Sun Youyue (399–489), abbot of the Xingshi guan (Abode for a Flourishing World) in the capital and a former senior disciple of Lu Xiujing. It was during this time that Tao first saw a Highest Clarity manuscript. Tao was enchanted by the calligraphic style and would dedicate a substantial portion of his life to collecting, transcribing, and classifying the extant Highest Clarity textual corpus. Over the next five years, he traced the manuscript owners and collected various manuscripts, especially those associated with Yang Xi and the Xu family.

Tao Hongjing retired to Mount Mao in 492 at the age of 36. There he lived in Huayang guan (Abode of Flourishing Yang) with some of his direct disciples as well as among other Highest Clarity adherents. The Mount Mao community included solitary and celibate members as well as communal and married members. That is, there were different paths to spiritual attainment, and renunciant and married adherents lived side by side. While it is unclear what Tao himself thought about these different models, he must have been fairly supportive. This is based on the fact that Zhou Ziliang (fl. 480–520), one of his senior disciples, moved to Mount Mao with his entire family. In addition, as the mountain grew in fame, Mount Mao became an object of pilgrimage and tourism for both the pious and curious. The mountain was only some 30 miles from the imperial capital; writing in 499, Tao describes the multitudes that annually flocked there on the two festival days associated with the Mao brothers. The community of permanent residents also continued to grow, with the mountain becoming populated by entire households, including young children. Tao's seclusion involved residence in a mountain temple, study and compilation of Daoist scriptures, and decoction of elixirs of immortality. In the process, Tao describes his aesthetic appreciation of the landscape and the esoteric topography of Mount Mao as particularly conducive for the compounding elixirs. These two dimensions commingle in Tao's frequent visits to a northward ridge and an adjacent scenic spot with a bubbling spring.

Thus, on the Mount Mao of Tao Hongjing, we find an inclusive, place-specific Daoist community. This community included men, women, children, and domestic animals. It included individuals following eremitic, quasi-monastic, or householder religious paths.

It allowed space for various Daoist activities: from scholarship and meditation, through alchemical experimentation, to popular devotion and pilgrimage. Such, perhaps, is the most Daoist of models of community and social organization. Respecting traditional Chinese values and rooted in traditional Chinese culture, Mount Mao Daoists accepted both individualistic and family-centered paths to the Dao. As an expression of foundational Daoist values and views, the Mount Mao community was inclusive, flexible, minimalist, and relatively egalitarian in terms of recognizing potential. At the same time, there were clearly degrees of adherence and commitment. The community was organized hierarchically, recognizing differences of affinity, aptitude, and effort. We must also note that there are other Daoist minority and dissenting views that understand spiritual capacities as endowed, as is the case in some alchemical discussions of "immortal bones." While there are many paths to the Dao, some are recognized as more efficacious, advanced, and esteemed.

The Mount Mao community also reveals some of the challenges of inclusion, especially in terms of a daily life of cohabitation and shared place. Fame and public interest frequently lead to the diminishment of the very aesthetic and spiritual dimensions that created elevation. People came to Mount Mao with different motivations, including materialist, tourist, devotional, and soteriological ones. Following a pattern in many contexts and traditions, increases in membership led to a decrease in commitment among the Mount Mao community. This was so much the case that Tao Hongjing relocated to more secluded parts of the mountains later in life, and eventually departed incognito to an area farther east where he hoped to complete his alchemical transformation.

Monastics

Daoist monasticism developed under the influence of Buddhism, which had been introduced to China during the first and second centuries CE and became increasingly influential from the fourth century forward. Both the Northern Celestial Masters community of Kou Qianzhi and the Mount Mao community of Tao Hongjing were quasi- or proto-monastic. These Daoist communities included unmarried, celibate practitioners, married priests and religious administrators, and disciples of various persuasions. They were thus not monastic in the strict sense of the word. They were not religious communities where celibate monastics (monks and/or nuns) lived according to a strict rule and schedule in a tightly knit religious community. The earliest Daoist monastery was roughly contemporaneous with the Mount Mao community (Kohn 2003, 2004b). After the Toba-Wei theocracy ended, Louguan (Lookout Tower Monastery; a.k.a., Louguan tai; Zhouzhi, Shaanxi) rose to become the major Daoist center in northern China and, in the early sixth century, also served as a refuge for southern Daoists who were persecuted under Emperor Wu (r. 464–549) of the Liang dynasty. Located in the foothills of the Zhongnan mountains and still a flourishing Complete Perfection Daoist monastery today, Lookout Tower Monastery was identified by Daoists as the place where Laozi transmitted the *Scripture on the Dao and Inner Power* to Yin Xi, the Guardian of the Pass. This version of the transmission legend arose in the mid-fifth century through Yin Tong (398–499?), a self-identified descendent of Yin Xi and owner of the estate. During the early sixth century, a group of Daoists, primarily members of the Northern Celestial Masters, apparently lived within a monastic framework, specifically according to ethical guidelines, communal celibate living, and standardized daily schedule. Members of the early Lookout Tower Monastery practiced longevity techniques, observed the five precepts adopted from Buddhism, venerated Laozi and the *Scripture on the Dao and Inner Power*, and honored Yin Xi as their first patriarch. They also composed and compiled various texts, such as the influential *Taishang Laojun jiejing* (Precept Scripture of the Great High Lord Lao; DZ 784). Regardless of the degree to which this Daoist community was fully monastic, the sacred site became one of the most important Daoist monasteries from the Northern Zhou dynasty and Tang dynasty to today.

Lookout Tower Monastery and other early Daoist monasteries prepared the way for later fully developed monastic systems, such as those of the Tang, late Song and Yuan, and Qing. While the actual social organization of the early Louguan community remains unclear, we have detailed information on later Daoist monastic life (Kohn 2003, 2004b, 2004c). Medieval Daoist monasticism was characterized by distinctive ordination rites, training regimens, distinctive vestments, ritual implements, as well as buildings and compounds. During the Tang, there was a nationwide monastic system, with large and small monasteries inhabited by celibate monks and nuns adhering to ethical codes and following a standardized daily schedule. In this way, Daoist monasticism paralleled the Chinese Buddhist system. Daily monastic life included hygiene practices, abstinence, meal regulations, ceremonial meals and associated foods, eating procedures, ritual performances, obeisances, and audiences with senior monastics, especially one's spiritual director.

While fully systematized Daoist monasticism thus emerged during the Tang dynasty, the most influential Daoist monastic tradition, Complete Perfection, was established during the late Song-Jin period and early Yuan (Komjathy 2013a). Complete Perfection monasteries and temples were established throughout northern China and its clerical membership grew, so that by the late thirteenth century there were some 4,000 Complete Perfection sacred sites and 20,000 monks and nuns. From records dating to the Yuan dynasty we know that late medieval Complete Perfection monastic life was characterized by intensive meditation, spiritual direction, and a set daily schedule. According to the *Quanzhen qinggui* (Pure Regulations of Complete Perfection; DZ 1235), the standard daily monastic schedule was as follows:

3 a.m.–5 a.m. Wake-up

5 a.m.–7 a.m. Morning meal

7 a.m.–9 a.m. Group meditation

9 a.m.–11 a.m. Individual meditation

11 a.m.–1 p.m. Noon meal

1 p.m.–3 p.m. Group meditation

3 p.m.–5 p.m. Individual meditation

5 p.m.–7 p.m. Formal lecture or interviews

7 p.m.–9 p.m. Group meditation and tea

9 p.m.–11 p.m. Individual meditation

11 p.m.–1 a.m. Scripture recitation

1 a.m.–3 a.m. Personal time

(DZ 1235, 6a)

Some Daoist monasteries functioned as semi-independent communities, while others were part of a vast, interconnected network of temples. Like the Mount Mao community of Tao Hongjing, many of these temples attracted tourists and pilgrims, and some received imperial recognition. Patronage from lay supporters, regional magistrates and aristocratic families, and the imperial court was essential. It is one thing to attempt to maintain a single monastery, but ensuring the flourishing of a nationwide monastic system with thousands of monks and nuns is a different matter entirely. As court Daoist and monastic leaders formed working relationships and political connections with emperors and officials, state regulation also became a social dimension of Daoist monasticism. For example, during the Ming dynasty, Emperor Taizu (1328–98; r. 1368–98) established the Xuanjiao yuan (Court of the Mysterious Teachings), an independent body that dealt with the administration of all Daoists throughout the empire (De Bruyn 2000). This court was abolished in 1371, after which Daoists were governed by the Daolu si (Bureau of Daoist Registration). This organization was a subdivision of the Libu (Ministry of Rites), responsible for the supervision of all levels of Daoist activity. It controlled the Daoji si (Bureaus of Daoist Institutions) on the provincial level, Daozheng si (Bureaus of Political Supervision of Daoists) on the prefectural level, and Daohui si (Bureaus of Daoist Assemblies) on the district level. There were, in turn, various policies associated with these state-sponsored administrative agencies. In addition to regulating the ages and total numbers of Daoists, the Ming administration continued the system of ordination certificates first established during the Tang, through which the state certified monks and nuns after an official examination taken after three years of study. The certificates contained the names of the monastic, his or her religious affiliation, date of ordination, as well as their various appellations. The Ming administration also created the Zhouzhi ce (Register of Complete Comprehension), an official list that contained the names of all Daoists who had ever passed time in any monastery. The Qing dynasty continued the Board of Rites and Bureau of Daoist Registration (Esposito 2000), and in certain ways it was the precursor to the modern PRC Bureau of Religious Affairs. In these bureaucratic institutions, we find another dimension of Daoist social organization, namely its ties to the Chinese imperial court and state control.

Further reading

Despeux, Catherine and Livia Kohn. 2003, *Women in Daoism*. Cambridge, MA: Three Pines Press.

Goossaert, Vincent. 2007, *The Taoists of Peking, 1800–1949: A Social History of Urban Clerics*. Cambridge, MA: Harvard University Asia Center/Harvard University Press.

Porter, Bill. 1993, *Road to Heaven: Encounters with Chinese Hermits*. San Francisco, CA: Mercury House.

Schipper, Kristofer. 1993, *The Taoist Body*. trans. Karen C. Duval. Berkeley, CA: University of California Press.

CHAPTER THREE

Identity

Daoist religious identity and adherence include many "ways to affiliation." "Ways to affiliation" refers to the traditional ways in which individuals have become Daoists. Such paths also relate to the ways in which Daoism has become a tradition, especially the emergence of new movements and lineages. In addition, it draws our attention to the ways in which Daoists have established and extended parameters of inclusion and participation. Here it is important to recognize that Daoists are adherents of Daoism, members of the indigenous Chinese and now global religious community. We may, in turn, make a distinction between "Daoist adherents," those with formal commitment to and/or affiliation with the religious tradition, and "Daoist sympathizers," those who find some aspect of that tradition appealing. While Daoists are individuals for whom the Dao is their most important concern, an orientation toward the Dao is a necessary, but not a sufficient condition for being a Daoist. As Daoism is not characterized by orthodoxy, the parameters of participation and inclusion are varied and multifaceted.

Daoist ways to affiliation are diverse and complex. While there can be no doubt that lineage and ordination have occupied a major place in the Daoist tradition and throughout Daoist history, overemphasis on these institutional dimensions of Daoist religious identity may obscure one's understanding. Considered comprehensively, Daoism is a tradition comprised of ascetics, hermits, ordained householder and celibate priests, monastics, as well as the larger lay membership, and there are diverse models of community within its contours. While many Daoist priests and monastics have located themselves in specific movements and lineages, and in the process privileged lineage affiliation and ordination, many "ordinary Daoists" did not. These were individuals and families who made up the vast majority of Daoists throughout Chinese history, and who supported the clerical elite, temple networks, and monasteries. While little has been written on the lives of "ordinary Daoists," their own paths into and within the tradition deserve consideration. This includes the ways in which they expressed their own religiosity and sense of commitment. In many cases, this occurred under the guidance of Daoist elders and teachers as well as established Daoist families. However, we do not know the specific motivations for their affiliation. Much of their lives probably centered on the cultivation of basic Daoist commitments, including ethical reflection and application, and on involvement with the larger Daoist community. In this respect, we must recognize that the situation of Daoism in traditional Chinese contexts was radically different than in the contemporary world, wherein Daoism has become a global religious tradition. Within the global tradition, specifically with respect to patterns of conversion, we must recognize affinity, orientation, practice, study, and transmission as central. At the same time, lineage, revelation, and ordination are key features of Daoist religious identity, adherence, and affiliation.

Lineage

Lineage has occupied a central place in the Daoist religious tradition from its earliest beginnings in the Warring States period. Here lineage refers to a particular line of spiritual ancestry, a line passed from teachers to students. In Daoism, this line may be biological, spiritual, and/or institutional. Daoist lineage is about connection, connection to the Dao and to a specific religious community and teacher. It is genealogical in the sense that one remembers and remains committed to ancestral origins. In this way, Daoist lineage affiliation and recollection might be understood as one expression of the Daoist principle of "returning to the Source" (*guigen*)—the source of the teachings, the community, and the tradition.

Like any religious tradition, Daoism may be mapped according to its conception of the sacred, the names that designate that tradition, as well as the specific movements that comprise the tradition. The diagram of Daoist locatedness below is a cosmological one that privileges the Dao, the sacred or ultimate concern of Daoists (Figure 3.1). From this perspective, the Dao manifests in/as/through the cosmos, world, life, and self. This suggests that it is possible for "non-Daoists" to have an affinity with the Dao, but there are specific paths and forms of relationship that are specifically Daoist, that are connected to the Daoist tradition. It is through this tradition that the Dao is re-membered and expressed. Moreover, Daoist communities provide spiritual guidance for "returning to

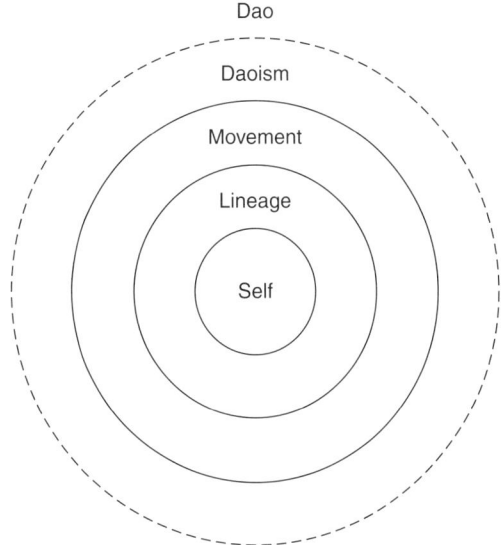

FIGURE 3.1 *Daoist Locatedness.*

the Source." Viewed from a Daoist perspective, the Dao is also that from which of all individual beings originate and in which they participate. The Dao is their innate nature. Finally, viewed from a socio-historical and cultural perspective, the Dao might be located in the innermost circle, as it is a Chinese character (道) and Daoist cosmological and theological conception. To invoke it is to invoke the tradition on some level.

The traditions of the Dao, the specific communities, movements and lineages that comprise Daoism, also receive other designations. These are usually associated with particular "founders," revelations, scriptures, and often places. Such movements are streams flowing into and out of the larger tradition, with the latter comparable to a river flowing toward the ocean of the Dao. Lineages are the tributaries that flow into and out of the streams of the Daoist movements. These are usually associated with major teachers or systems of practice. Members of specific movements and lineages in turn often understand their affiliation in terms of ancestry.

The earliest evidence of Daoist lineages is found in the *Book of Master Zhuang* and other texts of classical Daoism. These are the inner cultivation lineages, the master–disciple communities, of classical Daoism, and careful study and reading show that they were at least as diverse as the movements of organized Daoism. In addition to the textual evidence discussed below, we know about these earliest Daoist lineages through the compilation and transmission of classical Daoist texts. This point specifically relates to the *Book of Venerable Masters* and the *Book of Master Zhuang*, both of which are anonymous multi-vocal anthologies with a variety of textual and historical layers.

One extremely noteworthy feature of the *Book of Master Zhuang* is the presence of various teachers and students. Some key Daoist masters who appear in the text include Songrongzi (Master Dwelling-in-Beauty; Chapter 1), Liezi (Master Lie; Chapter 1), Lian Shu (Joined Brother; Chapter 1), Nanguo Ziqi (Adept Dissimilarity of South Wall; Chapters 2, 4, and 24), Changwuzi (Master Enduring Hibiscus; Chapter 2), Cook Ding (Chapter 3), Bohun Wuren (Uncle Obscure Non-identity; Chapters 5, 21, and 32), Nüyu (Woman Yu; Chapter 6), Huzi (Master Gourd; Chapter 7), Thief Zhi (Chapters 10 and 29), Guangchengzi (Master Expansive Completion; Chapter 11), Tian Zifang (Adept Square Field; Chapter 21), Gengsang Chu (Chapter 23), Xu Wugui (Ghostless

Xu; Chapter 24), Zeyang (Sudden Yang; Chapter 25), Lie Yukou (Chapter 32), and, of course, Lao Dan (a.k.a. Laozi; Chapters 3, 5, 7, 11, 12, 14, etc.) and Zhuang Zhou himself (see also Mair 1998). Of these, Ziqi is identified as a member of the Nanguo (South Wall) community, which also included other adepts such as Ziyou (Adept Wanderer; Chapter 2), Zikui (Adept Sunflower; Chapter 6), and Yanchengzi (Master Flourishing Completion; Chapter 24), an alternate name for Ziyou. One may, in turn, create corresponding lineage charts.

Now, if we wish to understand classical Daoism on a deeper level, specifically in terms of lineage-based teachings, we would read the relevant texts much more carefully. For example, when Nanbo Zikui (Adept Sunflower of Southern Elders) asks the female master Nüyu (Woman Yu), rendered as "Woman Crookback" by Burton Watson and also translatable as "Feminine Self-reliance" or the "female recluse," about Daoist practice, she recounts her instructions to Buliangyi (Divining Beam-support).

Nüyu's instructions to Buliangyi

I began explaining and kept at him for three days, and after that he was able to put the world outside himself. When he had put the world outside himself, I kept at him for seven more days, and after that he was able to put things outside himself. When he had put things outside himself, I kept at him for nine more days, and after that he was able to put life outside himself. After he had put life outside himself, he was able to achieve the brightness of dawn, and when he had achieved the brightness of dawn, he could see his own aloneness. After he had managed to see his own aloneness, he could do away with past and present, and after he had done away with past and present, he was able to enter where there is no life and no death. (*Zhuangzi*, Chapter 6; see also *Daode jing*, Chapter 20)

Following these practice instructions, most likely stages of realization attained through Daoist apophatic meditation, Adept Sunflower asks Woman Yu, "Where did you learn this?" The female Daoist elder in turn traces her lineage: It begins with

Yishi (Copying-the-Beginning); extends from Canliao (Merged Solitude) to Xuanming (Mysterious Obscurity), Yu'ou (According-with-Songs), Xuyi (Anticipated Application), Niexu (Whispered Oath), Zhanming (Revering Luminosity), and a grand-disciple of Luosong (Repeated-Recitation); and then becomes transmitted to a disciple of Fumo (Aided-by-Ink), who is the teacher of Woman Yu. It is open to debate if any of these names refer to real people; one might prefer to understand them as symbolic representations of spiritual insights and religious commitments. However, even if the names are imaginary, many of the stories and teachings appear to derive from actual master–disciple communities, from classical Daoist lineages. Especially noteworthy here is the fact that the text identifies the later part of the lineage as deriving from a "grand-disciple" (lit., "grandchild") of Luosong (Repeated-Recitation) and from a "disciple" (lit., "child") of Fumo (Aided-by-Ink). Here is a prototypical lineage construction that would become central in organized Daoism. In addition, a number of the classical Daoist masters receive various honorific titles designating an "elder."

Although the personages of the *Book of Master Zhuang* are often identified as "characters" in some kind of proto-fiction, I would thus suggest that in many cases they were either actual Daoist adepts or characters based on actual individuals, many of whom would have been community elders. It is especially noteworthy that we find the classical Chinese grammatical construction related to lineage connection: teachers are identified by their surname or religious name followed by "master" (zi), while their disciples are identified by a nickname preceded by "adept" (zi), the same character. That is, when one is a student, zi precedes a nickname; when one becomes a teacher, zi is attached to one's surname or religious name. This relationship is determined by context, whether textual or social.

These various details demonstrate that classical Daoism was a religious community, a series of master–disciple lineages. It consisted of individuals and communities, albeit diverse and only loosely associated ones, aimed at "cultivating the Dao." In this sense, they were individuals oriented toward the Dao ("Daoists") and part of an emerging tradition of the Dao ("Daoism"). That tradition had foundational views, values and commitments, practices, and models of attainment, some of which are discussed in the chapters of the present book. We might, in turn, understand the indigenous category of *daojia*, "Family of the Dao," as referring to these inner cultivation lineages. Evidence of its own sense of community, as an alternative to other early Chinese cultural movements, may be found in Chapters 15, 23, and 33 of the *Book of Master Zhuang* and in Chapter 41 of the *Scripture on the Dao and Inner Power*. The former includes a hierarchical ordering of practice models, with Chapter 15 beginning with five inferior forms of practice, including health and longevity practitioners, and culminating with the privileged and advocated Daoist approach. This is the classical Daoist commitment to apophatic meditation and mystical praxis. We also find an emphasis on the importance of practice and attainment in Chapter 41 of the *Scripture on the Dao and Inner Power*, wherein the most committed practitioners are characterized by consistent and prolonged training with an orientation toward the Dao.

The early Daoist community, like any religious community, consisted of people with varying degrees of affinity and commitment. So, we find some unnamed "venerable master" complaining, like so many Daoists after him, about his fellow adherents not understanding and practicing the teachings (*Daode jing*, Chapter 70). These adherents are referred to as "adepts" (*shi*), which eventually became the technical term for an ordained Daoist priest (*daoshi*) in organized Daoism. With various degrees of formality, lineage remained central to both early and later organized Daoism. Unfortunately, at present, we do not have much information on the fate of the classical inner cultivation lineages, including the degree to which such lineages survived into the Han dynasty. We do know that lineages and communities of Fangshi ("formula masters"), or magico-religious practitioners, occupied a central place in the Han (Csikszentmihalyi 2000, 2002; DeWoskin 1983), but little work has been done on the origins and influences of these networks.

Some hints at connections with classical Daoist lineages come from a number of sources and cultural developments. First, Lie Yukou ("Master Lie"), the figure mentioned in five chapters of the *Book of Master Zhuang*, became the basis of the pseudonymous *Liezi* (Book of Master Lie; DZ 733), which was most likely compiled around the third century CE. Second, the *Shenxian zhuan* (Biographies of Spirit Immortals), one of the most important early Daoist hagiographies (biographies of saints) partially compiled by Ge Hong, includes an entry on Guangchengzi (Master Expansive

Completion), a figure mentioned in the *Book of Master Zhuang*, the *Book of the Huainan Masters*, and later Ge's *Inner Chapters of Master Embracing Simplicity*. Moreover, in texts such as the second-century *Laozi bianhua jing* (Scripture on the Transformations of Laozi; DH 79; S. 2295), Guangchengzi became identified as an incarnation of Lord Lao, the deified Laozi.

Thirdly, Ge Hong also represents an important Daoist lineage. He was the grandnephew of Ge Xuan, a central figure in the formation of the Great Clarity movement of external alchemy and later associated with the Numinous Treasure movement. Ge Xuan traced his lineage through an obscure Fangshi named Zuo Ci. According to Ge Hong, the Great Clarity lineage was transmitted from Zuo Ci through Ge Xuan to Zheng Yin, Ge Hong's own master. These details draw our attention to two unanswered questions: (1) Who were Zuo Ci's teachers and how far back can this Fangshi lineage be traced? (2) Was the inclusion of Guangchengzi and similar figures in the *Biographies of Spirit Immortals* an attempt to claim ancestral connections with the classical Daoist inner cultivation lineages? If so, were these actual or retrospectively constructed?

While Masters Lie, Guangcheng, and Baopu are familiar names in Daoist history, there are also obscure and previously unidentified lineages. These lineages partially remain concealed in the annals of history because of various assumptions at work in Daoist Studies, most notably a neglect of continuities and connections among apparently distinct teachers, practitioners, and communities. For example, one possible bridge-figure between the classical inner cultivation lineages, Han-dynasty Fangshi lineages, and the beginnings of organized Daoism is Heshang gong (Master Dwelling-by-the-River). A semi-legendary figure, the real identity of Heshang gong is unknown, but he is identified as a recluse, most likely during the Later Han dynasty. He is most well known as the attributed author of the *Laozi zhangju* (Chapter-and-Verse Commentary on the *Laozi*; DZ 682), one of the most influential Daoist commentaries. Drawing upon the work of Alan Chan (1991b), the "legend of Heshang gong" points toward two distinct Daoist lineages that became conflated during the early medieval period. The first line is the most complex. It begins with Yue Yang (fl. 408 BCE), passes through Yue Yi (fl. 284 BCE), his ancestral descendent, Anqi Sheng (fl. 260 BCE), Ma Xigong (d.u.), Yue Xiagong (d.u.), Yue Jugong (Yue Chengong; fl. 230 BCE), and finally arrives at Tian Shu (fl. 210 BCE), who in turn becomes the teacher of Cao Can (d. 190 BCE).

There are a number of noteworthy dimensions of this lineage. First, Yue Yi was an adherent of Huang-Lao, a syncretic political philosophy that combined elements of Daoism and Legalism and that became highly influential during the Early Han dynasty. Second, Anqi Sheng was a famous Fangshi and legendary immortal who eventually became associated with both Great Clarity and Highest Clarity. That is, this lineage indicates multiple source-points and cross-pollination. As interesting in terms of geography and migration, the members of the Yue and Tian families eventually relocated to the state of Qi and Hanzhong. The former was the location of the Jixia Academy, which played a major role in the development of classical Daoism (Kirkland 2004; Roth 1999a). The latter was a key center of the early Celestial Masters movement (Kleeman 1998). All of these details point toward the importance of particular, previously unidentified Daoist families. As Alan Chan suggests, "the Way of the 'Old Lord' (Lao-chün Tao [Laojun dao]) as it is reflected in the Ho-shang Kung legend may be regarded as a transition from the Huang-Lao school of the early Han to the later Taoist religion" (1991b: 125).

The second line associated with Heshang gong traces the lineage from Xu Laile (d.u.) to Ge Xuan. As discussed above, Ge Xuan was a key figure in the emergence of Great Clarity. As is the case for Master Guangcheng, Ge Hong's *Biographies of Spirit Immortals* contains a biographical entry on Heshang gong. Regardless of the accuracy of the actual lineage, these details demonstrate a "sense of tradition" and further connections with Fangshi lines. All in all, the combined dimensions of the "legend of Heshang gong" reveal key lines of transmission and major Daoist families. One of these families, the Yue, goes back to a time contemporaneous with the classical Daoist inner cultivation lineages. Moreover, we find the intersection of ancestral lines, spiritual lineages, and geographical proximity among the Yue, Tian, Ge, and Li families. This occurred in Qi and Hanzhong, key locations for the emergence of organized Daoism. Moreover, the "legend of Heshang gong" includes the claim that the associated commentary on the *Scripture on the Dao and Inner Power* was transmitted to four individuals: Wu Guang (d.u.), Xianmen Zigao (d.u.), Qiuzi (d.u.), and Emperor Wen (r. 179–157 BCE), with

Xianmen Zigao and Qiuzi being major Fangshi (Chan 1991b: 123). Moreover, the *Gaoshi zhuan* (Biographies of Eminent Masters) identifies Heshang gong as "an ancestor of the Family of the Dao (*daojia zhi zong*)" (cited in Campany 2002: 307).

These are just some details that reveal the importance of lineage in the formative moments of organized Daoism and that hint at a greater degree of connection between the emergence of an institutionalized tradition and the earlier inner cultivation lineages. As discussed in previous chapters, most of the major Daoist movements trace their origins to specific teachers, including divine beings. With respect to early organized Daoism, there was also a sense of connection and succession among many of the most important movements (Figure 3.2).

During this period Daoists used the term *daojia* as a designation for the Daoist religious tradition in general and for the Daoist clergy in particular. On the one hand, Daoists were members of a spiritual lineage that emphasized the transmission of a tradition, but on the other hand, early organized Daoism was comprised of *actual families*. In keeping with the Chinese term, we might speak of these groups of ancestrally related individuals as "*families* of the Dao." In early organized Daoism, the Zhang family, associated with the hereditary, patrilineal position of the Celestial Master, became

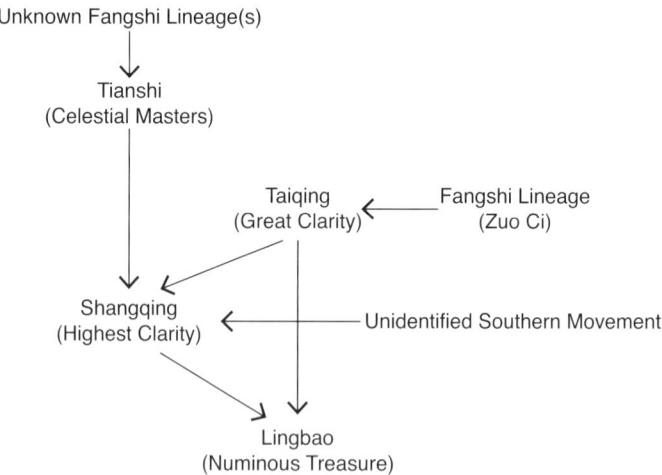

FIGURE 3.2 *Lineage Connections in Early Organized Daoism.*

especially prominent. This is so much the case that some scholars, partially under Christian-influenced constructions of religion and later Taiwanese Zhengyi influence, would (problematically) identify Zhang Daoling, the first Celestial Master, and/or Zhang Lu, his grandson and the third Celestial Master, as the "founder of Daoism." In fact, such individuals are more appropriately understood as "founders of the Celestial Masters movement;" our account of the origins of Daoism must be plural, rather than singular. With respect to the actual position of the Celestial Master, the movement claims a line of succession from Zhang Daoling to the present Celestial Master. Although the development and characteristics of this line are complex, and although the line was most likely broken and then reconstructed during the Tang dynasty (Kirkland 2004; Kohn and Kirkland 2000), members of the contemporary movement identify a continuity between Zhang Daoling and the most recent Celestial Masters: Zhang Yuanxu (1862–1924; 62nd), Zhang Enpu (1904–69; 63rd), Zhang Yuanxian (1930–2008; 64th) (Kleeman 2008), and possibly Zhang Jiyu (b. 1962; 65th).

While early organized Daoism evidenced the central importance of both actual biological families and spiritual lineages, later organized Daoism shifted from a householder model of community to a monastic one. In that context, Daoists developed lineage-based name systems. In contrast to their Chinese Buddhist counterparts, who change their surname to Shi (Śakya) upon ordination, Daoist monastics retain their ancestral surname, but change their given name. In some cases, religious names are self-chosen; in other cases, they are bestowed by one's teacher. An example of the former is the Complete Perfection founder Wang Zhe's adoption of the religious name of Chongyang (Redoubled Yang). This name indicates Wang's connection to the earlier immortals Zhongli Quan and his student Lü Dongbin, whose religious names are Zhengyang (Aligned Yang) and Chunyang (Pure Yang), respectively.

Regarding religious names bestowed by one's teacher, a good example appears in contemporary Complete Perfection. In contemporary mainland China, this monastic order consists of seven primary lineages, each of which is associated with one of the Seven Perfected, Wang Zhe's senior disciples. Each lineage has its own associated 100-character lineage poem (*paishi*), which are often hand-written by one's teacher and transmitted during ordination. They are also memorized by Complete Perfection monastics, as they are used to identify other Daoists' lineages. Let us take the example of the Dragon Gate lineage poem, specifically characters 30 through 40.

世	景	榮	惟	懋	希	微	衍	自	寧
Shi	Jing	Rong	Wei	Mao	Xi	Wei	Yan	Zi	Ning
World	Bright	Flourish	Only	Mindful	Rare	Subtle	Overflow	Natural	Serene

Suppose that a particular adherent's teacher is a member of the thirtieth generation (*dai*), his or her religious name would begin with Shi. This teacher's students would receive religious names beginning with Jing. The latter's students would, in turn, receive religious names beginning with Rong and become part of the thirty-third generation. In this imagined expression of Dragon Gate lineage affiliation, the individuals might be named Shiqing (Global Clarity), Jingshi (Bright Recognition), and Rongzhao (Flourishing Illumination). From the latter's perspective, he or she would be a "disciple" (*dizi*; *tudi*) of the former: Shiqing would be his "master-grandfather" (*shiye*), and Jingshi would be his "master-father" (*shifu*). Here we see the continued use of terms from family ancestry, but in a monastic setting in which ordinary family life and biological reproduction have been renounced. After Complete Perfection Daoists learn another monastic's name, they will frequently inquire concerning the names of that person's master-grandfather and master-father. If the characters correctly line up according to the lineage poem, then the claim of lineage affiliation is usually accepted.

Revelation

Revelation and mystical experience also have been ways to Daoist religious affiliation (Kohn 1991a; Komjathy 2007a). These categories are most often associated with "religious experience," but they are also important for understanding how Daoist identity and tradition have been established. Revelation refers to sacred communications between hidden dimensions of the cosmos, usually gods or divine entities, and human beings. Revelation usually results in the recipient claiming some special status and privileged position with respect to the sacred, and this position involves a spiritual message or teachings deemed essential for humanity. Mystical experience refers to an experience of that which a given individual or community identifies as sacred. There is no single, essential, and "ultimate" form of mystical experience; there are, rather, many types of mystical experiences, which differ according to the community and tradition involved and which assume different soteriologies and theologies.

Many influential Daoist religious movements originated in revelations or mystical experiences. Zhang Daoling, the founder of the Celestial Masters movement, received a revelation from Lord Lao. Yang Xi, a spirit-medium hired by the southern aristocratic Xu family, received a series of revelations and spiritual transmissions from a variety of Daoist gods and Perfected; in concert with his own spirit journeys to Daoist sacred realms and hidden regions of the cosmos, these revelations became the foundation for the emergence of the Highest Clarity movement. Wang Zhe had a number of mystical experiences with immortals, which may be considered a primary influence on the formation of Complete Perfection, a Daoist renunciant community and subsequent monastic order. For the moment, one key point must be emphasized: none of these individuals were ordained Daoists, and none of them probably had physically embodied Daoist teachers. That is, the "founders" of many of the most important Daoist religious communities were not "Daoists" strictly defined. These details suggest that there are multiple source-points for entry into the Daoist religious tradition, including not only lineage and direct association with Daoist teachers and communities, but also divine communications and mystical experiences.

According to traditional accounts, in 142 CE Zhang Daoling received a revelation from Lord Lao, the "deified" (divine form of) Laozi and anthropomorphic manifestation of the Dao, on Mount Heming (Crane Cry; Dayi, Sichuan). During Lord Lao's revelation, Zhang was appointed as terrestrial representative, the "Celestial Master," and given healing powers as a sign of his empowerment. The movement became patrilineal, passing from Zhang Daoling to his son Zhang Heng and then to the latter's son Zhang Lu. Following this precedent, the position of Celestial Master ideally passed from father to elder son within the Zhang family.

The founding revelation of Celestial Masters Daoism

Suddenly a celestial being descended, accompanied by a thousand chariots and ten thousand horsemen, in a golden carriage with a feathered canopy. Riding dragons and astride tigers, they were too numerous to count. At times the being referred to himself as the Scribe below the Pillar [Laozi], sometimes others called him the Lad from the Eastern Sea. He transmitted the Covenant of Orthodox Unity Newly Revealed to [Zhang Dao]ling. Having received this, Ling was able to heal illness. (*Taiping guangji* 8; adapted from Kleeman 1998: 67)

Similarly, Highest Clarity Daoism traces itself to a series of revelations from divine beings. There is an account of these revelations in the *Zhen'gao* (Declarations of the Perfected), an anthology of the original Highest Clarity revelations compiled by Tao Hongjing.

The initial revelation of Highest Clarity Daoism

The first appearance of the scriptures of the Perfected of Highest Clarity occurred in the second year of the Xingning reign period of the Jin Emperor Ai, the first year of the sexagesimal cycle [364]. It was then that Lady Wei of the Southern Marchmount [Wei Huacun], the Primordial Goddess of Purple Vacuity and Highest Perfected Directress of Destiny, descended from the heavens and bestowed these texts to her disciple Yang, Household Secretary to the King of Langye, [who was concurrently] Minister of Instruction. She had him transcribe them in standard script for transmission to Xu [Mi] of Jurong, Senior Officer to the Defensive Army, and his son [Xu Hui], Assistant for Submission of Accounts. The two Xus in turn set to work at transcribing them again, put them into practice, and attained the Dao. (*Zhen'gao*, DZ 1016, 19.9b; adapted from Strickmann 1977: 41)

In the 360s, members of the aristocratic Xu family, Xu Mi and his son Xu Hui, hired the spirit-medium Yang Xi to establish contact with Xu Mi's deceased wife, Tao Kedou. Through a series of revelations, Yang Xi described the organization and population of the subtle realms of the cosmos, particularly the heaven of Highest Clarity (Figure 3.3). In the process, Yang came in contact with the deceased female Celestial Master libationer Wei Huacun, the "Lady Wei of Southern Marchmount" mentioned above. Here Nanyue (Southern Marchmount) refers to the southern sacred peak of Hengshan (Mount Heng; near Hengyang, Hunan). The revelations were, in turn, written down by Yang Xi and the Xu family in a calligraphic style that seemed divine. Early Highest Clarity Daoism reveals another path to Daoist identity and religious affiliation: through a series of revelations, members of Highest Clarity established a new Daoist community and movement. In its formative moments, Highest Clarity's claim to religious authority and Daoist pedigree derived from three sources: (1) Secret teachings bestowed by various divine beings, including a former Celestial Masters libationer; that is, the connection with

FIGURE 3.3 *Yang Xi Receiving Revelations from Wangzi Jin.*
Source: *Tongbo zhenren zhentu zan*, DZ 612.

Daoism, via the Celestial Masters movement, came not from the terrestrial Celestial Masters community, but from connection with its early ancestors, now divine beings; (2) Access to higher sacred realms, and thus more advanced spiritual insights; specifically, Shangqing refers to the middle of the Three Heavens, which is located between Yuqing (Jade Clarity; highest) and Taiqing (Great Clarity; lowest); and (3) Possession and understanding of revealed scriptures. Such patterns continued in later movements in Daoist religious history.

Daoist movements have also been established through the transformative effect of mystical experiences. One of the most famous examples is that of Wang Zhe, the nominal founder of Complete Perfection. In 1161, at the age of forty-eight, Wang had a mystical encounter with one or more Daoist immortals, sometimes identified as the immortals Zhongli Quan and his spiritual disciple Lü Dongbin. This occurred on a bridge in Ganhe (near present-day Huxian, Shaanxi). The Complete Perfection tradition claims that one of these immortals transmitted a "secret formula in five sections."

These details regarding Daoist revelations and mystical experiences demonstrate that there are diverse ways to religious identity in the Daoist tradition. From a certain perspective, revelation and mystical experience may be seen as alternatives to organized and institutionally sanctioned forms of religious inclusion. While such phenomena may support tradition, they also force members of that tradition to make space for new expressions. The importance of revelation and mystical experience problematize easy explanations about Daoist religious identity and affiliation based solely on institutional frameworks. Some Daoists have found their connection through things such as lineage and ordination, but other Daoists have discovered this through revelation and mystical experience.

The key point here is that many founders of major Daoist movements were not ordained Daoists and had no formal standing within the tradition. In some sense, many of them were not even "Daoists" (members of the Daoist religious tradition); rather, they were incorporated into its historical annals retrospectively. The major "ways" (*dao*) of Daoism most often derived from the religious experience of unique individuals, while the lineages (*pai*) were created by descendants or disciples of these. While theologically speaking there may be almost an infinite number of paths to the Dao, not all paths may be recognized as Daoist, that is, as authentic expressions of Daoist religious orientations. Daoist ways to affiliation have recognizable patterns and characteristics, especially in terms of the virtue (*de*) and numinous presence (*ling*) that is manifested in the individual.

Ordination

As Daoism became more complex in its membership and organization, Daoists began creating integrated models of religious participation and ordination systems. This partially occurred under the influence of Buddhism, specifically through the Daoist adaptation of Buddhist monasticism.

Tang dynasty Daoists created one of the earliest fully integrated ordination systems, and there was also an increasing systematization of monasticism. As documented in the seventh century *Fengdao kejie* (Rules and Precepts for Worshipping the Dao; DZ 1125), one of the earliest Daoist monastic manuals, the ordination system included seven ranks (Figure 3.4). The first three ranks were those of lay masters, while the last three were monastic, and the middle rank (Disciple of Eminent Mystery) signified a transitional stage that could be held either by a householder or a renunciant (Kohn 2003, 2004b).

Ordinations into these ranks began early, with Daoist children initiated first into the Celestial Master level and receiving registers of protective generals. After that, each level required extended training, the guidance of an ordination master, and community sponsors. Once established, Daoists could serve as priests in larger communities, take up residence in a hermitage to pursue self-cultivation, or remain in a monastic institution to perform rituals both in-house or for lay donors, pray for the empire, and continue to strive for greater purity and immortality. That is, to be a Daoist in the late medieval period meant to participate in a tradition, to have commitments to the religious community, and to locate oneself in a hierarchically ordered training regimen. One's authority and affiliation were partially determined by this. The same is true with respect to lineage connections, or relationships to spiritual ancestors, in the larger tradition.

Rank	School	Texts	Affiliation
1. Register Disciple	Celestial Masters	See *Fengdao kejie*, section 13	Lay/Householder
2. Disciple of Good Faith	Great Mystery		Lay/Householder
3. Disciple of Cavern Abyss	Cavern Abyss		Lay/Householder
4. Disciple of Eminent Mystery	Laozi		Transitional (either)
5. Disciple of Cavern Spirit	Three Sovereigns		Monastic
6. Preceptor of Highest Mystery	Numinous Treasure		Monastic
7. Preceptor of Highest Perfection	Highest Clarity		Monastic

FIGURE 3.4 *Seven Ordination Ranks of the Tang Monastic System.*

Daoists continued to reformulate norms of affiliation throughout Daoist history. One enduring model was that of the Dragon Gate lineage of Complete Perfection Daoism advocated by Wang Changyue (Kohn 2004c; Komjathy 2013a). Although the Dragon Gate lineage is most often traced to Qiu Chuji and his supposed lineage-successor Zhao Xujing (Daojian [Resolute-in-the-Way]; 1163–1221), the official, "orthodox" Dragon Gate lineage was codified by Wang Changyue and his successors (Esposito 2001, 2004). While abbot of White Cloud Monastery in the late 1600s, Wang systematized the Dragon Gate ordination system and monastic regulations into three levels (ordination rank/precept text/ritual vestment): (1) Wondrous Practice and Initial Perfection/*Precepts of Initial Perfection*/Devotion Robe of Initial Perfection; (2) Wondrous Virtue and Medium Ultimate/*Precepts of Medium Ultimate*/Pure Robe of Lightened Dust; and (3) Wondrous Dao and Celestial Immortality/*Precepts of Celestial Immortality*/Mist Robe of Celestial Immortality. The first level, open to both monastics and laypeople, centered on the Five Precepts and 10 Precepts of Initial Perfection; the second level, specifically for monastics, consisted of the 300 Precepts of Medium Ultimate; and the third level was less clearly defined, but included the 10 Virtues of Celestial Immortality and the 27 Virtuous Activities of Celestial Immortality. According to Dragon Gate accounts, Wang Changyue compiled, or at least disseminated, the three corresponding monastic manuals, namely, the *Precepts of Initial Perfection*, *Precepts of Medium Ultimate*, and *Precepts of Celestial Immortality*, as guidebooks for Complete Perfection monastic life. They evidence a late-imperial Dragon Gate monastic hierarchy, with the ethical requirements, expectations, and types of adherence becoming increasingly strict as individuals progressed through the levels of commitment.

Although there are many self-identified Dragon Gate communities throughout the modern world, many with only tenuous connections with the mainland Chinese lineage, that lineage remains one of the most visible organized communities in contemporary Daoism, as Dragon Gate monastics function as administrators for most major Daoist sites in mainland China. For present purposes, Dragon Gate is fascinating for the way in which it preserves a monastic system based on ordination and lineage. In addition to its employment of large-scale public ordination ceremonies, which recommenced at White Cloud Monastery in 1989, Dragon Gate is noteworthy for a number of features. First, its ordinands receive the three precept texts and monastic manuals mentioned above. They ideally study and apply the ethical commitments and values advocated in the texts. Second, like most of the major Complete Perfection lineages in contemporary China, Dragon Gate ordinands receive religious names based on the corresponding lineage-poem contained in the *Xuanmen gongke* (Liturgy of the Mysterious Gate), the contemporary Complete Perfection liturgy that is usually chanted daily in the morning and evening at Complete Perfection temples. The Dragon Gate lineage poem consists of 100 Chinese characters, and ordinands receive a "generation-name" based upon their master-father's (*shifu*) name.

As we saw in the example of the hypothetical Daoist master Shiqing (Global Clarity) and his disciple Jingshi (Bright Recognition) and grand-disciple Rongzhao (Flourishing Illumination), this naming convention indicates not only Dragon Gate lineage-affiliation, but also relationship to a particular teacher. This coupled with possession of the lineage poem and the three monastic manuals, and sometimes of ordination certificates, in combination with adherence to the core Complete Perfection commitments to celibacy (no sex), sobriety (no intoxicants), and vegetarianism (no meat), indicates that the person's claim to lineage affiliation is verifiably authentic. This process is sometimes complicated by corruption in the monastic order (one can buy ordination certificates for the right price), fabrication of lineage, and lack of corresponding study, training, and attainment. Nonetheless, if we understand lineage and ordination as paths to and expressions of a religious vocation, then we are forced to ask much more difficult questions. These questions take one into the Daoist tradition as a path to spiritual transformation and as an all-encompassing religious way of life.

Further reading

Kohn, Livia. 2003, *Monastic Life in Medieval Daoism*. Honolulu, HI: University of Hawaii Press.

Kohn, Livia and Harold Roth, eds. 2002, *Daoist Identity: History, Lineage, and Ritual*. Honolulu, HI: University of Hawaii Press.

Saso, Michael. 2012 (1978), *The Teachings of Daoist Master Zhuang*, 3rd rev. edn. Los Angeles, CA: Oracle Bones Press.

Silvers, Brock. 2005, *The Taoist Manual: Applying Taoism to Daily Life*. Nederland, CO: Sacred Mountain Press.

CHAPTER FOUR

View

Daoist views refer to the various commitments, concerns, principles, and values that inform, express, and become embodied in Daoist ways of being-in-the-world. They are the worldview and "symbol system" that express Daoist perspectives on "reality." This is the doctrinal dimension of Daoism. Here it is important to recognize the complex interplay among view, practice, and experience. Daoist views inform Daoist practice and experience, while Daoist practice and experience embody, quite literally, such views. Similarly, Daoist practice leads to specific kinds of Daoist experience, and Daoist experience informs Daoist views. At the same time, Daoists have tended to place primary emphasis on practice and experience. One cannot fully understand Daoist views without understanding the practices that inspired, are informed by, and express those views. These dimensions of the Daoist tradition, in combination with the central importance of the Dao, reveal some of the reasons why Daoist views are better understood as "religious" rather than "philosophical." In addition, Daoist views have tended to emphasize the inherent limitations of conceptualization, intellectualism, knowledge, language, rationality, and so forth. Thus, if there is such a thing as "Daoist philosophy," it is philosophy rooted in embodied being-in-the-world and an orientation toward the sacred. It is primarily existential, ontological, practical, soteriological, and theological.

Daoist views encompass anthropology (discourse on human being), existentialism (discourse on existence, including meaning and purpose), psychology (discourse on *psyche*), soteriology (discourse on ultimate human purpose), cosmogony (discourse on the origins of the universe), cosmology (discourse on the structure of the universe), and theology (discourse on the sacred). Ethics may be considered in terms of both the doctrinal and practical dimensions of Daoism. These various Daoist concerns may be concisely understood through the framework of being, cosmos, and sacrality. They are rooted in an orientation toward the Dao, the sacred or ultimate concern of Daoists. On the most subjective level, Daoist views center on human being-in-the-world. They encompass the commitments, concerns, principles, and values that inform a Daoist way of life. In this respect, they relate to aliveness and existence, especially Daoist meaning and purpose. Daoist views also address the origins as well as the underlying principles and process of the universe. Such views inform and express the central Daoist concern of cosmological attunement. In addition, Daoists have addressed the nature and characteristics of the sacred, the Dao. Such theological views recognize an impersonal "reality" as well as individual beings that participate in and are manifestations of the sacred. Daoist views in turn tend to be more cosmocentric and theocentric, less anthropocentric. Daoist views thus encompass being, cosmos, and sacrality.

Being

Daoist being-in-the-world is rooted in and expressed through specific Daoist views, including various commitments, concerns, principles, and values. While Daoist worldviews are diverse, often varying according to different practitioners and communities, one way to approach Daoist being centers on Daoist ideals. The ideal of classical Daoism is the sage (*shengren* 聖人), while that of organized Daoism tends to be the immortal (*xianren* 仙人) or

Perfected (*zhenren* 真人). Each of the Chinese phrases includes *ren* 人 ("human being"). The Chinese character *sheng* 聖 in sage consists of "mouth" (*kou* 口) and "ear" (*er* 耳) over "great" (*ren* 壬). A sage is someone who listens to the sonorous patterns of the universe and whose spiritual insights may be listened to by others. From a classical Daoist perspective, a sage is someone who embodies the Dao and the teachings. They have merged with the Dao's transformative process and are attuned with its unending oscillations. Viewed etymologically, the Chinese character *xian* 仙 in immortal consists of "human being" (*ren* 人) and "mountain" (*shan* 山), while the variant character (僊) consists of "human being" and "to fly" (*qian* 䙴). An immortal is someone who dwells in the mountains, or at least someone who embodies the mountains, and someone who has the ability to fly. On a metaphorical level, immortals dwell in a state of seclusion from mundane concerns and live beyond the lowlands of human entanglements. In the later Daoist tradition, immortals are individuals who have completed a process of rarification, refinement, and perhaps self-divinization. Similarly, under one reading, the Chinese character *zhen* 真 in Perfected depicts an alchemical vessel. Perfected are individuals who have transmuted the negative aspects of self into their positive counterparts. This includes transcending mortality and attaining a state of timelessness. Such transformed beings have attained a transpersonal state in which they continuously participate in the Dao. One might, in turn, think of sages as individuals who have disappeared into the Dao, and immortals as individuals who have become pervaded by the Dao.

We may examine some classical Daoist descriptions of sages and higher-level adepts as an entry-point into foundational Daoist views and commitments.

DAOIST BEING-IN-THE-WORLD

Considering those in primeval times skilled at being adepts,
They were subtle, wondrous, mysterious, and connected.
Their depth was such that they could not be recognized.
It is only because they could not be recognized
That here we force ourselves to describe them.

> Cautious, as if crossing a river in winter.
> Hesitant, as if fearing neighbors everywhere.
> Impeccable, as if a guest.
> Expansive, as if ice on the verge of melting.
> Sincere, as if an uncarved block.
> Vast, as if a valley.
> Commingled, as if turbidity.
>
> (*Laozi*, Chapter 15)
>
> * * *
>
> The highest adeptness resembles water.
> Water is adept at benefiting the ten thousand beings,
> But it has no need to compete with them.
> It resides in the places that people avoid.
> Therefore, it is close to the Dao.
> > In dwelling, be adept at groundedness.
> > In cultivating the heart-mind, be adept at deepness.
> > In giving, be adept at humaneness.
> > In speaking, be adept at sincerity.
> > In rectifying, be adept at regulation.
> > In doing, be adept in abilities.
> > In moving, be adept at timeliness.
> Only one who does not compete is free from blame.
>
> (Ibid., Chapter 8)

As many Daoists have done throughout Daoist history, one might read the *Book of Venerable Masters* as a manual for self-cultivation. While sages are revered as embodiments of tradition, they also serve as models for human possibility, especially for those committed to Daoist practice and attainment. The above two sets of "seven aptitudes" represent a sample of an almost unlimited number of foundational Daoist principles found in classical Daoist texts. Aspiring Daoist adepts, individuals committed to a Daoist way life, endeavor to develop groundedness in place, depth in perspective, kindness in assistance, sincerity in speech, regulation in rectification, aptitude in action, and appropriateness in responsiveness. They embody attentiveness, carefulness, impeccability, expansiveness, sincerity, vastness, and connectedness. They also cultivate the "three treasures" of compassion, frugality, and deference or humility (*Laozi*, Chapter 67). Sages in turn resonate with the Dao, and this musicality of being creates further patterns of reverberation in other lives. There is a symphony of relational being based on mutual benefit and transformation.

Such commitments are rooted in an orientation toward the Dao, the sacred or ultimate concern of Daoists. From a foundational Daoist perspective, the Dao is the innate nature (*xing* 性) of human beings. The associated Chinese character consists of "heart-mind" (*xin* 心) and "to be born" (*sheng* 生): Innate nature is the heart-mind with which one was born. It is one's original being free of social conditioning, familial obligation, and personal habituation. For Daoists, the ground of one's being is innately "good," although various Daoists have expressed reservations about conventional, socially constructed notions of morality. Instead, Daoists tend to emphasize *de* 德, which has been translated variously as "inner power," "integrity," "potency," "virtue," and so forth. The Chinese character consists of "step" (*chi* 彳) and "upright" (*zhi* 直) over "heart-mind" (*xin* 心): To embody *de* is to have an aligned heart-mind that is expressed as embodied activity, activity that reveals one's degree of self-cultivation and exerts a transformational influence on others. *De*, or inner power, is the Dao manifested in human beings as numinous presence and as embodied activity in the world, especially as a beneficial and transformational influence that might be categorized as "good." From this perspective, "morality" and "ethics" are natural outcomes of Daoist practice, natural expressions of Daoist ontological conditions or ways of being. Specifically, spiritual attainment is rooted in the practice of stillness-based meditation and results in mystical union with the Dao. Such meditative absorption then manifests as embodiment, participation, and transmission. Viewed from a later Daoist perspective, one might think of *de* in terms of a talisman, with the Dao and one's innate nature being two halves of a talisman that, when joined, reveal original connection and integrity. For Daoists, each individual's *de* is manifested in diverse and unique ways, but Daoist *de* is rooted in and expressed through Daoist commitments, principles, and values. It is a specific way of being-in-the-world.

Famous exemplars of inner power in the *Book of Master Zhuang* include, among others, Master Zhuang himself, who knows the way to the Village of Nothing-Whatsoever (Chapter 1) and the joy of fish (Chapter 17); Changwuzi (Master Enduring Hibiscus), who knows how to tuck the universe under his arm and instructs on the Great Awakening (Chapter 2); Cook Ding, who cuts apart an ox with complete effortlessness (Chapter 3); Nüyu (Woman Yu), who teaches a stage-based training regimen that results in freedom from the bounds of life and death (Chapter 6); Huzi (Gourd Master), who, in emptiness, allows the not-yet-emerged-from-the-ancestral to manifest through him (Chapter 7); Liezi (Master Lie) and Guangchengzi (Master Expansive Completion), both of whom live in seclusion to cultivate the Dao (Chapters 7, 11, 28, and 32); Gengsang Chu, who commits himself to follow the teachings of Lao Dan and the Way of Heaven (Chapter 23); and Thief Zhi, who transcends the limitations of conventional, obligation-based morality and turns Kongzi's (Confucius') mind inside out (Chapter 29).

While most classical Daoist discussions of inner power focus on human beings, there are a few passages that indicate that every being has the potential to manifest the Dao. Examples in the *Book of Master Zhuang* include the Great Peng-bird, which wanders carefree above the cares of the world (Chapter 1); an ancient, gnarled tree, which teaches the value of uselessness (Chapters 1, 4, and 20); fish, which flow with the currents, abide in the shadows, and rest at ease with their place in water (Chapters 6 and 17); magpies and wasps, which embody the Dao's transformative process (Chapter 14); tortoises, which enjoy dragging their tails in the mud (Chapter 17); and sea turtles, which have the experience of swimming in the ocean's vastness (ibid.). Many Daoists have, in turn, studied such beings as models for Daoist practice and attainment. In the later Daoist tradition, this includes recognition of egrets (*guan*), who observe unseen or barely visible presences in stillness, as models for the Daoist practice of attentiveness and observation (*guan*).

The two most well known Daoist values associated with innate nature and inner power are "non-action" (*wuwei*) and "suchness" (*ziran*). From a Daoist perspective, the terms are intricately related: the *practice* of *wuwei* leads to a *state* of *ziran*. *Wuwei* is effortless activity, the practice of not doing anything extra or unnecessary; we may think of it in terms of conservation and non-attachment. In certain contexts, it may be understood as "non-intervention" and "non-interference," as letting be, as allowing space for existential freedom. *Ziran* (*tzu-jan*) is frequently translated as "self-so," "naturalness," or "spontaneity." The latter two renderings are problematic if not interpreted contextually. Returning to or attaining the state of *ziran*, which is the Dao as such, presupposes four dimensions mentioned in Chapter 19 of the *Book of Venerable Masters*: appearing plain, embracing simplicity, lessening personal interest, and decreasing desires. *Ziran* is not "going with the flow" in the sense of following one's own selfish desires. Rather, it refers to an ontological condition beyond the limitations of egoistic identity and states of psychological habituation, including desire-based ontological modes. *Ziran* is best understood as "suchness," or "being-so-of-itself," to use a phrase from the German philosopher Martin Heidegger (1889–1976). It is simultaneously one's "natural" condition and the manifestation of the Dao through one's being. However, too often *wuwei* is misunderstood as apathy or atrophy, while *ziran* is misunderstood as the reproduction of habituation. Within the Daoist tradition, there is actually much discussion of and different perspectives on the relationship between "fate" (ontological givenness) and freedom, or the capacity for independent action and the possibility and desirability of "perfection." This includes a creative tension and dialectic between notions of wildness and cultivation. *Wuwei* involves allowing each being to unfold according to its own nature and connection with the Dao. It involves allowing space for *ziran* to appear. One might, in turn, link non-action and suchness to other classical and foundational Daoist practices and ways of being. These include "being carefree" (*xiaoyao*), "making all things equal" (*qiwu*), "non-contention" (*wuzheng*), "non-knowing" (*wuzhi*), "uselessness" (*wuyong*), and so forth.

In later Daoist history, Daoists continued to reflect on and attempt to embody such classical and foundational Daoist principles. Some Daoist traditions formulated precepts and practices based on these classical foundations. For example, in the early Celestial Masters movement, community members applied Nine Practices (*jiuxing*).

The nine practices of early Celestial Masters Daoism

1 Practice non-action (*wuwei*).
2 Practice softness and weakness (*rouruo*).
3 Practice guarding the feminine (*shouci*). Do not initiate actions.
4 Practice being nameless (*wuming*).
5 Practice clarity and stillness (*qingjing*).
6 Practice being adept (*zhushan*).
7 Practice being desireless (*wuyu*).
8 Practice ceasing with sufficiency (*zhizu*).
9 Practice yielding and withdrawing (*tuirang*).

(*Laojun jinglü*, DZ 786, 1a)

Deriving from various chapters of the *Scripture on the Dao and Inner Power*, the Nine Practices may be understood as effortlessness, flexibility, receptivity, anonymity, serenity, aptitude, non-attachment, contentment, and deference. For anyone familiar with the *Scripture on the Dao and Inner Power*, the genius of the distillation is clear, and these prescriptive "precepts" reveal strong connections between classical Daoism and early organized Daoism. In this respect, it is also noteworthy that the *Scripture on the Dao and Inner Power* had a central position in this movement (Bokenkamp 1997). Zhang Lu, the third Celestial Master, may have written a commentary to the text, which is titled the *Laozi xiang'er zhu* (Commentary Thinking Through the *Laozi*; DH 56; S. 6825). The *Xiang'er* commentary is only one of over a hundred extant Daoist commentaries on the *Scripture on the Dao and Inner Power* in the Daoist Canon (Robinet 1998, 1999), almost none of which have unfortunately been studied or translated. The early Celestial Masters community also extracted precepts, the 27 Xiang'er Precepts, from their early commentary. These conduct guidelines, in turn, became collected in various Daoist precept texts (Kohn 2004c).

Daoist being-in-the-world is thus rooted in and expressed through specific Daoist views and ways of being. This includes a commitment to community, cultivation, embodiment, energetic aliveness, place, and so forth. Deeper Daoist practice and attainment becomes expressed as a recognizable pattern, as Daoist presence. From a more encompassing perspective, such presence is characterized by a connection with the Dao. This connection manifests as numinosity that pervades the Daoist's life and being. Through cosmological attunement, energetic listening, and transformative practice, Daoists become aligned with and pervaded by the Dao. One may then listen to the deeper dimensions of existence and follow the openings that are the unfolding of one's own life. This open receptivity and responsiveness often manifest as trust. Each and every moment is an opportunity for self-cultivation and an endowment from the Dao. Such infusion may, in turn, become a means to recognize others with similar affinities, commitments, and orientations. It may also become transmitted, whether through embodiment, movement, teachings, or some other activity. Regardless, whether known or unknown, hidden or visible, recognized or forgotten, Daoists endeavor to live through an orientation toward the Dao, an orientation rooted in commitment, contemplation, presence, sincerity, and reverence. This is concisely expressed in the "Neiye" (Inward Training) chapter of the *Guanzi* (Book of Master Guan): "Inwardly still and outwardly reverent" (*neijing waijing*) (Chapter 22).

Cosmos

The fundamental Daoist view of the universe centers on an impersonal transformative process (*zaohua*). This includes distinctive perspectives on cosmogony (origins of the universe) and cosmology (underlying principles and patterns of the universe). The primary Daoist cosmogony involves an impersonal and spontaneous process of manifestation and emanation. One dimension of the Dao manifests in and as the universe as cosmological process ("Nature"). Generally speaking, Daoists do not believe in intentionality, agency, or inherent and transcendent meaning in the cosmos. That is, in contrast to many monotheists, Daoists believe in neither a creator god nor "creation" as such. The foundational Daoist cosmogony involves a spontaneous transformation that led from primordial non-differentiation to differentiation.

According to various classical Daoist cosmogonic accounts, especially as appearing in the *Book of Venerable Masters, Book of Master Zhuang*, and *Book of the Huainan Masters*, the Dao represents primordial non-differentiation or pure potentiality. In a pre-manifest "state," the Dao is an incomprehensible and unrepresentable "before," also understood as original qi, the primordial "energy" of the universe. Through a spontaneous, unintentional, and impersonal process of unfolding or differentiation, this non-differentiation became the "One" or unity. That is, even unity or the wholeness of Being-before-being is not the Dao in its ultimate sense. The One represents the first moment or stage of differentiation. From this unity, separation occurs. In the next phase of differentiation, the one divides into "two," yin and yang. Here yin also relates to terrestrial qi or the qi of the earth (*diqi*), while yang relates to celestial qi or the qi of the heavens (*tianqi*). According to one account, at this moment of cosmogonic unfolding, the clear and light rose to become the heavens, while the heavy and turbid sank to become the earth. At this moment yin and yang have not yet formed patterns of interaction. The interaction of yin and yang is referred to as "three;" this moment involves yin and yang in dynamic and continual interaction, resulting in further differentiation. This further differentiation leads to the emergence of materiality as well as to more individuated beings and forces, including human beings. Human beings, as vertically aligned beings, are often seen as the life form with the clearest capacity to connect the heavens and the earth. This is a structural and organizational distinction, not an ontological or theological one. In the later Daoist tradition, the three dimensions of the heavens, earth, and human beings are referred to as the "Three Powers" (*sancai*).

Within the larger contours of the Daoist tradition, the foundational and primary cosmogonic account, the movement from non-differentiated Source and primordial unity to differentiation, is spoken of in terms of Wu wuji ("without non-differentiation"), Wuji ("non-differentiation") and Taiji ("differentiation"), which may be represented in a chart (Figure 4.1). Taiji, which literally means the "Great Ridgepole," or the "Great Ultimate" by extension, refers to the dynamic interaction of yin and yang. It is a cosmological category. Etymologically speaking, *ji* is the "ridgepole" or the center beam in an architectural structure. Applied to yin and yang, it suggests both distinction (a center dividing point) and connection (a center meeting point). This

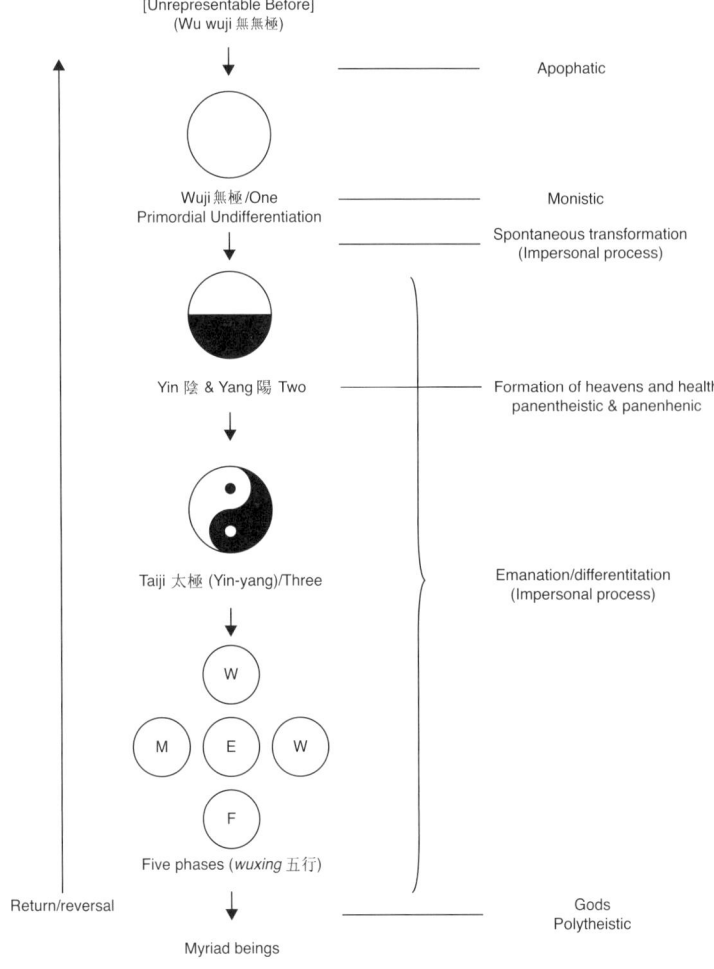

FIGURE 4.1 *Classical and Foundational Daoist Cosmogony.*

cosmogonic and cosmological process, involving yin and yang in continual, dynamic interaction, is not just in the past; it also represents the context of being and becoming, the unending process that is the world and being-in-the-world. Yin-yang interaction may be further mapped according to the Five Phases (*wuxing*), which are represented cosmogonically in the above chart. That is, they are located in their associated directions (Water/north; Wood/east; Fire/south; Metal/west; and Earth/center).

As the above illustration indicates, one of the primary Daoist soteriologies, or views on the ultimate purpose of human existence and goal of religious practice, involves "returning the Source" (*guigen*), to the Dao as primordial origin. This is a movement from differentiation to non-differentiation. Daoists in turn use various technical terms when referring to the Dao as primordial non-differentiation. These include "source" (*yuan*), "root" (*gen*), "mother" (*mu*), "beginning" (*shi*), and "ancestor" (*zong*). Here we must recognize that the Daoist view of the Dao is primarily impersonal, especially when considering the Dao as primordial Source and in its own suchness. Thus, Dao as "mother" does not refer to a compassionate and loving being, a personal divine consciousness. Rather, it refers to that which gave birth to the world, to life, and to all beings. It is the source of life and that which nourishes all beings without conscious concern. It is neither an actual mother (or father) nor gendered in any essential respect. While this may be depressing for some, Daoists generally identify the Dao as a supportive matrix that continuously and effortlessly gives without loss or diminishment. One also might recognize that the Dao as impersonal Source also manifests through beings who express personal concern and consideration. This includes humans who embody humaneness.

In terms of the structure and function of the universe, the foundational Daoist cosmology parallels that of pre-modern Chinese society and culture, and it centers on yin-yang and the Five Phases. This cosmology is not Daoist per se. It is best understood as "traditional Chinese cosmology" or part of the dominant "traditional Chinese worldview," as it was the primary cosmological viewpoint in traditional China. This cosmology is based on the principles and forces of yin-yang, which we encountered above in the classical Daoist cosmogonic account. Etymologically speaking, yin 陰 depicts a hill (*fu* 阜) covered by shadows (*yin* 侌), while yang 陽 depicts a hill (*fu* 阜) covered by sunlight (*yang* 昜). At the root level, yin and yang are ways of speaking about the same place at different times or moments of the day. Yin and yang are not "polar opposites" or antagonistic substances; they are, in fact, complementary principles, aspects, or forces. As the characters suggest, yin and yang are used to represent different dimensions of the same phenomenon or situation. By extension, there are various associations:

yin/female/earth/moon/dark/death/cold/moist/heavy/turbidity/ descent/rest/inward

yang/male/heavens/sun/light/life/hot/dry/light/clarity/ascent/ activity/outward

At times, "yin" is also used to designate "negative" or harmful aspects of life more generally (immorality, ugliness, disease, etc.), while "yang" becomes related to "positive" or beneficial aspects of life (morality, beauty, health, etc.). What must be emphasized is that these are relative associations, not absolute characteristics. They do not parallel conventional views of so-called "good" and "evil" as distinct ontological categories. Just because women are considered "yin" in one respect or in one context, it does not follow that they are also "immoral" or "turbid." There are also varying degrees of yin and yang in every phenomenon, in each moment or experience, and in every being. So, certain men may be more yin than certain women, and vice versa. People in one context may be more yang (e.g. talkative or hot), while in another that same person may be quite yin (e.g. quiet or cold). Because the universe is understood as a transformative process, this also means that any negative or harmful pattern or manifestation may be transformed into a positive or beneficial pattern or manifestation. In the context of a classical Chinese worldview in general and Daoism in particular, life is seen as depending on the mutually beneficial interaction of yin and yang. Even when Daoists speak of entities like "demons" (*mo*) or "ghosts" (*gui*), "yin entities," they generally understand them to be a momentary, unresolved energetic pattern capable of transformation into a more beneficial pattern. Generally speaking, such beings are not irrevocably lost or distorted. A skilled Daoist priest may assist their transformation.

Here we should also note that yin and yang take on specific and alternative meanings in certain contexts. For example, in many internal alchemy (*neidan*) lineages, yin appears to be defined negatively, while yang appears to be defined positively. A distinction must be made between yin-yang as cosmological principles, and yin-yang as alchemical map, specifically as a map of alchemical transformation. That is, there are cosmological and alchemical interpretations and applications of yin-yang, with the associations varying depending on system and context. The cosmological dimension cannot be changed—it is the underlying structure of cosmos. However, on an existential and alchemical level, yin may designate mortality, defilements, delusion, and so forth; yang may designate immortality, purity, realization, and so forth. Internal alchemists thus frequently speak of transforming yin into yang, of becoming a yang-spirit, a pure yang being. This does not mean that one transcends the foundational cosmological harmony of yin and yang. In fact, classical Daoism and the foundational Daoist worldview urge one to "embrace the feminine," understood as correlative with "yin qualities" (flexibility, passivity, receptivity, silence, etc.). Rather, it means that the internal alchemist works to become a perfected being in which all negative characteristics have been transformed into their positive counterparts.

The foundational Daoist cosmology also centers on the so-called Five Phases (*wuxing*), also rendered as Five Elements or Five Agents. Integrated into a single system, yin-yang and the Five Phases are referred to as "correlative cosmology" and the "system of correspondences." This again is best thought of as "traditional Chinese cosmology." The Five Phases include Wood, Fire, Earth, Metal, and Water, and the sequence is important. In terms of yin-yang, Wood is minor or lesser yang, while Fire is major or greater yang. Metal is minor yin, while Water is major yin. Earth is generally thought to be a balance of the two forces or a transition between them.

Conventionally rendered as "Five Elements," *wuxing* literally means something like "five activities" or "five movements." This dynamic and process-orientated aspect becomes more satisfactorily rendered in the designation of "Five Phases." While these five do, in fact, relate to actual substances as well as related phenomena and energetic qualities of the "phases," the system is much more complex and dynamic than "elements" would lead one to believe. Also referred to as "naturalistic medicine," this system of correspondences consists of various associations, charts of which may be found in almost any textbook on Traditional Chinese Medicine (TCM). Some examples include the following:

Wood/spring/east/wind/liver/gall bladder/ethereal soul/eyes/humaneness/anger

Fire/summer/south/heat/heart/small intestine/spirit/tongue/respect/hatred

Earth/—/center/dampness/spleen/stomach/thought/mouth/honesty/worry

Metal/autumn/west/dryness/lungs/large intestine/corporeal soul/nose/righteousness/grief

Water/winter/north/cold/kidneys/urinary bladder/will/ears/wisdom/fear

Here it is important to recognize that these are, from a traditional Chinese and Daoist perspective, actual correspondences. Each association directly relates to, and often may be substituted for, the others. For example, eye problems frequently appear or become exacerbated during spring; heart issues may manifest in problems with arteries; feelings of grief and depression may be more pronounced during autumn; kidney problems may manifest as a groaning voice; and so forth.

The Five Phases, including their various associations, are, in turn, understood to relate to each other in patterns of dynamic interaction. The so-called "production cycle" is as follows: Wood→Fire→Earth→Metal→Water→Wood→. Then there is the "destruction cycle": Wood→Water→Metal→Earth→Fire→Wood→. Finally, there is the "control cycle": Wood→Earth→Water→Fire→Metal→Wood→. In contemporary TCM, these sequences are often represented as a circle (the production cycle) with a pentagram inside (the control cycle). As the patterns of interaction are interrelated, dynamic, and mutually influential, each association or correspondence may be placed in such a diagram. Viewed in the production cycle, the liver (Wood) influences the heart (Fire), which influences the spleen (Earth). Viewed in the same cycle, intense grief (Metal) may lead to fear (Water). Viewed in the control cycle, honesty (Earth) may help to alleviate fear (Water). These are just some examples of the patterns of dynamic interaction drawn from the above list of correspondences.

The final element of traditional Chinese cosmology, and of foundational Daoist cosmology by extension, is qi (*ch'i*). Etymologically speaking, the standard character for qi 氣 consists of *qi* 气 ("vapor") above *mi* 米 ("rice"). Qi is like steam derived from the cooking of rice, with the latter often seen as paralleling vital essence (*jing*) in the human body. Interestingly, there is also a Daoist esoteric character for qi 炁, which consists of *wu* 无 ("non-being") above *huo* 灬/火 ("fire"). From this perspective, qi is a subtle (lit., "non-existing") heat in the body. In Western language sources, qi has been rendered relatively accurately as "subtle" or "vital breath," anachronistically as "energy," and obfuscatingly as "pneuma." While it does have some similarity with the Indian notion of *prāṇa* and the Greek concept of *pneuma*, qi, like "Dao" and "yin-yang," is best left untranslated. Qi refers to both material breath as well as subtle breath. With respect to the former, it is associated with the lungs and with physical respiration. In terms of the latter, it circulates through the universe and the human body as a subtle force or energetic presence. The notion of qi moving through the body relates to the organ-meridian system, subtle networks and channels throughout the body, and to the various vital functions of the organs. In combination with the Daoist notion of "elixir fields" (*dantian*), this system became an essential component of internal alchemy practice.

As an animating force or sacred wind, qi bridges the apparent divide between the "material" and "spiritual," "body" and "mind," and so forth. From a traditional Chinese and Daoist perspective, everything consists of qi; everything is qi. Everything may be mapped along a spectrum of qi, from the most substantial (rocks and bones, for example) to the most rarified (cosmic ethers and gods, for example). However, qi is not simply an undivided or unified quasi-substance. There are types of qi. As we saw above, on the most basic level, qi may be distinguished in terms of "celestial qi" (*tianqi*), the subtle breath associated with the sky and heavens, and "terrestrial qi" (*diqi*), the subtle breath of the earth. These are related to yang and yin, respectively. In the human body, they are thought to enter through the crown-point (Baihui) and soles of the feet (Yongquan), respectively. Although conventionally associated with "celestial qi," there are also other cosmological influences, such as from the sun, moon, stars, and so forth. Such attentiveness was especially prominent in early Highest Clarity and related visualization practices. Daoism and Chinese medicine also distinguish so-called "prenatal qi" (*xiantian qi*), which literally means "before heaven qi," from so-called "postnatal qi" (*houtian qi*), which literally means "after heaven qi." Prenatal qi refers to the qi that one receives from the universe and one's ancestors, especially one's parents, before birth. Postnatal qi refers to the qi that one acquires and gathers after birth, specifically from breath and food. Other types of qi include ancestral qi (*zongqi*), nutritive qi (*yingqi*), protective qi (*weiqi*), and original qi (*yuanqi*). From this perspective, qi is part of the vital substances of the body. On a more specifically Daoist level, there is *daoqi*, the qi of the Dao, which is mentioned, for instance, throughout the standard Complete Perfection liturgy. While one might be inclined to think of all qi as the "qi of the Dao," we must remember the above-mentioned cosmogonic account. There are some forms of qi that are less differentiated and closer to the Dao in its primordial suchness (*ziran*). Often discussed as "original," "primal," or "primordial qi" (*yuanqi*), *daoqi* is a "purer" form of qi, a sacred presence. It is not simply manifest in the universe and world; it is also activated and actualized through Daoist religious practice. From a Daoist perspective, its presence may be embodied, recognized, and transmitted within and among Daoists. From an emic ("insider") or adherent perspective, this is one of the ways in which Daoist being would be understood and identified. Daoists frequently refer to its presence as "connection" (*tong*) and/or as "numinosity" (*ling*).

Sacrality

Daoist theology, or discourse on the sacred, primarily centers on the Dao (Tao), albeit in diverse manifestations. The Dao is the sacred and ultimate concern of Daoists. It is, first and foremost, a Chinese character as well as a Daoist cosmological and theological concept. Etymologically speaking, the character *dao* 道, probably pronounced something like *d'ôg* in archaic and ancient Chinese (Karlgren 1964: 272), consists of *chuo* 辵 ("to walk") and *shou* 首 ("head"). It is a road that one travels, and a religious or existential path by extension. *Dao* may thus mean "path," "way," "to walk," and "to speak." Like "qi" and "yin-yang," Dao is best left untranslated, though it has been rendered as "Way." Here it is important to recognize that *dao* was part of the shared intellectual and conceptual repertoire of ancient China. In that context, various individuals and movements discoursed on *dao*. However, more often than not, such individuals meant their specific "way" or "path." In contrast, the inner cultivation lineages of classical Daoism elevated the concept of *dao* to designate that which is ultimately real ("the Way"), that which transcends and encompasses all of the small *dao*s ("ways").

The Dao cannot be separated from the religious tradition which is Daoism. It is a Daoist cosmogonic, cosmological, and theological concept. From a Daoist perspective, veneration of the Dao and commitment to realizing the Dao involve both recognition of the character as a place-holder for [   ] and reflection on Daoist theological views. To mistake "Dao" for [   ] is either idolatry or a mistaken view. For example, the first line of Chapter 1 of the *Book of Venerable Masters* reads *dao kedao feichang dao*, which literally means, "The *dao* that can be *dao*ed (i.e. made into 'dao') is not the continuous Dao." That is, the labeling of [   ] as "Dao" limits its suchness. In addition, the second to the last line of the same chapter reads *xuan zhi you xuan, zhongmiao zhi men*, which literally means, "The even more mysterious within the mysterious is the gate to all wonders." That is, the Dao as such is a twofold mystery, a mysteriousness that even "mystery" cannot express. Similarly, in Chapter 25 of the *Book of Venerable Masters*, we are informed: "Forced to name it, I call it 'great'." Here *da* 大, the character rendered "great," depicts a human being (*ren* 人) with outstretched arms (–). The Dao as *da* is beyond the human capacity for comprehension (encompassment), especially through linguistic, conceptual, and intellectual frameworks. As a further expression of such views, the anonymous, eighth-century *Qingjing jing* (Scripture on Clarity and Stillness; DZ 620) comments, "Forced to name it, we call it 'Dao'." That is, even "Dao" is simply an approximation of that which is ultimately real. Moreover, as one can see from these various Daoist theological insights, there is a strong skepticism in the Daoist tradition concerning language, conceptualization, and the human tendency toward "knowing." As Chapter 1 of the *Book of Master Zhuang* explains, "Names are the guest of reality." In addition, in Chapter 2 of the same text, which is titled "On Making Things Equal," we find a major Daoist theological and existential perspective: The commitment to abiding in a state of "non-knowing" (*wuzhi*). This relates to apophatic discourse (based on negation, or more accurately "beyond") as primary, and kataphatic discourse (based on affirmation) as secondary. This dimension of classical Daoism has been labeled "relativism" and "skepticism," but such characterizations fail to recognize the ways in which such views are rooted in meditative praxis and the resulting mystical experiences and spiritual insights. That is, Daoist apophatic discourse is primarily soteriological and theological, rather than merely intellectual and philosophical. It is primarily existential (about existence) and ontological (about being), and only conventionally epistemological (about knowing).

From a Daoist perspective, that which is referred to as "Dao," has four primary characteristics: (1) Source of all of existence; (2) Unnamable mystery; (3) All-pervading sacred presence; and (4) Universe as cosmological process. This is the foundational Daoist theology. As discussed above, everything emerged from and through the Dao's spontaneous and impersonal process of cosmogonic unfolding and emanation. In this respect, the Dao represents an unrepresentable and incomprehensible before. From its cosmogonic emanation, all differentiated existences came into being: from invisible realms and cosmic ethers to solar systems, stars, and sentient life. As mentioned above, this is the Dao as "mother," as impersonal origination process. Daoists generally believe that this emanationist process moved from more undifferentiated and subtle cosmological dimensions to more differentiated and material dimensions. That is, Daoists do not have a developmental model that privileges later forms of "evolution" (e.g. the emergence of humans on earth); such life forms are, cosmogonically speaking, more distant from the Dao as Source, as primordial unity. Various Daoist texts in turn urge practitioners to "return to the Source" (*guigen*). At the same time, Daoists understand the universe, world, and ultimately each of the myriad beings (*wanwu*) as manifestations of the Dao. The Dao is immanent in the universe, and this is so much the case that it is difficult to draw a distinction between the Dao and Nature as such. The Daoist reverence for the cosmos, and the human body by extension, is expressed in various admonitions to practice seasonal attunement, specifically through attentiveness to solar and lunar cycles. As a famous Daoist oral saying has it, "Out of step with the times, but not with the seasons." The second characteristic of the Dao, as unnamable mystery, suggests that the Dao as such is beyond human linguistic and conceptual expression and intellectual comprehension. It is a mystery so mysterious that it is beyond mysteriousness. Thus, classical Daoist texts speak of the Dao as "dark" (*xuan*), "subtle" (*miao*), "dim" (*hu*), "indistinct" (*huang*), and so forth. The Dao is the darkness that encompasses all light. At the same time, the Dao is an all-pervading sacred presence in the world. It can be directly experienced and participated in, and humans can cultivate a greater sensitivity to its presence, in whatever form it takes. This can occur as and through mountain summits, oak trees, extraordinary dogs, immortals, spiritual teachers, and so forth. However—and this cannot be stressed enough—there are degrees of presence. Although everything is the Dao in some sense, and everything expresses the Dao in certain respects, the sacred presence of the Dao (*daoqi*) has different degrees of intensity and clarity. Finally, the Dao is understood as the universe as cosmological process, specifically as expressed in the constant patterns of oscillation between yin and yang. In this respect, the Dao is the universe, but it is a universe of constant change and transformation. The Dao's manifest patterns are most clearly observed in the shifts of the constellations and seasons. The alterations of yin and yang, rest and activity, darkness and light, cold and heat, are literally the Dao.

From this brief account, one may recognize the ways in which the primary Daoist theology is monistic (one impersonal Reality), panenhenic (Nature as sacred), and panentheistic (sacred in and beyond the world). With respect to a monistic view, everything is the Dao. The Dao is Oneness, the primordial unity before the manifest cosmos and the totality of that universe. This includes all beings in all places at all times. Here one encounters the Dao-centered perspective that many Daoists endeavor to realize. Such is primarily an impersonal or transpersonal existential approach, although it does manifest through some sentient beings as love and compassion. With respect to the panenhenic view, the universe and Nature are the Dao. To be alive as an embodied being in the world is to participate in the Dao. Here one encounters the world-affirming and cosmocentric dimension of Daoism. On the one hand, the universe and its constant transformative shifts are primary; on the other hand, that universe is manifest in and expressed through each individual being. For Daoists, one problem with being human is an overemphasis on that category of being and an obsessive concern for one's individual life. Finally, in terms of the panentheistic view, the Dao is simultaneously immanent and transcendent, neither immanent nor transcendent. Although the universe is the Dao, the Dao will not cease to exist when the universe goes out of being. Daoists hold that the Dao is both Being and Nonbeing. While there is some question as to whether the universe is deemed eternal in the Daoist tradition, careful study seems to indicate that the dominant view is a finite universe that will one day end. In this way, the classical and foundational Daoist cosmogonic account seems to parallel the contemporary Big Bang theory to some extent; after the expansion (yang) reaches its extreme, contraction (yin) will increase until all returns to primordial unity. Daoists often compare this to human respiration. From a Daoist panentheistic perspective, we cannot know either what the Dao was before this manifestation or what it might be afterwards. Such a Daoist view would, in turn, emphasize the nature of embodiment, and one's location in a universe functioning according to yin-yang interaction.

The secondary Daoist theology is animistic (gods or spirits in Nature) and polytheistic (multiple gods). That is, the vast majority of Daoists throughout Chinese history believed in gods and spirits, and this remains true in contemporary Daoism. On some level, Daoists are polytheists, although one must consider Daoist conceptions of such deities. Daoist polytheism recognizes both place-specific deities, usually referred to as "locality-gods" (*dishen*; *tudi gong*), as well as cosmic, divine beings. The former includes mountain-gods, such as the gods of the Five Marchmounts, and the gods of the five directions. Many of these deities were adopted from the Chinese popular pantheon; they are not "Daoist gods" as such. Cosmic deities may be primordial gods, early emanations of the Dao, or apotheoses, human beings who went through a process of divinization.

Daoists also generally accept the standard Chinese distinction among gods (*shen*), ghosts (*gui*), and ancestors (*zong*). Gods are divine beings. Ghosts are disenfranchised and anomalous dead, usually those who fall outside the family structure, such as orphans or widows, or those who died unexpectedly or strangely, such as suicides. Ancestors are person-specific; they are the people from whom one descends. Ghosts are usually associated with unsettled corporeal souls (*po*), while ancestors are usually associated with settled ethereal souls (*hun*). To this tripartite structure, we should also add demons (*mo*), important in certain Daoist movements, and immortals (*xianren*) and Perfected (*zhenren*). Demons are usually viewed as malevolent entities, disoriented spirits and/or unresolved qi patterns. Depending on the Daoist sub-tradition, they are more or less permanent and fixed. Immortals and Perfected tend to be understood as individuals who completed a process of self-divinization, who made themselves into "gods." However, they differ from gods as such because they are outside the bureaucratic structure and are free from obligations.

As a final Daoist theological point, many individuals find it difficult to reconcile the primary Daoist theology (monistic, panenhenic, panentheistic) with the secondary one (animistic and polytheistic). However, if one understands Daoist emanationist cosmogony, such diverse theological views are easily reconciled. The Daoist cosmogonic account does not simply address the appearance of the visible universe; it also claims an earlier cosmogonic moment during which invisible or subtle realms formed. Within the dominant Daoist theological tradition, the universe contains multiple sacred realms inhabited by multiple gods. The unseen universe is as diverse as the seen universe. As the *Laozi xiang'er zhu* (Commentary Thinking Through the *Laozi*; DH 56; S. 6825) explains, "The One exists beyond the heavens and earth. When it enters the space between the heavens and earth, it simply comes and goes in the human body. It resides within the entire skin; it does not dwell in just one place. The One scatters its form as qi; it assembles its form as Taishang Laojun (Great High Lord Lao), who constantly governs Mount Kunlun." Deities are thus simply differently differentiated aspects of the Dao, and worshipping deities is not, in and of itself, different than having reverence for the unnamable mystery which is the Dao. At the same time—and this is centrally important for understanding the Daoist tradition— gods may be "higher" on some level, but Daoist panenhenic and panentheistic commitments recognize the ways in which the Dao may manifest through everything. So, some Daoists focus on divine immortals, while others venerate embodied teachers. Both may be manifestations of the Dao. Similarly, encountering a cherry tree blooming in spring may be as much of an encounter with the Dao's sacred presence as the appearance of Lord Lao or Lü Dongbin.

The Daoist pantheon is large and complex (see, CDA 1995; Little 2000a; Silvers 2005), and different Daoist gods and divine beings have been worshipped by different Daoists at different times. That is, Daoist gods and pantheons have a specific history and are often associated with specific movements. That being said, the most important "gods" of the modern Daoist pantheon are the Sanqing (Three Purities), namely, Yuanshi tianzun (Celestial Worthy of Original Beginning), Lingbao tianzun (Celestial Worthy of Numinous Treasure), and Daode tianzun (Celestial Worthy of the Dao and Inner Power; a.k.a. Laojun). They correspond to the Three Heavens of Yuqing (Jade Clarity; highest), Shangqing (Highest Clarity; middle), and Taiqing (Great Clarity; lowest), respectively. One finds them represented as three old Chinese men, usually sitting on elevated platforms (Figure 4.2). Celestial Worthy of Original Beginning sits in the center, with Celestial Worthy of Numinous Treasure on his left and Celestial Worthy of the Dao and Inner Power on his right. From a traditional Chinese perspective, this corresponds to the positions of host, first guest, and second guest, respectively. Here we may note a theological issue: Laojun (Lord Lao), formerly the "high god of Daoism," has become located in a triad in which he is technically in the lowest position. Whereas in earlier Daoist history he was a single high god, here he stands in relation to the other two members of the Three Purities. One explanation is that Celestial Worthy of the Dao and Inner Power is a more primordial, less differentiated presence, which becomes manifest in the personal deity of Lord Lao. This conception parallels modern Daoist views of Yuhuang dadi (Jade Emperor), the high god of the Chinese popular pantheon.

FIGURE 4.2 *The Three Purities.*

Source: Frontpiece of *Daozang*; *Duren jing*, DZ 1.

In terms of iconography, Celestial Worthy of Original Beginning usually holds a sphere or circular object in his hand, which represents unity. Celestial Worthy of Numinous Treasure holds a Ruyi scepter, which represents cosmic power and a wish-fulfilling capacity. Celestial Worthy of the Dao and Inner Power holds a fan, which usually depicts his celestial paradise and represents immortality. In a correct altar configuration, the scepter and fan extend out and away from the center as a sign of respect to Celestial Worthy of Original Beginning. Different Daoists have different interpretations of the Three Purities. Some hold that they are personal, and will respond to petitions, including personal prayers. However, many modern Daoists believe that the Three Purities are impersonal and represent the three primordial ethers or energies of the cosmos. They are usually placed on the central Daoist altar because they are the earliest emanation of the Dao and closest to the Dao as Source. Beyond them, the Dao as primordial undifferentiation cannot be represented iconographically. The Three Purities also receive additional correspondences, including the external Three Treasures of the Dao, scriptures, and teachers, and the internal Three Treasures of spirit, qi, and vital essence. That is, from a Daoist self-cultivation perspective, the Three Purities reside in the three elixir fields (*dantian*) of the human body, namely, head, heart, and lower abdomen.

The Daoist pantheon includes many other Daoist gods, immortals, and Perfected, and Daoist temple and altar configurations are also quite diverse. In terms of immortals, Lü Dongbin (b. 798?) as an individual and the Eight Immortals as a group probably receive the most veneration. From a Daoist theological perspective, the Dao, the universe, as well as individuated beings in the universe, including gods, immortals, humans, animals, and so forth, are sacred, albeit in varying degrees of connection and pervasion.

Further reading

Kohn, Livia. 2002, *Living with the Dao: Conceptual Issues in Daoist Practice*. E-dao (electronic) publication. Cambridge, MA: Three Pines Press.

Little, Stephen. 2000, *Taoism and the Arts of China*. Berkeley, CA: Art Institute of Chicago/University of California Press.

Major, John, Sarah Queen, Andrew Seth Meyer, and Harold Roth. 2010, *The Huainanzi: A Guide to the Theory and Practice of Government in Early Han China*. New York, NY: Columbia University Press.

Silvers, Brock. 2005, *The Taoist Manual: Applying Taoism to Daily Life*. Nederland, CO: Sacred Mountain Press.

CHAPTER FIVE

Personhood

Daoist anthropology, or discourse on human being, is a central aspect of Daoist worldviews. Human personhood and subjective experience consist of various dimensions, including corporeal, psychological, cognitive, spiritual, inter-subjective, and cultural aspects. That is, a comprehensive understanding of "self" acknowledges personhood as psychosomatic, relational, and social. On the most foundational level, Daoist views of personhood tend to be body-affirming and psychosomatic. This is expressed in various Daoist technical terms, including the Three Treasures and "innate nature and life-destiny." While each term has a nuanced meaning, they draw our attention to the interrelated nature of physical, psychological, energetic, and spiritual dimensions of human being.

Different Daoist views of self emerge in different contexts and are related to different Daoist models of practice and attainment. It is thus important to consider the ways in which specific Daoist views inform and become expressed in specific Daoist practices, including naturalistic, contemplative, ascetic, and alchemical approaches to human being. Daoist anthropology in turn relates to Daoist views of death, dying, and the afterlife, with the transformative process of dissolution, the actualized state of immortality, and, later under Buddhist influence, the ontological givenness of reincarnation being most common. Daoist conceptions of human personhood begin with deep attentiveness to corporeality, including unfamiliar and hidden layers of the body. Interestingly, the "Daoist body" often becomes discussed as landscape, mountain, and cosmos. Daoist body awareness involves recognition of the ways in which physicality cannot be separated from other aspects of self. Here embodiment consists of more apparently substantial dimensions (e.g. organs, sense organs, and vital substances) and more apparently immaterial dimensions (e.g. emotions, cognitive abilities, and spiritual faculties). Within this map of personhood, one also finds a sophisticated Daoist psychology, which centers on the heart-mind as emotional and intellectual center. On a more subtle level, Daoist views of personhood include recognition of energetic and spiritual, in the sense of related to spirit, aspects. This energetic view claims that there is a subtle body within the material body, which is awakened and actualized through Daoist alchemical practice. These various aspects of Daoist personhood may be explored through the framework of embodiment, psychology, and transformation.

Embodiment

Embodiment refers to the ontological givenness of somatic experiencing, specifically the fact we are endowed with physicality and express ourselves through kinesthetic being-in-the-world. At the same time, embodiment may be understood in a larger sense of what one cultivates and transmits through one's being and presence. In the case of Daoism, this relates to distinctively Daoist values and commitments, such as those discussed in the previous chapter. Such Daoist views also encompass the various dimensions of personhood, including views of the body and subjectivity. On the most physical level, this includes various associations related to correlative cosmology, specifically the five yin-organs (liver, heart, spleen, lungs, kidneys), five sense organs (eyes, tongue, mouth, nose, ears), five tissues (sinews, vessels, muscles, skin, bones), and five activities (walking, talking, sitting, reclining, standing).

Daoism is one of the more world-affirming and body-affirming religious traditions. Here it is important to note that, comparatively speaking, different religious adherents and communities have different conceptions of the world and body. Generally speaking, Daoists have tended to recognize the Dao as manifest in/as/through the world and the body. In terms of embodiment, classical and therefore foundational Daoist views emphasize the sacredness of embodiment. Physicality and organicism are generally viewed as positive dimensions of existence.

Daoist organicism

Master Dongguo addressed Master Zhuang: "Considering the Dao, where does it exist?"

Master Zhuang said, "There's no place it doesn't exist."

"Come on," said Master Dongguo, "be more specific!"

"It's in ants."

"As low as that?"

"It's in the grass."

"But that's lower still!"

"It's in tiles and shards."

"How can it be that low?"

"It's in piss and shit!"

(*Zhuangzi*, Chapter 22; see also Chapters 6 and 18)

For members of the inner cultivation lineages of classical Daoism, and for Daoists with affinities with such views, the Dao manifests in everything. This includes aspects of existence that are conventionally understood as "inferior," "impure," and "profane." Thus, one finds many Daoists discussing the body and world as "sacred vessels," as storehouses for the Dao's numinous presence. This even includes "piss and shit," the supposed waste products of digestion. Such Daoist organicism recognizes the universe as a compost system wherein everything participates in and contributes to the ongoing transformative process; it also recognizes each individual being as a microcosm of the larger cosmological system. The "waste" of some beings is the nourishment for others. On a more contemplative level, and especially in conditions of realization, Daoists see each aspect of existence as a manifestation of the Dao. The "grace" of the Dao is also found in the natural condition of the human body, in its effortless functioning. Like the universe, in a state of harmony and wellness, the body simply works in recurring beneficial patterns. This includes the often-unnoticed fact of unassisted digestion, nourishment, and elimination. Celebration of the natural transformative process of the body, which parallels that of the larger cosmos, is connected to the classical Daoist practice of apophatic meditation and the sage ideal of classical Daoism discussed in the previous chapter.

One way in which Daoists have explained embodiment and human aliveness centers on the concepts of "innate nature" (*xing*) and "life-destiny" (*ming*). In classical Daoism, these terms are roughly synonymous and often connected to "life" (*sheng*) more generally. From a foundational Daoist perspective, one's fundamental nature, including the fact of physical embodiment and existence, *is* the Dao. One has an innate connection to the sacred, and one's innate nature is "good" in a conventional sense. That is, we are fundamentally well. Human connection to the Dao manifests in the world as "virtue" or "inner power" (*de*), as beneficial and transformational influence. When abiding in a "natural condition," individuals participate in and express cosmological attunement and numinous pervasion. This map of human personhood in turn becomes more nuanced in the later Daoist tradition, especially in various systems of self-cultivation. Some Daoists focus on the "dual cultivation of innate nature and life-destiny" (*xingming shuangxiu*). Read etymologically, innate nature (*xing* 性) is the heart-mind (*xin* 心) with which one was born (*sheng* 生); it is associated with the heart, consciousness, and spirit. Life-destiny (*ming* 命) is a decree (*ling* 令) from the cosmos made manifest as one's corporeality; it is associated with the body, physicality, and one's foundational vitality. On a more Daoist esoteric level, *ming* depicts the kidneys viewed from the back. Although there are varying degrees of emphasis on these, the terms draw our attention to a Daoist psychosomatic view of human existence and religious practice; they reveal the importance of a holistic and integrated Daoist understanding of self, including corporeal, physiological, psychological, and spiritual dimensions. They also relate to specific types of training, with the cultivation of innate nature often associated with "stillness practice" (*jinggong*), or meditation, and the cultivation of life-destiny often associated with "movement practice" (*donggong*), or health and longevity techniques.

Another dimension of foundational Daoist views of human personhood and embodiment centers on the so-called organ-meridian system, which parallels classical Chinese medicine. From this perspective, the human body consists of 12 primary organs and meridians. As discussed in more detail below, this is an energetic view, with each organ having specific functions and relating to other organs in patterns of dynamic interaction. This occurs through "meridians," the channels and networks through which qi circulates in the body. Located in the system of correspondences discussed in the previous chapter, the five yin-organs (lit., "storehouse"; *zang*) are the liver, heart, spleen, lungs, and kidneys, while the six yang-organs (lit., "receptacle"; *fu*) are the gall bladder, small intestine, large intestine, stomach, urinary bladder, and Triple Warmer. Sometimes the pericardium is added to the five yin-organs in order to create parallelism with the six yang-organs as the paired organ of the Triple Warmer. The yin-yang associations here relate to the five yin-organs being more solid in nature and the six yang-organs being more hollow in nature. In addition, functionally speaking, the yin-organs are storehouses for essence, while the yang-organs serve as receptacles for things that pass through them. The body, and specifically the organ-meridian system, is often understood as a "country," with each "inhabitant" having a specific hierarchical position and functional role. For example, the heart is the "ruler," while the other yin-organs are understood as "ministers." Here we might also understand the body as ecosystem, microcosm, and world (Figure 5.1).

While the functions of each organ are vital for the harmony and wellness of the body, for present purposes a few examples must suffice. The liver is responsible for the smooth flow of qi throughout the body; the heart for the overall wellbeing of the body; the spleen for assimilation, including digestion; and so forth. In Daoist systems, the five yin-organs tend to be primary. For example, they are associated with the Five Marchmounts; the five cardinal sacred mountains; the Five Numinous Treasure Talismans, five protective cosmic graphs; the Five Qi and Five Spirits; and so forth. However, some systems, especially late medieval Daoist internal

FIGURE 5.1 *The Body as Mountain.*

Source: *Duren shangpin miaojing neiyi*, DZ 90; also DZ 1068.

alchemy, also emphasize the gall bladder or Triple Warmer. With respect to the former, one explanation is that the gall bladder is an "extraordinary organ," having a connection to marrow and thus to vital essence. In terms of the Triple Warmer, one interpretation suggests that it is basically synonymous with the elixir fields, three subtle locations in the body; it also relates to the circulation of original qi (*yuanqi*).

Again paralleling classical Chinese medicine, the Daoist body also consists of various substances and fluids. On the most basic level, there are five spiritual dimensions associated with the five yin-organs: liver/ethereal soul (*hun*), heart/spirit (*shen*), spleen/ thought (*yi*), lungs/corporeal soul (*po*), and kidneys/will (*zhi*). The ethereal soul is associated with dreaming and imagination; spirit with awareness more generally; thought with reflection; corporeal soul with habit; and will with volitional drive.

In a simplified expression, the ethereal soul and corporeal soul are paired in the so-called "two-soul model." From this perspective, the person consists of one *hun* and one *po*, though in the later Daoist tradition these are sometimes three and seven in number, respectively. *Hun* is conventionally translated as "cloud" or "ethereal soul," while *po* is conventionally rendered as "white" or "corporeal soul." The use of "soul" is misleading, as it implies something substantial and eternal. In understanding these terms, it is helpful to examine them etymologically. *Hun* 魂 consists of *yun* 云 ("cloud") and *gui* 鬼 ("ghost"), while *po* 魄 consists of *bai* 白 ("white") and *gui* 鬼 ("ghost"). The use of *gui* indicates that these aspects of self are ethereal, ephemeral, apparitional, and animating; the *hun* and *po* are best understood as animating forces or spiritual elements. "Cloud" is used for *hun* to suggest that it is more ethereal, while "white" is used for *po* to suggest that it is more material and physical. For clarity's sake, one may think of the *hun* as the yang-ghost and the *po* as the yin-ghost: the yang-ghost is associated with subtle and celestial aspects of self, while the yin-ghost is associated with the flesh and bones. According to the standard account, after death, the various composite aspects of self separate. The *hun* ascends into the heavens to become an ancestor, while the *po* descends into the earth, eventually dissipating as the body decomposes. In the standard account, one remains an ancestor for seven generations, though it is unclear to what extent this is a conscious and intentional post-mortem existence, rather than an "influence" partially maintained through the act of remembrance and ritual offerings by one's descendants. In any case, it is important to note that the *hun* and *po* are ephemeral, and eventually dissipate into the cosmos.

In a more specifically Daoist expression, especially prominent in internal alchemy, the spiritual dimensions of personhood become grouped in the internal Three Treasures (*nei sanbao*), namely, vital essence (*jing*), qi, and spirit (*shen*). Vital essence is one's foundational or core vitality as well as the blueprint for physical structure. It is associated with sexual reproduction, and specifically with menstrual blood in women and semen in men. Best left untranslated like "Dao" and "yin-yang," qi relates to both air derived from material respiration and vital breath, subtle currents that flow through the cosmos and the body. Although anachronistic, some people find it helpful to think of qi as "energy." Here it is important to recognize that there are different types of qi, with the "qi of the Dao" (*daoqi*), "perfect qi" (*zhenqi*), and "original qi" (*yuanqi*) being most important for Daoists. Often used synonymously, these types of qi are generally understood as more primordial and undifferentiated emanations of the Dao. Finally, spirit is even more subtle than qi; it is often associated with divine capacities and consciousness. Etymologically speaking, *shen* 神 consists of *shi* 示 ("omen") and *shen* 申 ("to extend"). Spirit is a capacity to connect with subtle realities. In the context of internal alchemy practice, the practitioner attempts to conserve and prevent the dissipation of these aspects of self. This often involves temporary or permanent celibacy. The standard, simplified alchemical process, in turn, involves three basic stages: (1) Transforming vital essence into qi, (2) Transforming qi into spirit, and (3) Transforming spirit into emptiness.

The Three Treasures also bring our attention to the central importance of body fluids and vital substances in Daoist views of personhood. In addition to the Three Treasures, fluids include blood, marrow, saliva, sweat, spinal fluid, tears, and so forth. In technical usage, fluids include "thin fluids" (*jin*), such as sweat and tears, and "thick fluids" (*ye*), such as cerebral spinal and synovial joint fluid. *Jin*-fluids exist at a more surface and outer level, while *ye*-fluids exist at a deeper and more inner level. These fluids are frequently compared to "dew," "mist," "rivers," and "ponds" in the body. While fluids are relatively straightforward, there are also more esoteric Daoist understandings. These include the Daoist view that alchemical practice produces clear and sweet saliva, which is contained in the Jade Pond (*yuchi*; mouth). Often referred to as Jade Nectar (*yujiang*), Spirit Water (*shenshui*), and Sweet Dew (*ganlu*), this saliva is swallowed during Daoist alchemical practice and is an essential component of "elixir formation." Blood also occupies a central place in certain Daoist practices, especially female alchemy (*nüdan*). For present purposes, it is noteworthy that blood is understood as a material dimension of spirit and that menstruation, as the loss of vital essence, is seen as a major source of dissipation for women.

In early medieval Daoist asceticism and external alchemy, one finds an even more esoteric Daoist view of personhood. According to this map, human beings consist of the Three Hun (*sanhun*), Three Death-bringers (*sanshi*), Seven Po (*qipo*), and Nine Worms (*jiuchong*). This view evidences ascetic tendencies as well. One of the standard sources on these various substances is the ninth-century *Chu sanshi jiuchong jing* (Scripture on Expelling the Three Death-bringers and Nine Worms; DZ 871), which includes illustrations. According to this text, the Three Hun are positive in nature, while the other three dimensions of self are negative influences. The Three Hun are the three yang and positive spirits associated with the liver (1ab). They are identified as Shuangling (Lively Numen), Taiguang (Terrace Radiance), and Youjing (Mysterious Essence). Here one is informed: "The Three Hun are located beneath the liver. They look like human beings and wear green robes with yellow inner garments. Every month on the third, thirteenth, and twenty-third, they leave the body in the evening to go wandering around" (1b). One of the main goals in early Daoist ascetic and alchemical practice was to keep the Three Hun within the body.

Alternatively rendered as "Three Corpses" and sometimes appearing as "Three Worms" (*sanchong*), the Three Death-bringers are conventionally understood as three biospiritual parasites residing in the human body. They reside in the three elixir fields (*dantian*), namely, Palace of Nirvana (center of head), Scarlet Palace (heart region), and Ocean of Qi (lower abdomen). The *Scripture on Expelling the Three Death-bringers and Nine Worms* (DZ 871, 7a–8a) contains illustrations of the Three Death-bringers, wherein they are identified as follows: Peng Ju (upper), Peng Zhi (middle), and Peng Jiao (lower). Thus, they are sometimes referred to as the "Three Pengs" (*sanpeng*). Other texts provide alternative names: Qinggu (Blue Decrepitude; upper), Baigu (White Hag; middle), and Xueshi (Bloody Corpse; lower). Various malevolent and harmful influences are attributed to them, including inciting people to become greedy, angry, forgetful, deluded, sexually deviant, and so forth.

From an early medieval Daoist perspective, the Seven Po are also bio-spiritual entities which exert negative influences on the individual and which lead to dissipation, and often to premature death. In the eleventh-century encyclopedia *Yunji qiqian* (Seven Tablets from a Cloudy Satchel; DZ 1032), they are identified as follows: (1) Shigou (Corpse Dog), (2) Fushi (Concealed Arrow), (3) Queyin (Sparrow Yin), (4) Tunzei (Seizing Thief), (5) Feidu (Negative Poison), (6) Chuhui (Oppressive Impurity), and (7) Choufei (Putrid Lungs) (54.7ab). Visual representations appear in the *Scripture on Expelling the Three Death-bringers and Nine Worms* (DZ 871, 3a). According to that text, "The Seven Po consist of yin and deviant qi. They are ghosts. They can make people into walking corpses, causing them to be stingy and greedy, jealous and full of envy. They give people bad dreams and make them clench their teeth. They command the mouth to say 'yes' when the heart-mind thinks 'no'. In addition, they cause people to lose their vital essence in sexual passion and become dissipated by hankering after luxury and ease. Through them, people completely lose their purity and simplicity" (2a). In late medieval Daoism, the Three Death-bringers and Seven Po become more psychologized.

Finally, the Nine Worms are nine material parasites residing in the human body. Visual representations appear in the *Scripture on Expelling the Three Death-bringers and Nine Worms* (DZ 871, 9a–14a). Here they are identified as follows: (1) Fuchong (Slinking Worm), (2) Huichong (Coiling Worm), (3) Baichong (White Worm), (4) Rouchong (Flesh Worm), (5) Feichong (Lung Worm), (6) Weichong (Stomach Worm), (7) Gechong (Diaphragm Worm), (8) Chichong (Crimson Worm), and (9) Qiaochong (Stilted Worm). This and related texts also provide the length (between one and four inches) and colors of the various worms, indicating that they were seen as material in nature.

As one might expect, the aspiring ascetic and alchemist aims to expel or transform the Three Death-bringers, Seven Po, and Nine Worms. One relevant formula appears in the *Lingbao wufu xu* (Explanations of the Five Talismans of Numinous Treasure; DZ 388), wherein one is advised to combine wild asparagus root (*tianmen dong*) with poke root (*shanglu*). In this respect it is difficult to separate specific views of self from their related practices and projected soteriological goals. Here the Daoist adept engages in ascetic and dietetic practice, specifically in what is known as *bigu*, "grain avoidance" or "abstention from cereals." It appears that *bigu* frequently refers to fasting more generally, rather than simply eliminating grains from one's diet (Campany 2002; Eskildsen 2004). In any case, from this dietetic and external alchemical viewpoint, one must expel "the worms," probably actual parasites in the present context, but possibly also the Three Death-bringers. The latter is possible because *bigu* practice often involves this informing worldview. Here one finds both a parasitological and possibly even demonological view of the body—it houses malevolent biospiritual parasites and actual worms, which must be expelled in order to attain longevity and immortality. This begs the question of the "natural condition" of the human body and the relationship between Daoist anthropological and theological views.

Psychology

As a comparative category, "psychology" refers to discourse on human subjectivity, especially from a lived emotional, intellectual, and behavioral perspective. The term derives from the Greek *psukhē* (*psyche*), meaning "breath," "soul," or "spirit." Psychology thus may relate to consciousness more broadly understood as well as spiritual dimensions of personhood. In addition, there are often tradition-specific psychologies, which include complex mappings of consciousness, human potential, and sometimes "numinous abilities."

The center of Daoist psychology is the heart-mind (*xin* 心). The ancient seal script version of the character (𢖾) is revealing, as it depicts the actual heart. Interestingly, in certain contexts *xin* also means "center." Along these lines, some Daoists interpret the Chinese character *zhong* 中 ("center") as depicting the chest cavity intersected by a central axis. The axis may be understood as the Thrusting Channel, which moves through the center core of the torso between the crown-point (heaven) and perineum (earth). From a classical and foundational Daoist perspective, the heart-mind is understood both as a physical location in the chest (the heart as "organ" [*zang*]) and as relating to thoughts (*nian*) and emotions (*qing*) (the heart as "consciousness" [*shi*]). For this reason, although sometimes translated as "mind" under Buddhist influence, *xin* is better translated as "heart-mind," thus indicating its psychosomatic nature. The heart-mind is the emotional and intellectual center of the human person. It is associated with consciousness and identified as the storehouse of spirit (*shen*). In its original or realized condition, the heart-mind has the ability to attain numinous pervasion; in its disoriented or habituated condition, especially in a state of hyper-emotionality or intellectualism, the heart-mind has the ability to separate the adept from the Dao as Source. The latter is often referred to as the "ordinary heart-mind" (*suxin*) or more poetically as the "monkey-mind" (*yuanxin*), while the former is often referred to as the "original heart-mind" (*benxin*). The ordinary heart-mind is characterized by chaos and instability, while the original heart-mind is characterized by coherence and constancy. In terms of classical Daoism, it is noteworthy that the received *Book of Master Guan* contains the four so-called "Techniques of the Heart-mind" chapters, with the "Inward Training" chapter being particularly important for clarifying classical Daoist apophatic meditation (Roth 1999a).

The heart-mind within the heart-mind

The Dao fills all under the heavens.
It is everywhere where people reside,
But people are unable to recognize it.
When you explore the whole meaning,
You extend up to the heavens above,
And stretch down to the earth below.
You pervade the nine inhabited regions.
What does it mean to investigate this?
The answer resides in the calmness of the heart-mind.
When your heart-mind is governed,
    The senses then are also governed.
When your heart-mind is calm,
    The senses then are also calm.
The heart-mind is what governs them;
The heart-mind is what calms them.
Store the heart-mind by means of the heart-mind;
Within the heart-mind, there is yet another heart-mind.
This inner heart-mind is an awareness that precedes language.

("Inward Training," ch. 14)

The notion of the "heart-mind within the heart-mind" suggests that there is mind within the actual, physical heart as well as that there is a purified form of consciousness within habituated psychological reactivity. Such a Daoist view is a form of "contemplative psychology" (DeWit 1991), meaning that it is a psychology informed by and manifested in contemplative practice. The "Inward Training" chapter in turn refers to this "inner heart-mind" as the "lodging place of the numinous." In the later Daoist tradition, it is often referred to as "awakened nature" (*wuxing*), "original nature" (*benxing*), and "original spirit" (*yuanshen*). More esoteric Daoist names include Central Palace, Numinous Tower, Scarlet Palace, and so forth. The original or purified heart-mind is understood as characterized by "clarity and stillness" (*qingjing*), one of the connective strands throughout various Daoist models of practice-realization. For example, according to the eighth-century *Qingjing jing* (Scripture on Clarity and Stillness; DZ 620), "The human spirit is fond of clarity,/But the heart-mind disturbs it./ The human heart-mind is fond of stillness,/But desires meddle with it./If you can constantly banish desires,/Then the heart-mind will become still naturally./If you can constantly settle the heart-mind,/Then the spirit will become clear naturally" (1b). Similarly, the thirteenth-century *Nei riyong jing* (Scripture on Daily Internal Practice; DZ 645) explains, "The Numinous Tower of the heart emptied of all things: This is called clarity. Not allowing even a single thought to arise: This is called stillness" (1a). In the standard account, through Daoist emptiness- and stillness-based meditation, turbidity and agitation are transformed into clarity and stillness. This parallels a return to an earlier cosmogonic moment when the clear and light rose to become the heavens (pure cosmic yang) and the heavy and turbid sank to become the earth (pure cosmic yin). By purifying the heart-mind of emotional and intellectual reactivity, one returns to an original state of clarity and stillness, which manifests as energetic sensitivity and spiritual insight.

Another dimension of Daoist psychological views centers on sensory engagement. Again rooted in contemplative practice, the primary psychological map identifies habituated sensory perception as a major source of dissipation. This involves a fairly standard view in which sensory engagement with the phenomenal world frequently creates emotional and intellectual turmoil. Decreasing these various forms of habituation also decreases dissipation and enables one to return to a state of internal harmony. Here one may remember the relevant associations in correlative cosmology, especially with respect to the sense organs: liver/eyes, heart/tongue, spleen/mouth, lungs/nose, and kidneys/ears. From this perspective, excessive visual stimulation (gazing) may injure the liver; excessive vocal stimulation (talking) may injure the heart; excessive gustatory stimulation (tasting) may injure the spleen; excessive olfactory stimulation (smelling) may injure the lungs; and excessive auditory stimulation (listening) may injure the kidneys. In the larger Daoist tradition, various technical terms are used to refer to sensory engagement as a potential source of dissipation and spiritual disorientation. Some of these include the Three Essentials (*sanyao*), Four Gates (*simen*), Five Thieves (*wuzei*), Six Roots (*liugen*), Seven Apertures (*qiqiao*), and Nine Apertures (*jiuqiao*). These referents are different ways of mapping the same corporeal constituents and capacities, while maintaining a certain nuance with regard to Daoist practice. Numerologically speaking, "three" most often refers to the eyes, ears, and mouth; "four" to the eyes, ears, nose, and mouth; "five" to the eyes (2), ears (2), and mouth (1); "six" to the eyes, ears, nose, mouth, body, and thought; "seven" to the eyes (2), ears (2), nose (2), and mouth (1); and "nine" to the previous seven plus the urethra and anus. In technical terms, the "body" has a different connotation than discussed above: Related to "touch," it is associated with sensual activity as another potential source of dissipation. For certain Daoists, the sense organs and associated sensory engagement are thus "gates" in the sense that they are the passageways into the body that allow entrance from outside to inside. They are "thieves" because they have the capacity to rob the Daoist adept of his or her vitality. In addition to being "apertures" or "cavities" (i.e. openings in the body), the sense organs are "roots" because, as causes of desire, they may generate defilements and vexations.

A natural question arises here: If the foundational Daoist anthropology sees embodiment as positive, as a manifestation of the Dao, then why are the senses sometimes viewed negatively? The answer is that various dimensions of human personhood have the capacity to connect or distance Daoists from the Dao. In the case of the senses, in a state of excessive use and habituation, they often create confusion and dissipation. However, in their "natural condition" and appropriate application, they provide one way of participating in the cosmological process and experiencing the numinous presence of the Dao. In this respect, it is noteworthy that Daoists tend to emphasize listening over the other senses. Here one may recall the previous discussion of the Daoist ideal of the sage (*shengren*). A realized Daoist embodies attentiveness and carefulness, especially with respect to deeper energetic dimensions of existence.

Emotionality is another dimension of foundational Daoist psychology. Like sensory engagement, emotionality, habituated emotionality in particular, is often viewed by Daoists as a source of dissipation. The associations of correlative cosmology are again relevant, especially the positive (yang) and negative (yin) emotions: liver/humaneness/anger, heart/respect/hatred, spleen/honesty/resentment, lungs/righteousness/grief, and kidneys/wisdom/fear. Under certain Daoist readings, the negative emotion of the heart is excessive joy or anxiety; the negative emotion of the spleen is rumination; and the positive emotion of the lungs is discernment. In Daoist systems that utilize this psychology, one's natural state of psychosomatic homeostasis manifests in a harmonious expression of the five positive emotions and a near absence of the five negative emotions. That is, there are clear emotional signs of subjective wellness. As individuals become more habituated and disoriented, there is a greater degree of negative emotionality, including various "composite" emotions. From this perspective, the five primary negative emotions become mixed together in complex and chaotic ways. Other Daoist systems also recognize the potentially harmful and dissipating effect of hyper-emotionality. This is again expressed in specific Daoist technical terms, such as the so-called Six Emotions (*liuqing*) and Seven Emotions (*qiqing*). The Six Emotions are usually identified as pleasure, anger, grief, happiness, selfish love, and hatred. The Seven Emotions are usually identified as pleasure, anger, worry, thought, grief, fear, and fright. Other harmful psychological states and ontological conditions singled out by Daoists include apathy, carelessness, desire, greed, insolence, judgment, obstinacy, profit-seeking, regret, selfishness, sorrow, willfulness, worry, and so forth. Here one may recall the previously discussed Daoist values of deference, flexibility, simplicity, and so forth. One also notices that emotions that are conventionally viewed as "positive" (e.g. happiness and pleasure) are defined negatively. This is because such emotions are object-centered, relational, and ephemeral. They are destined to disappear, and this "loss" frequently causes increased agitation and distress. Excess emotionality thus relates to "dissipation" (*lou*; lit., "leakage" or "outflow"), or the unnecessary loss of the Three Treasures. A central commitment in turn centers on "non-dissipation" (*wulou*; lit., "non-leakage" or "without outflow"), in which one refrains from engaging in any harmful activities. This results in increased psychosomatic integrity and aliveness.

However, in a manner paralleling Daoist views of the original condition of the heart-mind and appropriate sensory engagement, Daoists also recognize "natural emotionality" as beneficial and transformative. This is a form of emotionality that expresses internal harmony, interpersonal accord, and sacred connection.

Appropriate emotionality

Master Hui addressed Master Zhuang: "Can a human being really be without feelings?"

Master Zhuang replied, "Certainly."

Master Hui said, "But a person who has no feelings—how can you call him human?"

Master Zhuang responded, "The Dao gave him a face; Heaven gave him a form—why can't you call him human?"

Master Hui said, "But if you've already called him human, how can he be without feelings?"

Master Zhuang replied, "That's not what I mean by feelings. When I talk about having no feelings, I mean that a person doesn't allow likes or dislikes to get in and do harm. He just accords with suchness and doesn't try to help life along."

Master Hui said, "If he doesn't try to help life along, then how can he keep himself alive?"

Master Zhuang responded, "The Dao gave him a face; Heaven gave him a form. He doesn't let likes or dislikes get in and do harm. You, now—you treat your spirit like an outsider. You wear out your vital essence, leaning on a tree and moaning, slumping at your desk and dozing. Heaven picked out a body for you and you use it to babble on about making distinctions!" (*Zhuangzi*, Chapter 5; adapted from Watson 1968: 75–76)

In each and every circumstance, one naturally has an appropriate emotional response, which is further connected to the original condition of the heart-mind and innate nature. One expresses a psychological pattern that, while unique to oneself, also has recognizable characteristics with respect to Daoist cultivation. However, as ordinary human beings misunderstand hyper-reactivity and habituation as "being emotional," they are most likely to view Daoists as "emotionless." This apparent emotionlessness is actually an appropriate emotionality rooted in stillness. As the above passage indicates, it is beyond personal preferences. In a certain sense, it is transpersonal, as one becomes free of entanglements such as reputation and social acceptance. One cultivates something else. Daoists often refer to this "something else" as "true joy" (*zhenle*), that is, a state of spiritual freedom and bliss beyond the oscillations of gain and loss. This state is well represented in famous Daoist stories such as the "Great Peng-bird" and the "Joy of Fish." It also recalls the name for roving Daoists: "wandering clouds" (*yunyou*). Although non-attachment is one aspect of such Daoist existential modes, Daoists tend to be quite happy, playful, and jovial, to abide in a condition of carefree play.

Foundational Daoist psychology thus focuses on the heart-mind and innate nature, sensory engagement, and emotionality. In their appropriate expressions, these aspects of personhood may connect the Daoist practitioner to the Dao. However, in habituated or excessive conditions, they become major sources of dissipation and disorientation. It is also important to recognize that, while this is the foundational Daoist psychology, there are also other movement-specific and practice-specific Daoist psychologies. In addition, Daoist psychology clearly makes a distinction between pathological and realized states, with the latter including profound insights into human possibility. Beyond social conditioning, familial obligation, and personal habituation, one may live through spirit and a connection to the sacred. In this way, Daoism might be reasonably placed in dialogue with humanistic and transpersonal psychology, including claims about human potential, actualization, and a larger context of being. We might recognize such Daoist views of personhood as a "psychology of realization."

Transformation

As briefly touched upon above, Daoist views of personhood recognize more subtle dimensions of subjective being and existence. Such views relate to both embodiment and psychology because of the psychosomatic and interrelated nature of the various constituents of self. That which is "physical" has "psychological" dimensions, and vice versa. In addition, fundamental Daoist views include "energetic" and "spiritual" aspects. On the most basic level, these correspond to original qi (*yuanqi*) and original spirit (*yuanshen*). Like the "heart-mind within the heart-mind," there is a "body within the body." There is a subtle body within the physical body. Through various Daoist training regimens, especially internal alchemy (*neidan*), one may attain higher levels of cultivation and refinement. From this Daoist perspective and associated practices, one engages in a process of purification and transformation. This involves the attainment of a transformed ontological condition, the emergence of a new being. In more elitist Daoist expressions, while each being and every being ideally has the potential to become an immortal, some individuals have a greater propensity and perhaps innate endowment. This is sometimes referred to as "immortal bones" (*xiangu*) or "predestined affinities" (*yuanfen*).

Here we should also note that yin and yang take on specific and alternative meanings in such contexts. For example, in many internal alchemy lineages, yin appears to be defined negatively, while yang appears to be defined positively. A distinction must be made between yin-yang as cosmological principles, and yin-yang as alchemical map, specifically as a map of alchemical transformation. That is, there are cosmological and alchemical interpretations and applications of yin-yang, with the associations varying depending on system and context. The cosmological dimension cannot be changed—it is the underlying structure of cosmos. However, on an existential and alchemical level, yin may designate immorality, disease, mortality, defilements, delusion, and so forth; yang may designate morality, wellness, immortality, purity, realization, and so forth. Internal alchemists thus frequently speak of transforming yin into yang, of becoming a yang-spirit, a pure yang being. This does not mean that one transcends the foundational cosmological harmony of yin and yang. In fact, classical Daoism and the foundational Daoist worldview urge one to "embrace the feminine," understood as correlative with "yin qualities" (flexibility, passivity, receptivity, silence, etc.). Rather, it means that the internal alchemist works to become a perfected being in which all negative characteristics have been transformed into their positive counterparts.

The transformational dimension of Daoist views of human personhood thus relates to "alchemy," with alchemy being a term borrowed from Western esoteric and hermetic traditions to render a variety of indigenous Chinese terms. Just as alchemy broadly understood involves the transmutation of base metals into gold, so too parallel Daoist traditions involve the formation of an elixir through either the actual decoction of external ingredients (*waidan*; "external alchemy") or through psychosomatic transmutation (*neidan*; "internal alchemy"). As an approximation of a Daoist technical term, "alchemy" most often translates *dan*, which more literally means "cinnabar" or "pill."

In terms of Daoist anthropology, Daoist internal alchemy utilizes a complex mapping of human personhood. We may refer to this as the Daoist "alchemical" or "subtle body," and such views include subtle anatomy and physiology (Figure 5.2). The primary layer of the alchemical body centers on "elixir fields" (*dantian*). Sometimes referred to as the Three Islands (*sandao*), these are the somatic locations where "elixirs" (subtle substances) are formed and stored. When "elixir field" appears independently, specifically the "lower elixir field," it most often refers to the navel region. In the standardized expression, there are three elixir fields: Ocean of Qi (*qihai*; navel region; lower), Scarlet Palace (*jianggong*; heart region; middle), and Niwan Palace (*niwan gong*; center of head; upper). The technical meaning of *niwan* (lit., "mud-ball") is somewhat unclear. Under one reading, it derives from an earlier formula in external alchemy; in the context of internal alchemy, it is compared to a muddy pond out of which a pure lotus emerges. Under another reading, it is a transliteration of *nirvāṇa*; it is the place where enlightenment emerges. Sometimes the Niwan Palace is referred to as the Ancestral Cavity (*zuqiao*). In other maps, the Niwan Palace corresponds to the crown of the head. There is also an alternative system of three elixir fields: Earth Door (*dihu*; perineum region; lower), Ocean of Qi (middle), and Niwan Palace (upper). Sometimes the Earth Door is referred to as the Meeting of Yin

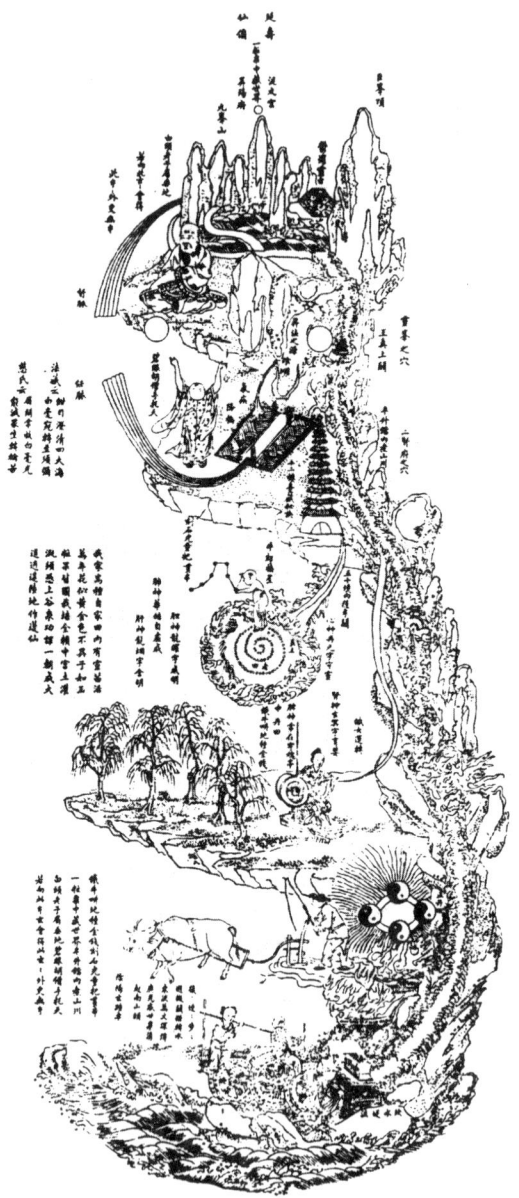

FIGURE 5.2 *The Daoist Alchemical Body.*

Source: Print of *Neijing tu* (Diagram of Internal Pathways; author's collection).

(*huiyin*). In both systems, the three elixir fields are associated with the Three Treasures mentioned above. These include vital essence, qi, and spirit. Generally speaking, vital essence is associated with the kidneys and perineum region, qi with the navel region, and spirit with the heart and head regions. On the most basic level, the aspiring internal alchemist must seal the body, prevent dissipation, and conserve the vital substances and spiritual dimensions of personhood in their corresponding corporeal locations.

In addition to the vital substances discussed above, there are many other key points and locations in the Daoist alchemical body. Here some of the most important ones must suffice. The spine contains the Three Passes (*sanguan*), namely, Tailbone Gate (*weilü*; coccyx), Narrow Ridge (*jiaji*; mid-spine), and Jade Pillow (*yuzhen*; occiput). This map is used in practices such as the Celestial Cycle (Microcosmic Orbit) in which one circulates qi up the Governing Vessel. The tongue is called the Crimson Dragon (*chilong*) and Descending Bridge (*jiangqiao*), while the throat is known as the Twelve Storied Tower (*shier zhonglou*). In many internal alchemy systems, one swirls the tongue around the mouth and gums, gathers clear saliva, and swallows the fluids down the throat to the Ocean of Qi. Some other key points utilized in Daoist Yangsheng and internal alchemy practice include the Hundred Meetings (*baihui*; crown-point; GV-20), Gate of Life (*mingmen*; between the kidneys; GV-4), Labor Palace (*laogong*; center of palms; PC-8), Bubbling Well (*yongquan*; center of balls of feet; KI-1), and Yellow Court (*huangting*). Many of these points parallel, and often derive from classical Chinese medicine. The Hundred Meetings is considered the primary entry-point of celestial qi into the body, while the Bubbling Well is the primary entry-point of terrestrial qi into the body. The latter is also connected with strengthening the kidneys and one's core vitality by extension. The Labor Palace is one of the locations where qi moves to the surface of the both; these points are used to guide qi. The Gate of Life is associated with the transformation of vital essence into qi. Finally, the Yellow Court is a more esoteric Daoist term. It derives from the famous third-century *Huangting jing* (Scripture on the Yellow Court; DZ 331; DZ 332), a scripture that provided much Daoist technical vocabulary to later movements. The standard location of the Yellow Court is the spleen, but sometimes it corresponds to the Ocean of Qi. There are many other Daoist esoteric names, and the actual locations often vary depending on the teacher, community, lineage, and texts. For example, in certain contexts, the Gate of Life corresponds to the Ocean of Qi, while the Mysterious Pass (*xuanguan*) may refer to Gate of Life or the Jade Pillow. Similarly, the Celestial Gate (*tianmen*) may refer to the crown-point, the third-eye, or the nose, while the Mysterious Female (*xuanpin*) may refer to respiration.

The Daoist alchemical body also includes meridians, the subtle channels, and networks through which qi circulates. Just as Daoist elixir fields parallel Indian Yogic *chakra*s on some level, so too the Daoist meridian-qi system parallels the Indian Yogic *nāḍi-prāṇa* system. In the standard classical Chinese medical system, there are the primary Twelve Meridians and the so-called Eight Extraordinary Channels. The former correspond to the 12 organs, while the latter correspond to "extra channels." In Daoist internal alchemy practice, the Eight Extraordinary Channels are central, and there is some question about whether or not they exist (beyond potentiality) in ordinary people. In terms of the subtle body, while Daoists also recognize the two extra arm and two extra leg channels, the Governing Channel (*dumai*), Conception Channel (*renmai*), Thrusting Channel (*chongmai*), and Belt Channel (*daimai*) are most important in Daoist practice. The Governing Channel basically moves from the perineum, up the centerline of the back to the occiput, around the crown-point, to the upper-lip; it is associated with the qi of the six yang-organs. The Conception Channel basically moves from the perineum up the front centerline of the torso to the lower lip; it is associated with the qi of the five yin-organs. The Thrusting Channel basically moves through the center of the body between the crown-point and perineum. Finally, the Belt Channel, the only horizontal meridian, moves around the waist between the Ocean of Qi and Gate of Life; it intersects all of the other meridians. Various Daoist practices employ this dimension of the somatic landscape, but the Celestial Cycle is representative. Here the Daoist adept circulates qi up the Governing Channel and down the Conception Channel. That is, one reverses the conventional movement of the Conception Channel, unites these channels, and establishes a state of energetic integrity. As with meridians in general, qi, comparable to flowing wind and water, circulates through the Eight Extraordinary Channels. However, in Daoist systems of self-transformation, this is not "ordinary qi." It is a purer and more primordial form of qi. Specifically, it is often infused with various cosmic vapors and locality influences. Such Daoist adepts literally ingest, cultivate, and circulate something different. The Dao's numinous presence circulates through one's body.

An even more esoteric dimension of the Daoist alchemical body is the Nine Palaces (*jiugong*). These are mystical cranial locations. The standard list is as follows:

1 Hall of Light (*mingtang*), located above the area between the two eyebrows and one inch (*cun*) in.

2 Grotto Chamber (*dongfang*), located two inches in.

3 Elixir Field (*dantian*), located three inches in. This palace is sometimes also called Niwan, literally meaning "mud-ball," but possibly a transliteration of nirvana.

4 Flowing Pearl (*liuzhu*), located four inches in.

5 Jade Thearch (*yudi*), located five inches in.

6 Celestial Court (*tianting*), located one inch above the Hall of Light.

7 Secret Perfection (*jizhen*), located one inch above the Grotto Chamber.

8 Mysterious Elixir (*xuandan*), located one inch above the Elixir Field. This palace is sometimes also called Niwan.

9 Great Sovereign (*taihuang*), located one inch above the Flowing Pearl.

(*Suling jing*, DZ 1314, 12b–22a; see also *Jiugong zifang tu*, DZ 156)

In some systems, each palace is also associated with a specific god, and each god also occupies a corresponding external sacred realm in the complex, multi-dimensional Daoist cosmos, which includes visible and invisible layers. In this respect, we must recognize that many Daoists understand the body as consisting of an "inner pantheon," specifically body-gods associated with various bodily constituents such as the hair and organs. In some cases, these appear to be actual "gods" (theistic entities), while in other cases they seem to be energetic dimensions of and numinous presences in the body. In addition, the Nine Palaces are noteworthy for their non-spatial or semi-spatial nature. This spatial mapping reveals another subtle or unknown dimension of the body. Specifically, the head region becomes a portal to the sacred characterized by perhaps infinite space. Beyond the apparent conventional physicality of the head, there is a series of inner corridors that are sequentially opened in specific Daoist practices. If we connect this to the previous discussion of the spiritual dimensions of Daoist personhood, we find that the Nine Palaces become lodging places for spirit. We might refer to this as the "Daoist mystical body." It is a form of "somatic mysticism" because the Daoist adept experiences the Dao as numinous presence in/as/through the body.

In Daoist internal alchemy, the culmination of alchemical transformation is referred to as the "body-beyond-the-body" (*shenwai shen*), "immortal embryo" (*xiantai*), and "yang-spirit" (*yangshen*). Through consistent and prolonged alchemical practice, specifically sequential, stage-based training, one transforms oneself into a pure yang being. One unites all of the disparate dimensions of composite personhood into a unified, transcendent spirit. What must be emphasized here is that such a transcendent spirit *is created*, not given. From a traditional Daoist perspective, immortality is not an ontological given; it is actualized through Daoist training. Daoist internal alchemists refer to the culmination using the language of "embryo/fetus" and "inner body." Vital substances are preserved; spiritual dimensions are unified; the subtle body becomes activated; and the emerging unity coalesces into a transcendent spirit. This occurs *within* the physical body, and there is a felt sense of energetic presence in the lower elixir field, the navel region. As the Daoist adept continues to nourish the "embryo," like a hen incubating an egg, the "fetus" eventually emerges. This is the transcendent spirit capable of leaving the ordinary body. The energetic presence in the lower elixir field is often depicted as a child inside the navel; while the transcendent spirit is often depicted as a Chinese aristocrat (immortal in court regalia) above the head. This is because at the hour of death the internal alchemist sends out the spirit through the crown-point in order to enter the Daoist sacred realms. This is the immortal (*xianren*) ideal of the later Daoist tradition.

Daoist views of personhood thus directly relate to death, dying, and the afterlife. The foundational Daoist anthropological view is that of a composite self destined to disappear into the universe upon or shortly after death. Within the transformative process of the universe, everything comes into and goes out of being. Upon death, individual beings dissipate, decompose, and become reabsorbed into other things. One can discover the same process while alive. This foundational Daoist anthropological view also informs Daoist alchemy, whether external or internal. As the ordinary fate of human beings is to dissipate upon death, Daoists have one of two choices: accept this ontological fact by merging with the Dao's transformative process, or attempt to attain immortality by completing a process of alchemical transformation. If successful, one creates a transcendent spirit capable of transcending death and entering the Daoist sacred realms. The first Daoist model of death is final unification and return to the Dao, while the second is continual participation. These Daoist views of death and the afterlife are connected to traditional Chinese culture. However, through the influence of Buddhism, Daoists increasingly accepted the standard Indian idea of reincarnation. That is, Daoists increasingly recognized an ontologically given aspect of personhood that transcends death and reincarnates. Such a view of self led to various reconceptualizations of Daoist practice, especially the purpose of internal alchemy. Nonetheless, Daoists continued and continue to follow the standard Chinese funeral practice of full body interment, thus revealing the strong psychosomatic dimension of Daoist personhood and reverence for the body.

Further reading

Kohn, Livia. 1991, "Taoist Visions of the Body." *Journal of Chinese Philosophy* 18: 227–52.

Komjathy, Louis. 2009, "Mapping the Daoist Body: Part II: The Text of the *Neijing tu*." *Journal of Daoist Studies* 2: 64–108.

—2011, "The Daoist Mystical Body." In *Perceiving the Divine through the Human Body: Mystical Sensuality*, ed. Thomas Cottai and June McDaniel, 67–103. New York: Palgrave Macmillan.

Schipper, Kristofer. 1993, *The Taoist Body*. Trans. Karen C. Duval. Berkeley, CA: University of California Press.

CHAPTER SIX

Practice

Daoist practice is complex and multi-dimensional. Considered from an integrated and comprehensive perspective, it includes aesthetics, art, dietetics, ethics, health and longevity practice, meditation, ritual, seasonal attunement, scripture study, and so forth. At the same time, it is important to recognize that different Daoists, Daoist communities, and Daoist movements have embraced and advocated different approaches to Daoist practice. This relates to models of Daoist practice and attainment. Such models are rooted in particular Daoist views, including those related to personhood, and they have different rationales, purposes, benefits, and objectives. Nonetheless, one connective strand is a commitment to self-cultivation. This includes recognition of the psychosomatic reality of human being and embodiment. In the larger Daoist tradition, this is sometimes referred to as the "dual cultivation of innate nature and life-destiny," with innate nature related to consciousness and life-destiny related to physicality. One may, in turn, develop the former through "stillness practice" (*jinggong*), or meditation, and the latter through "movement practice" (*donggong*), or health and longevity techniques. Such considerations reveal the importance of both stillness and movement in Daoist practice. This is movement rooted in awareness, and awareness expressed in movement.

Daoist practice thus involves embodiment, interiority, movement, and presence. It encompasses attentiveness to one's behavior, consumption, physicality, relationships, vitality, and so forth. The specific types of Daoist practice may, in turn, be approached through the categories of observation, ingestion, and expression. One may develop a root in stillness through the practice of meditation. This stillness becomes expressed as observation, specifically as purity of consciousness and spiritual discernment and insight. Free from contention and attachment, one becomes more receptive to life as it is. One becomes more attentive to the effects of one's existence and consequences of one's actions. Observation then applies to ethical reflection and application. At the same time, one recognizes that what one ingests becomes and expresses what one is. Daoist ingestion practices include attentiveness to diet and energetic influences. One may consciously transform oneself by interrupting habituated appetites and modifying intake patterns. At the higher levels of Daoist ingestion, one absorbs and circulates purer influences, including cosmic qi. Such refinement may also be cultivated and manifest through embodied and enacted expressions. This includes practices that strengthen the body, increase vitality, and facilitate numinous pervasion. Such is the applied and participatory dimension of Daoist practice. It becomes expressed in/as/through attunement, circulation, refinement, rarification, and transmission. It becomes cultivated through observation, ingestion, and expression.

Observation

A foundational Daoist religious commitment centers on observation. "Observation" translates the Chinese character *guan* 觀, which consists of "egret" (*guan* 雚) and "to perceive" (*jian* 見). *Guan* may be compared to the quality of an egret observing barely visible or unseen presences. This reminds us of the classical Daoist ideal of the sage as well as the foundational Daoist emphasis on deep listening. For Daoists, this deep listening is connected to energetic sensitivity, especially as expressed in spatial, temporal, geographical, seasonal, and cosmological awareness. Such Daoist attunement frequently centers on the lunar and solar cycles. The former especially relates to the new and full moon, while the latter especially relates to the so-called Twenty-four Nodes, with the beginning of the seasons and the solstices and equinoxes being particularly important. Daoist observation is, in turn, rooted in stillness, attentiveness, and presence. In terms of Daoist practice, "observation" most often refers to the late medieval Daoist meditation method of inner observation (*neiguan*), which was influenced by Buddhist insight meditation (Pali: *vipassanā*; Skt.: *vipaśyanā*) (Kohn 1987, 1989). However, in a broader sense, observation encompasses many, if not most Daoist practices, especially those in which interiority is central. Daoists ideally cultivate attentiveness and awareness in almost every activity, whether "mundane" or "religious." This includes attentiveness in thinking, speaking, and acting. It encompasses dietetics, ethics, meditation, ritual, and so forth. Such observation is an all-pervading existential approach. It may be applied to one's drinking, eating, sleeping, ways of relating, and so forth. Observation may thus involve self-care and other-care.

Considering specific Daoist practices, the inwardness at the root of observation especially relates to meditation. Along with ritual, meditation has been and remains one of the primary forms of Daoist practice. Daoists often refer to meditation as "stillness practice" (*jinggong*) and understand it as relating to the cultivation of innate nature. There are five major types of Daoist meditation. These include apophatic or quietistic meditation, which relates to a variety of Daoist technical terms; visualization (*cunxiang*); ingestion (*fuqi*); inner observation (*neiguan*); and internal alchemy (*neidan*). Daoists also developed a specific type of practice for women, known as "female alchemy" (*nüdan*), which was first systematized in the late imperial period. Historically speaking, these methods emerged during different periods and are often associated with specific movements. Apophatic meditation first emerged during the classical period and specifically within the inner cultivation lineages (Roth 1999a). Visualization and ingestion first emerged during early medieval period and are especially associated with Highest Clarity (Robinet 1989a, 1993). Inner observation emerged during the late medieval period under the influence of Buddhist insight meditation and is especially associated with the Tang dynasty monastic system (Kohn 1987, 1989). Finally, internal alchemy also emerged during the late medieval period and is associated with

Complete Perfection, the so-called Southern School, as well as a variety of other lineages (Boltz 1987; Komjathy 2007a; Needham et al. 1983; Pregadio and Skar 2000). In addition, internal alchemy incorporated many of the other Daoist meditation methods into a larger system. Considered more generally, apophatic meditation emphasizes emptiness and stillness; ingestion emphasizes connecting to and absorbing various energetic influences (e.g. solar and lunar qi); visualization emphasizes envisioning various dimensions of self and universe (e.g. spirits of the five yin-organs); inner observation involves exploring the inner landscape of the body; and internal alchemy involves stage-based training with the goal of complete psychosomatic transformation. Of these, apophatic meditation and internal alchemy are the most widely practiced and perhaps representative forms of Daoist meditation, so here we will concentrate on these.

Daoist apophatic meditation is first attested to in classical Daoist texts, wherein it receives various technical names. These include "embracing the One" (*baoyi*), "guarding the One" (*shouyi*), "fasting of the heart-mind" (*xinzhai*), "sitting-in-forgetfulness" (*zuowang*), and so forth. In contemporary Daoism, where the practice often incorporates internal alchemy dimensions, it is usually called "quiet sitting" (*jingzuo*), also translated as "tranquil sitting," "stillness meditation," or "sitting-in-stillness." Apophatic meditation emphasizes emptiness and stillness; it is contentless, non-conceptual, and non-dualistic. One simply empties the heart-mind of all emotional and intellectual content. The two most famous and influential passages appear in the *Book of Master Zhuang*.

Entering stillness

You must fast! I will tell you what that means. Do you think that it is easy to do anything while you have a heart-mind? If you do, the luminous heavens will not support you . . . Make your aspirations one! Don't listen with your ears; listen with your heart-mind. No, don't listen with your heart-mind; listen with qi. Listening stops with the ears, the heart-mind stops with joining, but qi is empty and waits on all things. The Dao gathers in emptiness alone. Emptiness is the fasting of the heart-mind. (*Zhuangzi*, Chapter 4)

* * *

I'm improving . . . I can sit in forgetfulness . . . I smash up my limbs and body, drive out perception and intellect, cast off form, do away with understanding, and make myself identical with Great Pervasion. This is what I mean by sitting-in-forgetfulness. (Ibid., Chapter 6)

Based on these and similar classical Daoist textual passages, we may reconstruct the practice. Although detailed information on pre-Buddhist meditation postures is rare in Daoism, the "Inward Training" chapter of the *Book of Master Guan* provides some hints. The text emphasizes aligning the body (*zhengshen*) and aligning the four limbs (*zheng siti*). Based on reasonable conjecture, especially drawing upon roughly contemporaneous texts and archaeological finds, it appears that the corresponding posture involved sitting on the heels in a fashion that parallels the later Japanese *seiza* position. The spine would have been elongated and erect, and the shoulders aligned with the hips. The hands probably rested on the lap. In addition, the practice seems to have been solitary, rather than communal. With respect to actual method, adepts sought to empty the heart-mind of emotional and intellectual activity; they endeavored to enter a state of stillness, wherein perceptual and cognitive activity decreased. This was a hypoaroused and hyperquiescent state, that is, a condition characterized by deep relaxation and decreased physiological activity. According to the texts of classical Daoism, apophatic meditation eventually leads to the dissolution of self, to the end of subject-object dichotomies and separate identity. Through dedicated and prolonged practice, one may attain a state of mystical union with the Dao and become an embodiment of the Dao in the world.

Classical Daoist texts established the foundation for later Daoist meditation practice. This is so much the case that an entire Daoist meditation manual was inspired by the second passage from the *Book of Master Zhuang*. The eighth-century CE *Zuowang lun* (Discourse on Sitting-in-Forgetfulness; DZ 1036), a central text of the later Highest Clarity movement written by Sima Chengzhen (647–735), provides the following instructions: "As a method, we refer to it as 'blunting the sharpness and untying the knots' [*Daode jing*, Chapters 4 and 56]. If you maintain constancy of cultivation, you will complete innate nature through practice. Smash up limbs and body, drive out perception and intellect, and experience detachment and forgetfulness. Unmoving in silence, you imperceptibly and subtly enter illumination" (section 6). The *Discourse on Sitting-in-Forgetfulness* in turn maps Daoist meditation in terms of seven stages or dimensions: (1) Respect and Trust; (2) Interception of Karma; (3) Taming the Mind; (4) Detachment from Affairs; (5) Perfect Observation; (6) Intense Concentration; and (7) Realizing the Dao. Sima Chengzhen thus infuses Daoist apophatic meditation with elements from Buddhism and the contemporaneous Daoist method of inner observation.

The increasing Daoist emphasis on stage-based practice reaches its culmination in internal alchemy. Internal alchemy (*neidan*), which literally means something like "inner pill" or "inner cinnabar" and which is also translated as "inner elixir," is a complex physiological practice aimed at complete psychosomatic transformation. Combining a variety of early traditions and dimensions of traditional Chinese culture, early internal alchemy was extremely complex. Considered as a whole, early internal alchemy includes elements from the following sources: classical Daoist texts, earlier meditational techniques, correlative cosmology, *Yijing* (Classic of Changes) symbology, Yangsheng views and practices, cosmological views and technical terms related to external alchemy (*waidan*), Chinese medical theory, and occasionally Buddhist soteriology. Generally speaking, early internal alchemy was a stage-based system that involved dedicated and prolonged practice of complex physiological techniques aimed at complete psychosomatic transformation. The goal was the creation of a transcendent spirit, usually referred to as the "immortal embryo" (*xiantai*), "yang-spirit" (*yangshen*), or "body-beyond-the-body" (*shenwai shen*). In this way, it employs both the composite view of personhood and the alchemical body discussed in the previous chapter.

Early internal alchemy systems utilize a wide variety of esoteric terminology and involve intensive training focusing on complex techniques (Komjathy 2007a, 2013a; Needham et al. 1983). Traditionally speaking, internal alchemy training takes place under a Daoist teacher, who provides person-specific guidance through oral instruction (*koujue*). Daoist internal alchemy systems also tend to be lineage-specific, and these dimensions lead to a certain degree of secrecy and circumspection. In terms of the practice itself, according to some late medieval texts, one begins by conserving the vital substances of the body. This usually involves temporary or permanent celibacy. After these vital substances have been stabilized, one begins internal alchemy proper. Typical methods include uniting the Five Qi; activating the subtle body, especially through the Celestial Cycle; sending out the yang-spirit; and so forth. Uniting the Five Qi involves visualizing the five yin-organs as orbs of light: liver/azure, heart/crimson, spleen/yellow, lungs/white, and kidneys/purple. These radiant orbs are then combined into a single orb of white or variegated light in the Ocean of Qi, the navel region. In the Celestial Cycle, also referred to as the Microcosmic Orbit or Waterwheel, one circulates qi up the Governing Vessel (centerline of back) and down the Conception Vessel (front centerline of torso). There are various visual depictions of the practice, including that of the *Diagram of Internal Pathways* in the previous chapter. Through these and other practices, often in a nine-stage sequence, one combines the disparate elements of ordinary personhood. One creates a transcendent spirit capable of transcending physical death. One becomes an immortal capable of entering the Daoist sacred realms by "casting off the husk and sending out spirit." This usually involves sitting in upright meditation at the moment of death and sending out the alchemically formed yang-spirit through the crown of the head. In late imperial and more modern texts, Daoist internal alchemy often becomes simplified as a three-stage process: (1) Transforming vital essence into qi, (2) Transforming qi into spirit, and (3) Transforming spirit into emptiness. However, the actual and complex process of "elixir formation" is obscured as much as revealed by this apparently simple formula.

A key dimension of Daoist meditation, and observation more generally, is virtue. Although often separated from other Daoist practices, ethical reflection and application are central aspects of Daoist cultivation. As discussed more fully below, Daoist ethics are one expression of Daoist practice. There are diverse Daoist views concerning virtue, especially with respect to the necessity of conscious cultivation. The classical and foundational Daoist view is that virtue is the natural condition of human beings and a natural expression of innate nature, which is understood as innately "good" on a conventional level. Thus, through the practice of apophatic meditation and non-action (*wuwei*), one returns to one's innate nature and intrinsic connection to the Dao. The Daoist technical term here being discussed as "virtue" is *de*. Under one etymological reading, the character *de* 德 consists of *chi* 彳 ("step") and *zhi* 直 ("direct," "straight," "upright," "correct") over *xin* 心 ("heart-mind"): To be virtuous is to have an aligned heart-mind that is expressed as embodied activity, activity that reveals one's degree of self-cultivation and exerts a transformational influence on others. *De*, which is also translated as "inner power," "integrity," and "potency," is the Dao manifested in human beings as numinous presence and as embodied activity in the world, especially as a beneficial and transformational influence that might be categorized as "good." From this perspective, "morality" and "ethics" are natural outcomes of Daoist practice, natural expressions of Daoist ontological conditions or ways of being. In addition, Daoists often speak of the "energetics of virtue," or the way in which ethical being-in-the-world leads to an increased sense of aliveness, fulfillment, and vitality. At the same time, Daoists have emphasized that ethical reflection and application, especially in the form of precept study, are expressions of alignment with the Dao. Daoist precepts express important Daoist concerns and commitments, and they help orient aspiring Daoist adepts toward the Dao. An ethical model of practice and attainment is one possible path to the Dao. This involves conscious moral self-cultivation, especially with respect to Daoist values. In many internal alchemy systems, the development of virtue is referred to as "establishing the foundations" (*zhuji*). Some Daoist teachers even go so far as to claim that internal alchemy practice without an ethical foundation will be fruitless. "Establishing the foundations" in turn involves "hidden virtue," merit, and beneficial deeds. One works selflessly to alleviate suffering and to assist beings without concern for recognition or reward.

Ingestion

Ingestion relates to what one consumes and absorbs. Daoists have tended to emphasize attentiveness to consumption patterns, especially in terms of energetic influences. What one ingests literally becomes what one is, and what one is becomes expressed in what one ingests. Daoist ingestion practices are thus rooted in observation, attunement, and energetic sensitivity. They are a form of Daoist self-cultivation and an expression of Daoist realization. This relates to our earlier examination of Daoist existential and ontological views, especially with respect to being and personhood. On a more mundane level, there are dimensions of ingestion that relate to habituated psychology, ancestral influences, and social conditioning. On a more realized level, there are dimensions of ingestion that relate to realized psychology, cosmological attunement, and sacred pervasion. Beyond, or perhaps most fully within, personal identity, one recognizes that one is located in a larger matrix of being, in a larger cycle of life. This includes community and place. Ingestion is not simply about self-cultivation in a narrow sense; it is also about responsibility and implication. It involves awareness that one participates in a larger cosmological and ecological process in which individual beings seek their own freedom and fulfillment. One may thus follow a way of life that exerts a beneficial and transformational influence on other beings, that respects and nourishes the flourishing of all life.

Within the larger contours of Daoist practice, ingestion relates, first and foremost, to dietetics (Kohn 2010; Komjathy 2011c). Generally speaking, Daoists emphasize the importance of nourishing food and good sleep. As discussed in previous chapters, food and air relate to postnatal qi, while ancestral and cosmological influences, embodied in one's constitution, relate to prenatal qi. There are, in turn, various types of Daoist diets and diverse relationships to food intake. These include conventional, therapeutic, cosmological, monastic, ascetic, and alchemical diets.

Daoist "Food Groups"

Eating everything is not as good as eating vegetables. Eating vegetables is not as good as eating grains. Eating grains is not as good as eating mushrooms and excrescences. Eating mushrooms and excrescences is not as good as eating gold and jade [metals and minerals]. Eating gold and jade is not as good as eating primordial qi. Eating primordial qi is not as good as not eating at all. By not eating at all, even though Heaven and Earth may collapse, one will survive forever. (*Fashi jinjie jing*, DH 80; Kohn 2004b: 124–5; Kohn 2010: 12)

One might in turn identify "basic Daoist food groups": (1) Vegetables, (2) Grains, (3) Mushrooms and fungi (wild and foraged foods), (4) Herbs, metals, and minerals (herbal and alchemical formulas), and (5) Qi (subtle breath and primordial vapor). These roughly correspond to the aforementioned types of Daoist diets. The conventional or standard Daoist diet parallels that of traditional Chinese society. It largely consists of vegetables, legumes, grains, and smaller amounts of meat. Along these lines, Daoists have also embraced a dietetic approach that parallels Chinese medicine. This involves a cosmological and therapeutic approach, specifically with respect to correlative cosmology. In this approach, one may utilize the Five Phase correspondences either to cultivate cosmological and seasonal attunement or to heal constitutional imbalances. One expression of the cosmological diet involves eating according to the seasons and the associated correspondences. In addition, Daoist monastics, under the influence of their Buddhist counterparts and earlier Daoist ascetic and purificatory practices, have embraced a dietary path that excludes intoxicants, meat, and the so-called five strong-smelling vegetables. Stated more positively, many Daoist monastics follow a way of life rooted in celibacy, sobriety, and vegetarianism. On a more esoteric level, Daoists have engaged in various forms of dietary modifications. These include "elimination diets," such as grain avoidance, as well as a shift from more mundane forms of nourishment to more subtle ones. Considered from a comprehensive and integrated perspective, Daoists have moved from agriculture-based diets to diets focusing on wild foods and alchemical substances. Here one finds another application of yin-yang cosmology. One transitions from a more "yin" diet, associated with the earth, physicality, heaviness, and mortality, to a more "yang" diet, associated with the heavens, subtlety, lightness, and immortality. According to certain Daoist systematizations, there is thus a hierarchical order to various ingestible substances and the associated diets. In simplified form, what unites more esoteric or "advanced" Daoist dietetics is a movement toward rarification.

One of the most well-known and representative expressions of Daoist ascetic diets is "grain avoidance" (*bigu*), which often includes alchemical dimensions as well. Daoist ascetic and alchemical diets became a central element of the Daoist tradition beginning in the early medieval period (Eskildsen 1998; Needham et al. 1976). Ascetic diets tend to emphasize purification and separation from ordinary society and ways of being. Here "alchemical diets" refer to those that incorporate elements from external alchemy (*waidan*), specifically the use of herbal and mineral formulas. In terms of grain avoidance, conventionally understood *bigu* involves eliminating grains from one's diet, that is, complete abstinence from eating any grain or grain byproducts. There are different rationales and motivations for the practice, but this ascetic approach to dietetics emerged in the context of early medieval Daoism. In medieval sources, the practice of *bigu* is associated with eliminating the Three Death-bringers discussed in the previous chapter. The Three Death-bringers are harmful bio-spiritual parasites that depend on cereals or grains for nourishment; they also attempt to bring the human being to early death. As the Three Death-bringers depend on grains for sustenance, grain abstention leads to their expulsion or extermination, and to increased freedom and longevity for the Daoist practitioner.

Certain *bigu* regimens also have cosmological and theological components. For example, many medieval Daoists claimed that the Three Death-bringers would leave the body on every *gengshen* (Jpn.: *kōshin*) day, the fifty-seventh day in the traditional Chinese 60-day cycle. On this day, they are believed to report one's moral transgressions to Siming, the Ruler of Life-destiny or Arbiter of Fate, who would deduct time from one's lifespan depending on the type of transgression. By staying awake on the *gengshen* day, one could prevent the Three Death-bringers from making their report. Much more effective, though also more exacting, was observation of a certain period of grain abstention, usually 100 days, which would eliminate the Three Death-bringers. From an early medieval ascetic perspective, grains seem to be among the lowest forms of nourishment, perhaps because of their connection to sedentary, agrarian civilization; they are below vegetables and wild foods, as indicated by the importance of various vegetal and herbal substances in ascetic, therapeutic, and alchemical dietetics. In addition, the ingestion of certain substances, such as poke root, was believed to expel or exterminate the Three Death-bringers and other, more physical parasites.

The power of poke root

Add one *dou* of wild asparagus root (*tianmendong*; *asparagus cochinchinensis*) powder to ten *jin* of yeast and three *dou* of rice. Place the gathered poke root (*shanglu*; *phytolacca acinosa*) [in this mixture] for six days. Thereupon, begin eating them, while observing ritual prohibitions. After six days, your food intake will decrease. After twenty days, grains will be eliminated and your intestines will be so large that they can only hold air. The various worms will leave. Your ears and eyes will hear and see clearly. All of your moles and scars will disappear. When the moon resides in the Yugui constellation on a *ding*-stem day, gather the poke root plant. Eat a piece the size of a jujube three times per day. Daoist adepts always grow this plant in a garden by their meditation chamber. It allows a person to communicate with gods. (*Lingbao wufu xu*, DZ 388, 2.11a; adapted from Eskildsen 1998: 61)

Here it is also important to note that although conventionally understood as "abstention from grains," in certain contexts *bigu* appears to designate fasting, that is, complete elimination of food (Campany 2002; Eskildsen 1998). As we saw in the above passage on Daoist "food groups," aspiring Daoist adepts seeking immortality endeavor to complete a process of rarification. This involves a movement away from ordinary types of nourishment and toward "cuisines of immortality."

Many Daoist dietetical regimens also emphasize the importance of virtue and moral purity (Kohn 2004c). There is an ethical dimension to certain Daoist dietary approaches. This is often expressed in guidelines and precepts. Many Daoist monastic manuals and precept texts contain guidance concerning ingestion, both with respect to proscribed substances and dining etiquette. For example, the possibly fourth-century *Laojun yibai bashi jie* (180 Precepts Spoken of Lord Lao; DZ 786, 4a–12b), an early medieval set of Celestial Masters precepts most likely intended for libationers, admonishes Daoists to avoid certain foods and activities related to eating (Hendrischke and Penny 1996; Schipper 2001). These include precepts against the following types of behavior: harming and killing sentient beings (4, 39); throwing food into fires (7); eating the five strong-smelling vegetables (10); using fancy utensils (15); drinking alcohol and eating meat (24, 172, 173); eating alone (26); hunting and fishing (79); commenting on the quality of food (90, 133, 151); eating fine food (131); and eating to excess (142, 155). The 180 Precepts also express bioregional and conservationist commitments, which are sometimes discussed in terms of "ecology" or "environmentalism." Some relevant precepts include those against burning fields, mountains, and forests (14); excessively cutting down trees (18); excessively picking flowers or herbs (19); polluting wells, ponds, and waterways (36, 100); excessively digging holes (47); abusing domestic animals (49, 129); draining waterways (53); digging up hibernating insects (95); plundering nests (97); catching or frightening birds and animals (98, 132); obstructing ponds and wells (101); setting dangerous fires (109); and urinating on plants or in water (116). In the context of the early medieval Celestial Masters, the 180 Precepts specifically related to ritual purity. In preparation for ritual and audiences with divine beings, Celestial Masters libationers observed temporary celibacy, sobriety, and vegetarianism. This ensured access to Daoist gods, considered to be pure emanations of the Dao, and Daoist sacred realms as well as ritual efficacy. As Daoist gods did not accept alcohol, blood, and meat offerings, so too Daoist priests needed to purify themselves of such mundane influences (Kleeman 2005). In later Daoist monasticism, such ritual purity became expanded as permanent celibacy, sobriety, and vegetarianism (Komjathy 2011c). This frequently includes a commitment to non-harm and animal welfare rooted in transhuman compassion. Thus, as discussed in more detail below, Daoist ethics may be considered in terms of "embodiment" and "expression." Recalling foundational Daoist values, Daoist dietary ethics emphasize simplicity and reverence.

One of the most subtle dimensions of Daoist dietetics is "qi ingestion" (*fuqi*), which is also practiced as a meditation method as well as a health and longevity technique (Robinet 1989a, 1993). Qi ingestion is particularly associated with the early Highest Clarity movement, but this type of practice also became incorporated into some systems of internal alchemy. One also finds qi ingestion practices in Qigong (Ch'i-kung; Qi Exercises), a modern Chinese

FIGURE 6.1 *Ingesting Solar Effulgences.*
Source: *Yuyi jielin tu*, DZ 435.

health and fitness movement often misidentified as "Daoist" (Komjathy 2006). From a Daoist perspective, at the highest "dietetical" level, one lives on subtle breath and cosmic vapors; one needs little or no ordinary food to survive. Qi ingestion involves the ingestion of seasonal and local influences as well as absorption of astral effulgences. That is, there are ecological and cosmological aspects of the practice, as well as different informing views. Some approaches to qi ingestion emphasize cosmological attunement, while others focus on rarification and self-divinization. Some representative qi ingestion practices include absorbing the qi of the five directions (east, south, center, west, north) and the energies of the sun, moon, stars, and planets (Figure 6.1).

For example, in the early medieval technique known as "Method of Mist Absorption," which involves ingesting the so-called "five sprouts" (*wuya*), one absorbs the qi of the five directions and locates the qi in the corresponding yin-organ (Robinet 1989a, 1993). The method begins with swallowing saliva while chanting invocations to the original qi of the directions. At dawn, one faces the associated direction, usually beginning with the east, and visualizes the qi of that direction in its corresponding colors (east/azure, south/ crimson, center/yellow, west/white, and north/purple). A general mist in the beginning, it gradually forms into an orb of light. It then becomes more concentrated, during which stage it decreases in size and approaches the adept's body. Eventually the size of a pill, the sprout is swallowed and directed to its corresponding yin-organ (liver, heart, spleen, lungs, and kidneys).

Here one notices the central importance of light in certain Daoist views and approaches to practice-realization (Miller 2003, 2008). This is so much the case that one might understand such qi ingestion practices as "nourishing on light" or "living on light." This is the Dao as the light that manifests within the more-encompassing darkness and mysteriousness. As discussed in the previous chapter, the Daoist adept literally ingests and circulates something else. This "something else" includes primordial cosmic ethers and the numinous presence of the Dao. The qi circulating through such Daoists is infused with solar, lunar, and stellar energies. This is a new form of embodiment and being activated through Daoist practice.

Expression

Expression refers to the ways in which Daoist practice becomes physically manifest and enacted in the world. Specifically, it relates to the outward expressions and externally observable dimensions of Daoist practice, and it brings embodied and kinesthetic elements into high relief. Daoist practice is expressed in applied, participatory, and performative activities. Such activities may be individual or communal, and they may be more or less internal and external. The physical and locomotive aspect, often referred to as "movement practice" (*donggong*), may be mapped in a variety of ways, including in terms of musculoskeletal, sensory (sights, sounds, smells), and symbolic dimensions. Recalling the Daoist emphasis on physical embodiment, one may consider bodily expression and engagement, specifically the "anatomy of movement" of particular Daoist practices. There are actual postures and movement patterns, which draw our attention to the physical aspects of any practice or activity.

In terms of Daoist expression, the most clearly related practices include ethics, health and longevity techniques, aesthetics and art, as well as ritual. Here it is important to recognize that Daoist expressive or performative practices often have particular characteristics and qualities. These are consciously cultivated, frequently under the guidance of a particular teacher and community and through intensive and prolonged training. In higher-level practitioners, such qualities may include excellence, effortlessness, fluidity, lightness, numinosity, spontaneity, refinement, and so forth. This is "mastery" as both an inward condition and external expression. Such mastery often manifests in a Daoist's being and presence. As the "Inward Training" chapter of the *Book of Master Guan* explains, "A complete heart-mind at the center cannot be concealed or hidden. It will be known through your appearance; it will be seen in the color of your skin. . . . The form of this qi and heart-mind is more luminous than the sun and moon" (ch. 18). One's activities and movement become infused with the numinous presence of the Dao. Such movement awareness may, in turn, become a specific type of Daoist transmission. At the same time, a practitioner's degree of cultivation may be "invisible;" he or she may be hidden and go unrecognized. As the *Book of Venerable Masters* explains, "the sage wears coarse

clothes on the outside, while hiding the jade within" (ch. 70). This
parallels the classical and foundational emphasis on formlessness,
namelessness and obscurity. There are degrees of manifestation
among different Daoists and within different Daoist activities, and
higher-level Daoist practitioners often have the ability to conceal
or reveal their connection depending on the situation. This recalls
Daoist emanationist cosmogony and theology, wherein the Dao is
simultaneously formless Source and manifest forms.

Ethics is one enacted form of Daoist practice (see Kleeman
1991; Kohn 2004c). As previously discussed, the classical and
foundational Daoist view is that human beings are originally and
"naturally" aligned with the Dao. This is one's original heart-mind
and innate nature. Free from social conditioning, familial obligation,
and personal habituation, one abides in a state of cosmological and
mystical integration. This manifests as "virtue" or "inner power"
(*de*), as uncontrived beneficial and transformational influence. One
is naturally and inherently "moral." One's being is infused with
the Dao's numinous presence, and one becomes an embodiment
of the Dao in the world. At the same time, Daoists have developed
sophisticated and nuanced ethical systems. Within an ethical model
of Daoist practice and attainment, reflection on and application of
Daoist principles is one path to the Dao. Ethical cultivation may
return one to the Dao. It may also help disoriented individuals,
especially those unwilling to engage in other types of practice, to
become more attuned. In the larger tradition, ethics most often
focuses on specific precepts, which frequently relate to specific types
of community. One thus finds precepts that are specifically intended
for lay adherents, householders, ordained priests, monastics, and
immortals. Among these, there are higher levels of involvement and
degrees of adherence, with corresponding ethical commitments and
responsibilities. "Ordinary Daoists" are frequently encouraged to
develop basic morality; priests and monastics are often directed to
become exemplars of the tradition; and sages and immortals abide
in a "transmoral" condition in which conscious ethical cultivation
becomes unnecessary. In any case, Daoists generally claim that
a greater degree of alignment with the Dao manifests in a more
beneficial energetic influence. This of course begs the question of
the degree to which conventional morality is a social construct and
distortion of human nature.

Precepts, or Daoist ethical principles and conduct guidelines,
first emerged in the context of early organized Daoism, specifically

in the early Celestial Masters movement. From the early medieval period into the modern period, most forms of organized Daoism included formalized ethical systems and precept texts. Daoist precepts express various Daoist ways of life and ethical commitments, including personal moral cultivation, bioregional locatedness, communal harmony, social engagement, and so forth. Here a representative example will have to suffice. The 10 Precepts of Initial Perfection, which are the first-level precepts for Dragon Gate initiates, both monastic and lay, begin by emphasizing that adepts should be familiar and proficient with the five foundational precepts against killing, stealing, lying, taking intoxicates, and sexual misconduct as well as the *Taishang ganying pian* (Treatise on Response and Retribution of the Great High [Lord Lao]; DZ 1167) before focusing on the 10 Precepts of Initial Perfection. According to the late imperial Dragon Gate ordination system, there are, in turn, three ranks with corresponding precept texts: (1) Initial Perfection and the *Chuzhen jie* (Precepts of Initial Perfection; JY 292; ZW 404), (2) Medium Ultimate and the *Zhongji jie* (Precepts of Medium Ultimate; JY 293; ZW 405), and (3) Celestial Immortality and *Tianxian jie* (Precepts of Celestial Immortality; JY 291; ZW 403). One practices each in sequence, and bestowal of the subsequent monastic rank requires proficiency in the former. The Dragon Gate novitiate or first-level ordinand begins formal, lineage-specific precept study with the 10 Precepts of Initial Perfection.

10 Precepts of Initial Perfection

1 Do not be disloyal, unfilial, inhumane or dishonest. Always exhaust your allegiance to your lord and family, and be sincere when relating to the myriad beings.

2 Do not secretly steal things, harbor hidden plots, or harm other beings in order to profit yourself. Always practice hidden virtue and widely aid the host of living beings.

3 Do not kill or harm anything that lives in order to satisfy your own appetites. Always act with compassion and kindness to all, even insects and worms.

4 Do not be debased or deviant, squander your perfection, or defile your numinous qi. Always guard perfection and integrity, and remain without deficiencies or transgressions.

5 Do not ruin others to create gain for yourself or leave your own flesh and bones. Always use the Dao to help other beings and make sure that the nine clan members all live in harmony.

6 Do not slander or defame the worthy and good or exhibit your talents and elevate yourself. Always praise the beauty and goodness of others and never be contentious about your own accomplishments and abilities.

7 Do not drink alcohol or eat meat in violation of the prohibitions. Always harmonize qi and innate nature, remaining attentive to clarity and emptiness.

8 Do not be greedy and acquisitive without ever being satisfied or accumulate wealth without giving some away. Always practice moderation in all things and show kindness and sympathy to the poor and destitute.

9 Do not have any relations or exchange with the unworthy or live among the confused and defiled. Always strive to control yourself, becoming perched and composed in clarity and emptiness.

10 Do not speak or laugh lightly or carelessly, increasing agitation and denigrating perfection. Always maintain seriousness and speak humble words, so that the Dao and inner power remain your primary concern. (*Chuzhen jie*, ZW 404, 9b–10a)

The second Dragon Gate ordination rank focuses on the 300 Precepts of Medium Ultimate. Rather than containing precepts per se, the *Precepts of Celestial Immortality*, corresponding to the third and highest Dragon Gate ordination rank, provides general encouragement for developing certain ethical qualities. These might be best understood as resolutions to cultivate the 10 Virtues of Celestial Immortality, namely, wisdom, compassion, forbearance, meritorious activity, mind-cultivation, positive karma, strong determination, self-concealment, removal of passions, and universal mind. By applying and embodying these virtues, the adept also engages in the 27 Virtuous Activities of Celestial Immortality, such as avoidance of verbal transgressions, sensory engagement, psychological impurity, deviant thinking, and so forth.

Health and longevity techniques are another expression of Daoist practice (see Kohn 1989, 2008a). Daoist health and longevity practice primarily involves specific techniques aimed at strengthening vitality, increasing wellbeing, and prolonging life. Traditional Daoist health and longevity practice is designated by a variety of technical terms, with Yangsheng ("nourishing life") and Daoyin ("guided stretching") being most common. Yangsheng is a more encompassing umbrella term. Daoist Yangsheng tends to focus on conserving vital essence and cultivating qi, both as physical respiration (breathing techniques) and as subtle or vital breath. There is thus some overlap with internal alchemy practice. Daoist Yangsheng practice involves physiological, psychological, and behavioral principles and includes daily behavior, dietetics, massage (*anmo*), qi circulation practices (*xingqi*), qi ingestion methods, and respiratory techniques. Daoyin is usually used in a more restrictive sense to designate physical practices involving stretching and breath-work, although there can also be cosmological, energetic, purificatory, and exorcistic dimensions. The technical term *daoyin* literally means "guiding and pulling" or "to guide and direct." It has been translated as "gymnastics" and "calisthenics," and more recently as "healing exercises," and most problematically as "yoga." None of these is satisfactory, so I will leave the term untranslated, but believe that "guided stretching" would be the best rendering. In a contemporary context, Daoists tend to designate moving, sequential, and qi circulation practices as Yangsheng; they tend to designate seated or stationary postures that involve stretching and breath-work as Daoyin.

Chinese health and longevity practices must be distinguished from Daoist Yangsheng and Daoyin in particular. Although there is frequent cross-pollination, Daoists have had and continue to have diverse views on the relevance or importance of such practice. In addition, traditionally speaking, Yangsheng and Daoyin are almost always located in a larger system. Here we must also note that in the modern world, Chinese health and longevity practices such as Qigong and Taiji quan (T'ai-chi ch'üan; Great Ultimate Boxing) are frequently misidentified as or conflated with Daoist practice; neither of these practices are Daoist in origin or essence, although there are Daoist forms of Qigong and some Daoists practice Taiji quan.

One way of thinking about the "Daoist connection" centers on historical origins, religious affiliation, and defining characteristics. Some health and longevity methods emerged in a Daoist context or were created by Daoists. Others cultivate specific Daoist principles and forms of embodiment. Still others utilize specifically Daoist views or have specially Daoist content, such as Daoyin sequences that utilize postures associated with particular immortals.

Generally speaking, there are different Daoist views concerning the appropriateness and relevance of Daoyin and Yangsheng. While some Daoists have engaged in such practice, many Daoists have not. For those who have utilized Daoyin and Yangsheng methods, they have often done so at a particular moment in their training. There also are varied rationales, motivations, and conceptions involved. Daoists have tended to understand Daoyin and Yangsheng practice as remedial, preliminary, and/or foundational. Daoists have tended to locate health and longevity practices in a larger religious and soteriological framework, a framework that may or may not involve such methods. In the case of the larger Daoist tradition, Daoyin and Yangsheng have tended not to be seen as a sufficient or advanced practice. They have been placed within larger ascetic, alchemical, and monastic training regimens. They are, perhaps, necessary for health, vitality, and longevity, but deficient in terms of immortality and mystical modes of being.

These qualifications notwithstanding, there can be no doubt that some Daoists and Daoist communities have engaged in health and longevity practice, and certain forms of Yangsheng and Daoyin are often part of a larger Daoist training regimen (Kohn 1989, 2008a). Some key health and longevity practices utilized and/or developed by Daoists include the Five Animal Frolics (*wuqin xi*), Seated Eight Brocades (*baduan jin*), Twelve Sleeping Exercises (*shier shuigong*), and Twenty-four Nodes Daoyin (*ershisi qi zuogong daoyin*). Here I will briefly introduce the Five Animal Frolics, the Seated Eight Brocades, and the Twelve Sleeping Exercises. This will be followed by a more detailed discussion of the Twenty-Four Nodes Daoyin. Associated with the semi-legendary physician Hua Tuo (ca. 145–208 CE), the Five Animal Frolics involves taking the postures and imitating the movements of five animals, namely, tiger, deer, bear, monkey, and bird (crane). Associated with the Daoist immortal Zhongli Quan (Zhengyang [Aligned Yang]; 2nd c. CE?), the Seated Eight Brocades is a series of eight stretches utilizing seated postures. Associated with the Daoist immortal Chen Tuan (Xiyi [Infinitesimal Subtlety]; d. 989), the Twelve Sleeping Exercises are, not surprisingly, a series of 12 sleeping exercises (*shuigong*), which are practiced primarily just before going to sleep while reclining on the right side. Historically speaking, the Five Animal Frolics are first attested to in the third century CE; the Seated Eight Brocades, not to be confused with the later Standing Eight Brocades, in the thirteenth century; and the Twelve Sleeping Exercises in the sixteenth century. While these methods survive into the modern world, with apparently earlier historical precedents and perhaps ancient pedigrees, it is important to consider the degree of actual connection as well as modifications of the practices, including alternative rationales and changing contexts.

Another important and influential Daoist practice is the Twenty-four Nodes Daoyin. The sequence is first attested to in the *Neiwai gong tushuo jiyao* (Collected Essentials and Illustrated Descriptions of Internal and External Exercises; JH 20; QYC 59), a collection of health and longevity practices possibly dating from the seventeenth century. Interestingly, like the Twelve Sleeping Exercises, the Twenty-four Nodes Daoyin is associated with Chen Tuan. The Twenty-four Nodes Daoyin is a set of 24 seated postures correlated to the 24 nodes, that is, the key seasonal and energetic times of the year (Figure 6.2). Here we must acknowledge that the 24 nodes are not specifically Daoist, but are best understood as part of "traditional Chinese culture." Like correlative cosmology and the stem-branch (*ganzhi*) system, the nodes are not Daoist in origin or essence; rather, Daoists, like most Chinese people in pre-modern China, utilized the system. The various postures of the Twenty-four Nodes Daoyin involve stretching with attentiveness to the associated time, season, organ and meridian, and seasonal imbalances that may appear. That is, this is a practice aimed at seasonal and cosmological attunement.

The ailments that they propose to heal tend to be associated with qi-blockages (one of the main sources of illness in Chinese medicine), including joint pain, digestive problems, and muscular weakness. The corresponding time for the practice is during the hour of *zi* (11 p.m.–1 a.m.) during winter (tenth, eleventh, and twelfth exercises), and after sunrise, during the hour of *mao* (5–7 a.m.), at the beginning and into the height of summer (fourth and fifth exercises). During the remainder of the year, it is ideal to

Mo	Period	Practice
1	Spring Beginning	cross-legged, press both hands on R/L knee, turn neck R/L, 15x
	Rain Water	press both hands on R/L thigh, turn neck and torso R/L, 15x
2	Insects Stirring	make tight fists, lift arms to elbow level, turn neck R/L, 30x
	Spring Equinox	stretch arms forward, turn neck R/L, look over shoulders, 42x
3	Pure Brightness	pull arms into shooting bow position R/L, 56x
	Crop Rain	lift arm up, palm out, place other arm across torso, turn shoulders, 35x
4	Summer Beginning	cross-legged, interlace fingers, hug knee into chest R/L, 35x
	Slight Ripening	lift arm up, palm out, press other arm on legs, press R/L, 35x
5	Seeds Sprouting	stand up, lift both arms to ceiling, slight back bend, 35x
	Summer Equinox	sit with legs out, lift one leg, hold with both hands, stretch R/L, 35x
6	Slight Heat	kneel on one leg, stretch other leg away, lean back, R/L, 15x
	Great Heat	cross-legged, lean forward over legs, push floor, turn neck R/L, 15x
7	Fall Beginning	cross-legged, press both hands on floor, push body up, 56x
	Last Heat	lifting the chest, turn the head R/L, drum fists on back, 35x
8	White Dew	press hands on respective knees, turn neck R/L, 15x
	Fall Equinox	interlace hands behind head, lean sideways R/L, 15x
9	Cold Dew	lift arms overhead in V position, pressing upward, 35x
	Frost Descending	sit with legs out, hold both feet, stretch and lift, 35x
10	Winter Beginning	cross-legged, stretch both arms to one side, turn head to the other, 15x
	Slight Snow	press one hand on knee, hold at elbow with other hand, R/L, 15x
11	Great Snow	stand up, cross legs at knees, open arms to the side, press, 35x
	Winter Equinox	sit with legs straight, press arms on knees with vigor, R/L, 15x
12	Slight Cold	cross-legged, push one arm up, looking at it, other arm on floor, 15x
	Great Cold	kneel on one leg, lean back, bend and straighten other leg, R/L, 15x

FIGURE 6.2 *Twenty-four Nodes Daoyin.*

Source. *Chinese Healing Exercises*, Livia Kohn, 171.

practice them at dawn. One is advised to alternate the postures to the right and left and to practice them on each side for a given number of repetitions.

Daoist practice also becomes embodied, enacted, and performed in the world through aesthetics, creativity, and material culture (see, Little 2000a). Daoist material expression includes architecture, art, calligraphy, clothing, devotional and liturgical objects, music, painting, ritual paraphernalia, sculpture, texts, and so forth. Historically speaking, many Daoist aesthetic expressions and artistic endeavors parallel those of traditional Chinese culture. We might refer to this aspect of Daoist being and lifeways as "art practice." One particularly important expression of Daoist aesthetics and art is calligraphy. Calligraphy, or writing Chinese characters using brush and ink on bamboo, silk, paper, and other materials, has been central in the Daoist tradition throughout Chinese history. Many Daoists have written calligraphy, and calligraphy has been used traditionally for a variety of purposes. These include various forms of commemoration, instruction, ritual, and transmission. Specifically, Daoists have used calligraphy to compose and transmit lineage-poems, ordination certificates, ritual announcements and petitions, talismans, temple boards, and so forth. In addition, Daoist texts, and specifically "scriptures" (*jing*), have primarily been hand-written in classical Chinese using calligraphy. Daoist scriptures are sacred texts written in classical Chinese using calligraphy, and most often transmitted in manuscripts. This point draws our attention to the corporeal and material dimensions of Daoist texts. It also highlights the ways in which our access to Daoist texts is indebted to the Daoist tradition, and the multiple sources of Daoist texts. The latter include specific revelations, teachers, communities, as well as language. Daoist texts have also occupied a central place in ordination and transmission. There is thus a history of material culture as embodied preservation and transmission behind the modern encounter with Daoist literature. Here we may recall that scriptures are one of the external Three Treasures, and Daoists often consider them to be manifestations of the Dao in the world. The various material expressions of Daoism thus inspire one to contemplate the aesthetic, material, and spatial dimensions of Daoist practice. Perhaps Daoist practices outside of a Daoist place and community, including in the absence of Daoist material culture, lacks key dimensions.

The final expression of Daoist practice is ritual (see Dean 1993, 2000; Lagerwey 1987; Saso 1972, 1978; Schipper 1993). Along with meditation, ritual has been and remains one of the primary forms of Daoist practice. Ritual involves prescribed, coordinated, and socially recognizable formal behavior and movement patterns. In terms of large-scale, public activity, ritual is orchestrated movement. Daoist ritual may be considered in terms of individual and daily ritual as well as communal and occasional ritual. Personal Daoist ritual includes such activities as hygiene practices, bowing, lighting incense, and so forth. Certain aspects of meditation, such as moving in prescribed ways, hitting the wooden fish-drum, and ringing the prayer-bell, could be considered as ritualistic. Daoist communal ritual involves various types of public performance. Such ritual includes announcement, atonement, commemoration, consecration, ordination, petition, purification, and so forth.

The two primary forms of large-scale public Daoist ritual are *jiao*-offering and *zhai*-purification rites. In its early Daoist formulations, it appears that *jiao*-offerings focused on subordinate spirits, while *zhai*-purifications focused on the highest deities. In more contemporary usages, *jiao*-offerings are large-scale Daoist ceremonies. The standardized, modern forms of Daoist ritual are particularly associated with Orthodox Unity communities. However, Complete Perfection Daoists also perform them, even though daily chanting of the morning and evening liturgy (*gongke*) is more common. The modern expression of Daoist ritual also has many historical layers, including elements that originated in Chinese court ritual, the early Celestial Masters, early Numinous Treasure, as well as various Song dynasty ritual movements. In terms of modern Orthodox Unity Daoism, public rituals are organized by local communities, and by religious associations, in order to define themselves on a religious level, and specifically in order to establish or confirm a semi-contractual relationship between the group and its tutelary (guardian or protector) deity. There are also calendrical, cosmological, exorcistic, petitionary, purificationary, salvific, and therapeutic dimensions. Modern Orthodox Unity ritual is performed by an officiant, the head-priest referred to as the "Master of Lofy Merit" (*gaogong*), and his or her assistants before a central altar (Figure 6.3). Each of these individuals is an ordained Daoist priest (*daoshi*) with formal ritual training. The standard

FIGURE 6.3 *Zhuang-Chen Dengyun Performing Jiao-offering.*
Source: Michael Saso.

Daoist altar, which may be a temporary outdoor or permanent indoor one, consists of statues, scrolls or paintings of gods; an incense burner; two candelabras; two red candles; as well as the prayer-bell and wooden fish-drum. Offerings of flowers and fruit are often present as well. A typical three-day Taiwanese Orthodox Unity *jiao*-offering consists of a variety of stages.

Typical modern Taiwanese Orthodox Unity *Jiao*-offering

Day 1

1 Announcement
2 Invocation
3 Flag-raising
4 Noon Offering
5 Division of the Lamps
6 Sealing the Altar
7 Invocation of the Masters and Saints
8 Nocturnal Invocation

Day 2

1 Morning Audience
2 Noon Audience
3 Evening Audience

Day 3

1 Renewed Offering
2 Presentation of the Memorial
3 "Ten Thousand Sacred Lamps of the Three Realms"
4 Orthodox Offering
5 Universal Salvation

(Schipper 1975: 10–11)

Such ritual involves various forms of orchestrated movement, including lighting and offering incense, bowing, chanting, and so forth. The chanting is either done from memory or utilizing liturgical texts in classical Chinese. One of the most distinctive elements of Daoist ritual involves offering "petitions," which are also referred to as "announcements" and "memorials." Written on pieces of paper using calligraphy, petitions often include information on the ritual's purpose and hope for the response, support, and efficacy. They are offered to Daoist deities through burning. In terms of material culture, Daoist ritual also utilizes a variety of liturgical implements and ritual paraphernalia. The officiant, assistant priests, and cantors wear liturgical vestments, which are highly ornate, hand-embroidered silk robes. The officiant also utilizes the audience tablet (*chaoban*), command placard (*lingpai*), ritual ruler (*fachi*), and ritual seal (*fayin*). The cantors employ a variety of ritual instruments, including cymbals, gongs, and drums. Most large-scale public Daoist ritual has a solemn and refined quality. The smell of aloeswood (*chenxiang*) or sandalwood (*tanxiang*) incense wafts through the air, as chanting, music, and orchestrated movement occurs in the central ritual space. The latter is known as the "enclosure of the Dao" (*daochang*), which is established and consecrated by Daoist priests in preparation for the ritual. While Daoist ritual may be described as "performative" and "thearatrical," there are also inner dimensions, including esoteric symbolism and internal alchemical practices.

In summation, Daoist practice is complex and multi-dimensional. A comprehensive and integrated understanding recognizes aesthetics, art, dietetics, ethics, health and longevity practice, meditation, ritual, seasonal attunement, scripture study, and so forth. These various types of Daoist practice may be approached through the categories of observation, ingestion, and expression. Daoists endeavor to cultivate attentiveness with respect to being and embodiment. This involves a psychosomatic approach that emphasizes conservation of vitality, purity of consciousness, integrity of character, enhancement of aliveness, and refinement of movement. It involves cosmological attunement, energetic sensitivity, numinous pervasion, and embodied participation. Viewed as an all-pervading existential approach, Daoists recognize everything as practice. Daoist practice is not reducible to technique. One's practice is one's life, and one's life is one's practice. Each and every moment is an opportunity for deeper self-cultivation. Thus Daoists frequently emphasize trusting in the Dao and accepting the unfolding of one's own life. Everything, even difficulty and apparent obstruction, is an "ingredient" for refinement and transformation, for the formation of the elixir.

Further reading

Kohn, Livia. 2004, *Cosmos and Community: The Ethical Dimension of Daoism*. Cambridge, MA: Three Pines Press.

—2010, *Daoist Dietetics: Food for Immortality*. Dunedin, FL: Three Pines Press.

Komjathy, Louis. 2008 (2003), *Handbooks for Daoist Practice*, 10 vols. Hong Kong: Yuen Yuen Institute.

Saso, Michael. 2012 (1978), *The Teachings of Daoist Master Zhuang*, 3rd rev. edn. Los Angeles, CA: Oracle Bones Press.

CHAPTER SEVEN

Experience

Experience refers to the subjective and lived dimension of human existence. It relates to various dimensions of personhood discussed in previous chapters, including corporeal, psychological, cognitive, spiritual, inter-subjective, and cultural aspects. As emphasized, there is a complex interplay and interrelationship between view, practice, and experience. One's experience is conditioned by specific views and practices. At the same time, experience influences views and practices. Practice and experience also may have a transformative effect on one's life. In the case of Daoism, "Daoist experience" refers to the types of experiences that occur in Daoist contexts or under Daoist influences. Here personal experience includes affinities, influences, interests, and so forth. These dimensions of experience may lead to a deeper sense of connection and belonging. Broadly understood, Daoist experience consists of a wide range occurrences, sensations, sentiments, and responses. These include those rooted in and manifested as diverse ways of life, such as those of ascetics, contemplatives, mystics, monastics, scholastics, and so forth. In this respect, Daoist experience relates to more "common" and "ordinary" events as well as to more "anomalous" and "extraordinary" events.

Daoist experiences include those related to specific aesthetics, teachers, communities, material culture, practices, and place. Daoist experience encompasses friendship, instruction, mysticism, participation, rarification, revelation, transmission, and so forth. There are also uniquely Daoist experiences such as "somatic mysticism," or the experience of the sacred in/as/through the body. This is the Daoist "mystical body" awakened through Daoist practice. Many Daoist experiences, in turn, have distinctive and recognizable qualities and characteristics. Taken as a whole, Daoist experience may be viewed through the framework of attunement, encounter, and pervasion. These roughly correspond to personal, relational, and transpersonal experiences, although the latter is problematic from a conventional view of "experience." Attunement principally refers to a feeling of connection with the Dao, especially a "felt sense" (Eugene Gendlin) of cosmological situatedness. Encounter refers to inter-subjective and relational experiences. Such experiences involve encounters with aesthetics, teachers, communities, places, and even immortals and deities. Pervasion relates to mysticism, numinosity, rarification, and immortality. It is an experience in which the individual disappears into the Dao and becomes infused with the Dao's numinosity. This frequently then becomes manifest as a transformed ontological condition expressed in embodied activity. One becomes a new being, perhaps residing in a different reality. We may thus explore Daoist experience through the lens of attunement, encounter, and pervasion.

Attunement

Although Daoist models of practice and attainment are diverse, alignment or attunement with the Dao is the primary goal, the fundamental expression of a Daoist way of life. This is a way of being infused with the Dao's numinous presence. It is a type of Daoist experience in which Daoists feel closer to the Dao. "Alignment" suggests that there are moments when one has a deeper sense of connection and support. Alignment relates to integrity in its myriad forms, including corporeal, psychological, and spiritual.

"Attunement" suggests that the universe is a resonant system, and there are moments when one has a deeper sense of accord and harmonization. Attunement relates to musicality in its myriad forms, including appreciation, attentiveness, and expression. Here one may recall the foundational Daoist emphasis on listening, especially energetic sensitivity. As we have seen in previous chapters, Daoists tend to believe that humans have an innate connection with the Dao, and thus an innate capacity for resonance (*ganying*). From a Daoist perspective, this is our original condition. There are various famous Daoist sayings to this effect. "Fish thrive in water; humans thrive in the Dao." "Human beings may be distant from the Dao, but the Dao is never distant from human beings." On an experiential level, one may feel closer and more connected to the Dao, or one may feel more distant and disconnected from the Dao. However, distance, disconnection, and disorientation are only apparent. If this is the case, then how does one return to the *felt sense* of alignment and attunement with the Dao? This relates to the various practices discussed in the previous chapter, and these practices lead to particular types of experiences. As the Dao manifests through everything, at least to a certain degree, there are many forms of "attunement with the Dao." Such attunement may be understood as specifically related to personal experience.

The experience of attunement may occur in various forms and activities: from more general pursuits, such as aesthetic engagement and nature immersion, to more specifically Daoist undertakings, such as meditation, ritual, scripture study, and so forth. The key point is that attunement usually emerges in connection to specific forms of embodied activity. In this way, attunement is connected to other dimensions of Daoist being-in-the-world. It relates to being, embodiment, and presence. This recalls both foundational Daoist views, including those related to psychosomatic aliveness, cultivation, and refinement. As discussed in more detail below, Daoist experiences of attunement often have specific and recognizable qualities, patterns, and benefits. Thus Daoist attunement is not simply about "belief," "doctrine," or "philosophy" (disembodied ideas and intellectual rumination); rather, practice-based experience is primary. One may directly experience attunement, and such experience is confirmed by the continuity of Daoist community and tradition. Daoist teachers and texts provide insights into and guidance concerning attunement. Of course, rigid attachment to and reification of another's experience is antithetical to fundamental Daoist principles; one must listen to and trust one's own experience. Moreover, as Daoists claim that human beings have an innate connection to the Dao, subjective experience, including corporeal indicators, is trustworthy. Recalling the Daoist energetic view of "reality," Daoists frequently refer to the "felt sense" of attunement in terms of "true qi" (*zhenqi*). There is a feeling of energetic connection and support, and this support leads to greater flourishing, vigor, and endurance/resilience/ perseverance/stamina. This Daoist view suggests that a life rooted in virtue and integrity has energetic support. Even when it appears that corruption, immorality, and distortion are succeeding, in the end endeavors with such characteristics lack a firm foundation. They eventually lead to dissipation and failure. One might think of this as the "energetics of virtue."

As the Dao is understood as Nature on some level, one representative form of Daoist experiencing is cosmological attunement. This relates to Daoist cosmology and theology, especially panenhenic and pantheistic theology, discussed in previous chapters. Here "Nature" refers to the universe as transformative process, including energetic cycles, and the manifestations of this transformative process in terrestrial existence. Specifically, it is Nature as animals, forests, lakes, moonlight, mountains, rain, rivers, streams, sunlight, and so forth. As discussed in the next chapter, such attunement often manifests in a "sense of place" and panenhenic mystical experiences in which the Daoist adept disappears in Nature. One may cultivate and realize attunement with Nature in many ways. Related Daoist practices include mountain contemplation, nature observation, Yangsheng practices that imitate animal movements, and so forth.

In the Daoist tradition, cosmological attunement is often referred to as following the Way of Heaven (*tiandao*). *Tian* literally refers to the "sky," and the "heavens" and "cosmos" by extension. In later Daoist theology, it also refers to hidden sacred realms that are part of the cosmic structure. One of the most influential admonitions appears in the sixth-century *Yinfu jing* (Scripture on the Hidden Talisman; DZ 31), "Observe the Way of Heaven. Attend to the activities of the heavens. And that is all" (1a). In Daoist contexts, the phrase *tiandao* first appears in chapters 9, 47, 73, 77, 79, and 81 of the *Book of Venerable Masters* and in various chapters of the *Book of Master Zhuang*, with the "Tiandao" (Way of Heaven) chapter (ch. 13) being especially important. There is also an important chapter, chapter 3, of the *Book of the Huainan Masters*, which is titled "Tianwen" (Celestial Patterns).

Cosmological attunement

The sage is still not because he takes stillness to be good and therefore is still. The ten thousand things are insufficient to distract his heart-mind—that is the reason he is still. Water that is still gives back a clear image of beard and eyebrows; reposing in the water level, it offers a measure to the great carpenter. And if water in stillness possesses such clarity, how much more must pure spirit (*jingshen*). The sage's heart-mind in stillness is the mirror of the heavens and earth, the glass of the ten thousand things.

Emptiness, stillness, lucidity, silence, and nonaction—these are the level of the heavens and earth, the substance of the Dao and inner power . . . . Resting, one may be empty; empty, one may be full; and fullness is completion. Empty, one may be still; still, one may move; moving, one may have attainment. Still, one may rest in nonaction; resting in nonaction, responsibilities and affairs will be fruitful. Resting in nonaction, one may be joyful; being joyful, care and anxiety will have no place to reside, and the years of one's life will be long. Emptiness, stillness, lucidity, silence, and nonaction are the root of the ten thousand things. (*Zhuangzi*, Chapter 13; adapted from Watson 1968, 142–3; see also Chapters 11, 17)

Through stillness, one attains a deeper level of cosmological attunement. This is a condition wherein on accepts what is and allows each being to unfold according to its own affinities and connections. Following the patterns of the universe, one abides in emptiness, stillness, lucidity, silence, and non-action. One is free from disruptive psychological conditions. One takes on the qualities of the heavens (pure yang) and earth (pure yin), specifically clarity and stillness (*qingjing*). Rooted in non-interference, open receptivity, and carefree play, one simply participates in the Dao's transformative process. Daoists frequently refer to such an ontological condition and way of experiencing as "true joy" (*zhenle*). This is joyfulness beyond the confines of gain and loss, unaffected by mundane concerns and apparent difficulties. As the same chapter of the *Book of Master Zhuang* continues, "So it is said, for one who understands celestial joy, life is the working of the heavens, and death is the transformation of things. In stillness, one shares virtue with yin; in motion, one shares flow with yang. Thus one who understands celestial joy incurs no injury from the heavens, no opposition from humanity, no entanglement from things, and no blame from ghosts. So it is said, one's movement is of the heavens, and one's stillness of earth."

Interestingly, chapter 2 of the *Huangdi neijing suwen* (Yellow Thearch's Inner Classic: Basic Questions; DZ 1018), a central text of classical Chinese medicine that appears to have some Daoist elements and that exerted some influence on specific Daoist movements, is titled "Siqi diaoshen lun" (Discourse on Harmonizing Spirit with the Four Qi). Here we are told that cosmological harmonization involves following the seasons. This specifically manifests as attunement with the energetic qualities and cycles of each season. One may recall the relevant Five Phase associations: Wood/spring/minor yang/birth/outward/planting; Fire/summer/major yang/adolescence/upward/tending; Earth/late summer/yin-yang balance/adulthood/centered/pausing; Metal/autumn/minor yin/maturation/inward/harvesting; and Water/winter/major yin/old age/downward/storing. Harmonizing with the solar cycles, following the movement of the sun, one naturally rests more during autumn and winter, and one naturally becomes more active during spring and summer. According to the *Basic Questions*, such seasonal attunement especially relates to sleep, with the longest periods of sleep occurring in the depth of winter and the shortest periods occurring in the height of summer.

There are other expressions of such Daoist temporality. One's body, specifically the organ-meridian system, returns to homeostasis. This type of attunement results not only in an experience of the yin-organs as energetic orbs, but also as a connection with the qi of the four directions. As mentioned in the previous chapter, this relates to the Five Sprouts. An expression of

Daoist microcosm/macrocosm correspondences, one's connection to the larger universe occurs through particular experiences of embodiment. This type of energetic attunement may be further experienced as celestial qi entering the body through the crown-point and terrestrial qi entering the body through the soles of the feet. In addition, one may become more sensitive to the lunar phases and the Twenty-four Nodes, the key seasonal and energetic times of the year. So, in certain expressions, attunement results in greater sensitivity to energetic openings and closings. This includes a higher facility and greater subtlety of spatial perception.

This form of Daoist cosmological attunement closely parallels mystical union with the Dao, including the post-unitive mode of mystical being-in-the-world in which one manifests and transmits the Dao's numinous presence. In classical Daoist texts, this state of attunement is compared to streambeds, useless trees, valleys, vessels, water, and so forth. From this perspective, attunement with the Dao manifests as emptiness, fluidity, modesty, simplicity, suppleness, and so forth. Water is especially significant here, as the *Book of Venerable Masters* explains, "The highest adeptness is like water. Water is adept at benefiting the myriad beings because it does not compete" (ch. 8), and "Nothing in the world is softer and weaker than water; But attacking with hardness and strength cannot overcome it. This is because nothing can change it. Weakness overcomes strength; Softness overcomes hardness" (ch. 78) (see also *Zhuangzi*, ch. 17). Here one may recall the Daoist practice of observation, with the lessons of water being especially important. As mentioned, the Dao is often compared to the ocean, while movements are compared to rivers and lineages to tributaries. Daoism is the watercourse leading back to the ocean of the Dao. This recalls various other classical and foundational Daoist principles and values, but on an experientially actualized level in this case. Merging with the Dao, one enters a state of desirelessness and namelessness. Mundane concerns, such as fame and reputation, no longer influence one. Here we see an overlap with the Nine Practices, Daoist contemplative psychology, and the qualities of Daoist sages discussed in previous chapters. In addition, classical Daoist texts suggest that attunement is characterized by hiddenness, invulnerability, and perhaps invisibility on some level.

Characteristics and benefits of attunement

It is said that those who are adept at protecting life
Travel on land without meeting rhinos or tigers,
Enter battle without the protection of armor or weapons.
Rhinos have no place to gore with their horns;
Tigers have no place to seize with their claws;
And weapons find no place to pierce with their blades.
Why is this?
Because such people have no ground for death.

(*Laozi*, Chapter 50; see also Chapter 55)

* * *

The authentic person of ancient times did not rebel against want, did not grow proud in plenty, and did not plan his affairs. A person like this could commit an error and not regret it, could meet with success and not make a show. A person like this could climb to high places and not be frightened, could enter water and not get wet, could enter fire and not get burned. His knowledge was able to climb all the way up to the Dao like this.

(*Zhuangzi*, Chapter 6; adapted from Watson 1968: 77; see also Chapter 17)

***

A complete heart-mind at the center
Cannot be concealed or hidden.
It will be known through your appearance;
It will be seen in the color of your skin.
If you encounter others with this exceptional qi,
They will be kinder to you than your brothers.
If you encounter others with harmful qi,
They will injure you with their weapons.
The reverberation of the wordless
Is more rapid than the drumming of thunder.
The shape of the qi and the heart-mind
Is more luminous than the sun and moon.

("Neiye," Chapter 18)

The infusion of the Dao manifests in the individual as numinous presence. Members of the inner cultivation lineages of classical Daoism had different views on the degree to which this could be concealed, but such qualities resulted in a different way of experiencing. Specifically, one's life becomes increasingly characterized by ease, harmony, serenity, and so forth, even if these are just internal qualities. One also apparently attains a greater degree of resiliency and protection, even to the point where one no longer needs "protection." One no longer encounters harm or difficulty. Anticipating later Daoist views and material expressions, it appears that one's own heart-mind and being become a talisman, which provides assistance, refuge, and benefit. Harold Roth of Brown University has identified the benefits of classical Daoist apophatic meditation, including physical, psychological, and spiritual benefits (see, Roth 1999a: 118–23, 140–2, 164–9). These include perceptual acuity, heightened vitality, energetic integrity, psychological equanimity, numinous pervasion, and so forth. The accomplished Daoist adept experiences life beyond the trials and tribulations of mundane concerns. This recalls the existential and ontological transformation discussed in previous chapters.

Encounter

If attunement is primarily about direct personal experience of the Dao, encounter is about inter-subjective, relational, and communal types of experience. This expression of Daoist experience is multidimensional and wide-ranging: from aesthetics and material culture through teachers and communities to places and even specific forms of mystical experience. That is, "encounter" may encompass the entire range of Daoist experience, from more "ordinary" to more "extraordinary" types. In this respect, encounter often relates to sources of personal affinity and connection, including those that result in deeper levels of adherence, commitment, and even conversion. Such sources may include particular teachers, views, practices, material expressions (e.g. scriptures), and so forth. These are some of the dimensions of Daoist religiosity that provide sustenance, consolation, and inspiration for Daoists.

In the previous chapter, we considered Daoist aesthetics and material culture as a dimension of Daoist practice. That discussion attempted to bring attention to the production of Daoist art, calligraphy, literature, painting, and so forth. Here we may examine the other side, namely, the encounter with and reception of such Daoist creative expression. While Daoism is frequently constructed as "thought" and "philosophy," Daoist material religion, such as the texts out of which "ideas" are extracted, remind us that particular Daoists and Daoist communities have been and continue to be involved. There is a lived and living dimension of Daoist aesthetics and material culture. Although these aspects are often presented in the modern world as fragments extracted or isolated from the larger Daoist tradition (e.g. in bookstores or museums), this is one form of encounter with Daoism. Many individuals may find an interest in Daoism through material culture, especially through Daoist literature. A typical example involves reading Daoist texts and having an affinity with the views and insights contained therein. As will be discussed in the last chapter of the present book, such phenomena bring the question of adherence and affiliation into high relief.

Individuals also encounter Daoism as manifested in place-specific communities with distinctive aesthetics, spatial organization, and material culture. Let us take the example of a typical visit to a Daoist temple, especially as experienced by committed Daoist adherents and pilgrims. The idealized Daoist temple is sited along a north–south axis. In this configuration, the temple faces south. Approaching the entrance, one usually encounters a large gate. This is followed by a series of halls and altars, with the highest altar being the northernmost. In modern Complete Perfection monasteries, the main altar is usually dedicated to the Three Purities. As one walks through the temple compound, one may notice various types of trees, stones, and wildlife. One may also recognize different dimensions of Daoist material culture, including distinctive art, dress, food, ritual implements, steles, temple boards, texts, and so forth. The temple boards are especially interesting, as they often consist of calligraphy engraved from that of famous calligraphers or influential Daoist teachers. "Clarity and stillness are the rectification of the world." "In cultivating the Dao, begin by observing the heart-mind." "When studying immortality, you must study celestial immortality." Individuals who take the time to read these "living texts" may find important Daoist principles and insights into Daoist practice-realization.

Beyond this idealized Daoist temple, there are also architectural features unique to specific temples and sacred sites. For example, Tianshi dong (Celestial Master Grotto), the mid-level temple on Qingcheng shan (Azure Wall Mountain; Guanxian, Sichuan), has a cavern identified as the place where Zhang Daoling received a revelation from Lord Lao. At Yuquan yuan (Temple of the Jade Spring), the base-monastery at Huashan (Mount Hua; near Huayin, Shaanxi), one finds a large Koi pond, where the local Daoists speak of observing the "joy of fish." One also finds a Complete Perfection monastic community adhering to a daily monastic schedule, wherein recitation of the morning and evening liturgy is the key religious event of the day. In addition to tending to altars, welcoming visitors, and administering to other monastic tasks, monastics often share afternoon tea and "discuss the Dao" (lundao). In such contexts, different participants have different experiences. Resident Daoists perhaps encounter these places as "home." However, in the process, because of their high degree of familiarity, they may overlook or take for granted the amazing aspects of habitation. Visiting Daoists may encounter such places as "pilgrimage sites." Their experience may be characterized by a higher degree of reverence, attentiveness, and appreciation, especially the rarity and distinctiveness of the place. Tourists may completely overlook much of the aesthestic and communal, the Daoist, dimensions, on their way to "peak ascents" or "nature appreciation." In any case, whether recognized or not, there is a place-specific Daoist community, a form of lived Daoist religiosity, that may be encountered. Such encounters include dense layers of materiality, including historical dimensions, and diverse levels of awareness. These may inspire deeper connection. They may lead to a deeper sense of tradition and Daoist locatedness.

Moving into more living forms of Daoist encounter, individuals may meet teachers and become involved with Daoist communities. This recalls the various types of Daoist adherence, commitment, and participation discussed in previous chapters. Teachers (shi), and the larger Daoist community by extension, are one of the external Three Treasures, with the Dao and scriptures (jing) being the other two. Traditionally speaking, Daoism has tended to function as an elder-based community. Such seniority is not simply a matter of age; it also includes level of insight, study, training, experience, and so forth. Agedness is not necessarily equivalent to wisdom. In any case, teachers, often referred to as *shifu* ("master-father"), are centrally important in the Daoist tradition. Daoist teachers have traditionally provided in-depth training and spiritual direction. In terms of the larger community, one may also receive insights, assistance, and support from one's spiritual friends, often referred to as "Companions of the Way" (*daoyou*) in Daoism. Affiliation with a particular teacher and community is, in turn, often expressed through lineage and ordination.

As a formal disciple and member of a particular lineage, one often gains access to esoteric materials, including specific texts and methods (Figure 7.1). Such training frequently includes "oral instructions" (*koujue*), in which teachers clarify more obscure or difficult dimensions of affiliation and practice. However, such secrecy may also create obstruction and confusion. Without discernment and carefulness, Daoist esotericism may lead to abuse of power, psychological manipulation, rigid hierarchies, personal mistrust, spiritual disorientation, and so forth. Nonetheless, higher levels of training often require acceptance by a teacher and lineage affiliation. Such experience frequently correlates to levels of ordination, training, and access. For example, commenting on modern (1970s) Taiwanese Daoist ritual, Michael Saso distinguishes dimensions and layers of Daoist ritual experience.

FIGURE 7.1 *Transmission of Scriptures.*
Source: *Wudou sanyi tujue*, DZ 765.

Inner dimensions of Daoist ritual

The ritual of religious Taoism [*sic*] is esoteric; that is, it is not meant to be directly understood and witnessed by all the faithful. The esoteric meaning of Taoist ritual and magic is concealed from all but the initiated; only after many years of training and a gradual introduction to religious secrets is the disciple deemed worthy of elevation to the rank of master and full knowledge of the esoteric meanings of religious ritual . . . . The expertise of a Taoist priest is judged by several criteria, the first one being his external performance of ritual . . . . The second criterion for judging a Taoist [priest], which determines his rank at ordination, is his knowledge of the esoteric secrets of the religion, including the ability to perform the meditations and breath-control techniques of internal alchemy (*nei-tan*), and to recite the classical orthodox lists of spirits' names [*lu*-registers] and apparel and the mantric summons found in the Taoist Canon. (Saso 1978: 325–6)

That is, one's degree of training (instruction and practice) depends on one's position within the community, one's level of adherence, and one's degree of commitment to the Daoist tradition. This training in turn most often leads to a different level of practice and experience, even when one is practicing the "same" technique or performing the "same" ritual. There is thus an inner (cultivation) dimension and an outer (performative) dimension of Daoist ritual. The former may remain completely unknown outside of Daoist clerical circles.

A more distinctive dimension of Daoist views of teachers centers on immortals (*xianren*). As previously discussed, Daoists generally understand immortals as individuals who have completed a process of alchemical transformation and self-divinization. Throughout Daoist history, Daoists have attained revelations from specific deities and had mystical encounters with immortals. In terms of experience, teachers may thus be embodied and disembodied. One may receive teachings from physical and divine beings. From a Daoist perspective, these are some of the sources of transmission. Here it is important to remember that immortality most often relates to the formation of the yang-spirit through alchemical practice. An interesting and representative example is Wang Zhe (1113–70), the founder of Complete Perfection. According to traditional historiography and hagiography, Wang had a number of mystical experiences with immortals, during which he was given secret transmissions (Komjathy 2007a, 2013a). These experiences became one inspiration for his decision to completely embrace a Daoist way of life. As interesting, Complete Perfection sources report a number of instances where Wang would send out his yang-spirit in order to provide instruction and spiritual direction to his disciples.

Disembodied transmission

[Wang Chongyang] was locked in the Hermitage of Complete Perfection for 100 days transforming himself. Sometimes he ate and sometimes he refrained from eating . . . [One night] Master Ma was sleeping on the second floor of his private residence. The doors and windows were all locked. Perfected [Chongyang] arrived during the night to have a face-to-face conversation. Ma did not know where he came from. [Later] a person wanted to draw his [Wang's] spirit. [However,] his left eye revolved to the right, while his right eye revolved to the left. At various moments he appeared as old and young, fat and skinny, yellow and vermilion, as well as azure and white. His form and appearance had no stability. (*Ganshui lu*, DZ 973, 1.2b–10a)

During these types of Daoist encounter, individuals receive personal transmissions. Such visitations from the yang-spirit of higher-level teachers and immortals may also occur in dreams. Many Daoist accounts report alchemically transformed practitioners "sending out spirit to enter dreams" (*chushen rumeng*). We may refer to this as "Daoist dream teachings." These are nocturnal visitations during which a teacher or immortal, specifically as a spirit-being, enters an individual's dreams to transmit specific instructions. The above description of Ma Yu's experience also highlights another dimension of Daoist experience: the appearance of higher-level Daoists as an ever-shifting qi field. As individuals attain higher levels of practice-realization, they become more rarified and infused with the Dao's numinosity. This numinosity may be perceived by others with similar abilities, and Daoists often use such qualities as a means of recognition and confirmation. That is, there is a specific "qi pattern" to Daoist religious identity and adherence, especially as the culmination of dedicated and prolonged cultivation.

Here we should also note that Daoist perspectives on dreams are complex. The classical and foundational Daoist view is found in the *Book of Master Zhuang*: "The authentic person sleeps without dreaming and wakes without cares" (Chapter 6). However, dreams also provide existential clarification and spiritual insights. Taken as a whole, Daoists seems to both downplay and celebrate dreams. It appears to depend on the individual person, type of dream, and stage of practice. Discernment and non-attachment are crucial, as dreams may be a source of both inspiration and distraction. As a final point in terms of Daoist inter-subjective experience and relationship, it is noteworthy that many individuals have converted to Daoism through mystical experiences, including encounters with immortals.

Pervasion

Just as attunement is about personal experience, and encounter is about inter-subjective and relational experience, pervasion may be understood as a form of transpersonal experience. Similarly, just as material culture may be viewed experientially from the side of artisan (expression) and audience (reception), so too pervasion relates to both encounter (interpersonal) and unification (transpersonal). The Daoist experience of pervasion may involve an inter-subjective dimension, in which one recognizes the numinous presence of the Dao in another being, or a transpersonal dimension, in which the individual becomes pervaded. In these types of experiences, Daoists overcome dualistic modes of being and subject-object dichotomies. Experiences of pervasion are more unitive, wherein the boundaries of personhood become more permeable. One transcends the limitations of separate identity, becomes infused with the Dao's numinous presence, and recognizes other layers of existence. The latter may include a deeper sense of interconnection.

Following Harold Roth of Brown University, we may, in turn, distinguish introvertive and extrovertive aspects of Daoist mystical experience (Roth 2000), or experiences of the sacred. In the present context, introvertive refers to the inner experience of pervasion, while extrovertive refers to the post-unitive expression of being-in-the-world. In this way, pervasion relates to various dimensions of Daoist religious identity discussed in previous chapters, especially being, embodiment, and transformation. Here it is important to recognize that there are different types of Daoist mystical experience, including disappearance into Nature, encounters with gods and immortals, rarification, and so forth. These types of mystical experience relate to the different types of Daoist theology, namely, monistic, panentheistic, panenhenic, polytheistic, and aniministic. Along these lines, we may also recall the importance of revelation in the Daoist tradition as well as the ideal of sages and immortals. Pervasion especially relates to unification with the Dao and self-divinization.

Let us begin with the introvertive and transpersonal dimension of Daoist mystical experience. The Daoist experience of pervasion principally relates to immortality and transformation. In this way, pervasion is the experiential dimension of various Daoist practices, with external alchemy (*waidan*) and internal alchemy (*neidan*) being particularly relevant. As mentioned, external alchemy involves the decoction and ingestion of "elixirs," or esoteric formulas made from rare, and often dangerous, herbal and mineral ingredients. Internal alchemy involves complex, stage-based training aimed at complete psychosomatic transformation. The goal is immortality. Immortals are individuals who have gone through a process of rarification and self-divinization. On some level, such beings have made themselves divine through alchemical transmutation. There are various aspects of such experience, including types of immortality, experiential confirmation, and the attainment of numinous abilities.

Daoists have recognized various types of immortals, with varying degrees of "immortality" (extended longevity) and "transcendence" (otherworldliness).

Types of Daoist immortals

Superior adepts who rise up in their bodies and ascend to the Void are called celestial immortals (*tianxian*). Mid-level adepts who wander among renowned mountains are called terrestrial immortals (*dixian*). Lesser adepts who first die and then cast off [their shell] are called corpse-liberated immortals (*shijie xian*). (*Baopuzi neipian*, DZ 1185, 2.11a)

* * *

The immortals have five ranks, including ghost immortal (*guixian*), human immortal (*renxian*), terrestrial immortal (*dixian*), and spirit immortal (*shenxian*). The celestial immortal (*tianxian*) is beyond rank. All of these are immortals. (*Chuandao ji*, DZ 263, 14.2b)

Recalling our earlier discussion of alchemical applications of yin-yang, this distinction relates to degrees of physicality/subtlety, defilement/purity, mortality/immortality, and so forth. There are degrees of sublimation, refinement, and perfection. In terms of a fairly standard distinction, "ghost immortals" are the most apparitional and ephemeral. Human immortals are embodied, so they also have a higher degree of temporality and finitude. Terrestrial immortals are spirit-beings who reside on earth, especially in wild places such as mountains; they also have a certain degree of limitation, as they are earthbound. Often used interchangeably, spirit immortals and celestial immortals are the most yang. They reside in Daoist sacred realms and have a long, perhaps infinite, celestial lifespan. Sometimes celestial immortals are ranked higher according to their ability to access the highest Daoist heavens. In terms of the present context, these ideals of immortality directly relate to Daoist experience. Daoists engaging in alchemical practice may experience degrees of subtlety. One goes through a process of rarification and transformation, in which one becomes less substantial, less distorted, and less entangled. One's body becomes lighter; one's heart-mind becomes purer; one's energetic sensitivity becomes heightened; and one's ability to connect to divine presences and sacred realities becomes actualized. As we saw in the discussion of personhood, immortality also relates to Daoist views of death, dying, and the afterlife. From an alchemical perspective, the fate of ordinary human beings involves dissipation into the cosmos or fragmented and transitory post-mortem existence as an ancestor or ghost. For those who complete alchemical training, their post-mortem experience will be radically different.

Another dimension of pervasion, especially in the form of rarification, is "experiential confirmation" (*zhengyan*), which is also referred to as "signs of proof" and "verification" (Eskildsen 2004; Komjathy 2007a). For example, the final section of the *Anthology on the Transmission of the Dao* is titled "Lun zhengyan" (On Experiential Confirmation). It informs the Daoist adept that specific training regimens may result in specific experiences. There will be signs of successful training. After one conserves vital essence, opens the body's meridians, and generates saliva, one begins a process of self-rarification and self-divinization. At the most advanced stages of alchemical transformation, one becomes free of karmic obstructions and entanglements, and one's name becomes registered in the records of the Three Purities. The embryo of immortality matures, which includes the ability to manifest as the body-beyond-the-body and to have greater communion with celestial realms. After the adept's bones begin to disappear and become infused with golden light, he or she may receive visitations from divine beings. This process of experiential confirmation is said to culminate as follows: "In a solemn and grand ceremony, you will be given the purple writ of the celestial books and immortal regalia. Immortals will appear on your left and right, and you will be escorted to Penglai. You will have audience with the Perfect Lord of Great Tenuity in the Purple Palace. Here your name and place of birth will be entered into the registers. According to your level of accomplishment, you will be given a dwelling-place on the Three Islands. Then you may be called a Perfected or immortal" (16.30a).

Closely associated with these signs of proof, Daoist practitioners have suggested that Daoist practice may result in certain "boons along the way," specifically in the acquisition of "numinous abilities" (*shentong*) and "numinous pervasion" (*lingtong*). The "Lun liutong jue" (Instructions on the Six Pervasions), a Yuan dynasty internal alchemy text, provides a clear description.

The Six Pervasions

1 Pervasion of Heart-mind Conditions, involving the ability to experience unified nature as distinct from the ordinary body.
2 Pervasion of Spirit Conditions, involving the ability to know things beyond ordinary perception.
3 Pervasion of Celestial Vision, involving the ability to perceive internal landscapes within the body.
4 Pervasion of Celestial Hearing, involving the ability to hear the subtle communications of spirits and humans.
5 Pervasion of Past Occurrences, involving the ability to understand the karmic causes and effects relating to the Three Realms of desire, form, and formlessness.
6 Pervasion of the Heart-minds of Others, involving the ability to manifest the body-beyond-the-body. (*Neidan jiyao*, DZ 1258, 3.12a–14a)

These parallel the Buddhist emphasis on the attainment of "supernatural powers" and "paranormal abilities" (Skt.: *siddhi*), including magical powers, the divine ear (clairaudience), penetration of the minds of others (clairvoyance), the divine eye (ability to see into time and space), memory of former existences, and knowledge of the extinction of karmic outflows. As is the case among Buddhists, Daoists have tended to identify such abilities as a natural outcome of practice. One should not pursue, elevate, or become attached to such abilities. Instead, one must recognize them for what they are: byproducts of practice. They are simply one possible form of experiential confirmation. Other forms include an increased sense of meaning and purpose, a teacher's recognition, or veneration by others. At the same time, none of these things may occur. It depends on one's affinities, constitution, and the time.

The Daoist experience of pervasion thus relates to mystical experience, numinosity, rarification, and immortality. Through internal alchemy, one may transmute the mundane and limited dimensions of self into their celestial and divine counterparts. This involves awakening the subtle body and the formation of the yang-spirit. From a Daoist perspective, the actualization of such hidden or latent layers of personhood provides the ability to become pervaded, to increase one's connection to the Dao and sacred realities. It also ensures post-mortem existence and entrance into the highest sacred realms upon death. At the same time, recalling the above-mentioned distinction between introvertive and extrovertive mystical experience, pervasion manifests as transformed being-in-the-world. Infused with the Dao's numinous presence, and connected with the larger matrix of life, one becomes a new being. This transformed ontological condition includes different ways of experiencing, including various forms of experiential confirmation and numinous abilities. Such anthropological views and their related experiences perhaps challenge the conventional distinctions between "natural" and "supernatural," "normal" and "anomalous," as well as "human" and "divine" If humans are originally connected to the Dao, and if the Dao pervades everything, then perhaps so-called "supernatural abilities" are, in fact, "natural." At the very least, according to Daoism, we have latent capacities. The experience of the fullness of our humanity includes a connection with the sacred, which manifests in ways that perhaps reveal normalcy as the anomalous experience. In keeping with Daoist insights, perhaps to be "normal" is to be "abnormal," and vice versa. The strange and exceptional may reveal something fundamentally important about being and existence.

Further reading

Herrou, Adeline. 2013, *A World of Their Own: Daoist Monks and Their Community in Contemporary China*. St. Petersburg, FL: Three Pines Press.

Kohn, Livia. 1991, *Early Chinese Mysticism: Philosophy and Soteriology in the Taoist Tradition*. Princeton, NJ: Princeton University Press.

Komjathy, Louis. 2007, *Cultivating Perfection: Mysticism and Self-transformation in Early Quanzhen Daoism*. Leiden: Brill.

Porter, Bill. 1993, *The Road to Heaven: Encounters with Chinese Hermits*. San Francisco: Mercury House.

CHAPTER EIGHT

Place

Daoism tends to center around place-specific communities, and places have been centrally important in the Daoist tradition and Daoist imagination. Daoists have lived and continue to live in a variety of locales, including urban, rural, and wild places. Daoist residences and sacred sites are found in urban centers, remote villages, dense forests, and mountain summits. There are also various types of abodes and habitation, including caves, hermitages, houses, monasteries, and temples. These usually relate to specific Daoist ways of life and forms of community: from ascetics and hermits to householders and monastics. One may, in turn, reflect on the ways in which specific Daoist commitments and religious pursuits are located in specific types of residency. This draws our attention to the central importance of place in Daoism in particular and religious traditions more generally.

There is a strong "sense of place" among Daoists. This sense of place includes awareness concerning location, dwelling, and spatiality. Daoists have been and continue to be attentive to the various dimensions of locatedness. Such awareness begins with landscape and surrounding locale, including the various influences (e.g. animals, moonlight, sunlight, trees, water, wind). One may then more efficaciously site buildings and situate oneself. Even in more urban settings, natural influences tend to be key characteristics of Daoist sacred sites; Daoist urban temples often have the feel of a nature sanctuary. The Daoist sense of place thus relates to specific places, types of residency, as well as aesthetics and architecture. Aesthetic and energetic sensitivity also relates to attentiveness to placement and relationality. Daoist places tend to have distinctive qualities, including cleanliness, harmoniousness, naturalness, openness, simplicity, and so forth. In this respect, one may consider the ways in which Daoist values inform and become expressed in Daoist aesthetics and habitation. These various dimensions of place may be understood through the framework of location, dwelling, and spatiality.

Location

While Daoists have lived in a variety of environs, including urban settings, rural villages, and even wild places, there can be little debate that mountains have occupied a special place in the Daoist tradition and Daoist imagination. As Ge Hong informs us in his *Inner Chapters of Master Embracing Simplicity*, "All of those cultivating the divine process and preparing medicines, as well as those fleeing political disorders and living as hermits, go to the mountains" (DZ 1185, 17.1a). In the Daoist tradition, mountains are seen as manifestations of the Dao, as portals into the sacred, as places to collect immortal substances, as ideal locations for self-cultivation, and so forth. Many Daoists have entered the mountains in order to engage in deeper Daoist practice. This perennial Daoist sentiment is echoed by Xue Tailai (1923–2001), one of the most prominent modern Huashan (Mount Hua) monastics and twenty-fourth-generation representative of the Huashan lineage: "Monks who live here [on Huashan] have to take care of visitors. We can't concentrate on our practice. No one can accomplish anything this way. People who want to practice have to go deeper into the mountains" (Porter 1993: 80).

For many Daoists, mountains are places where the heavens (yang) and the earth (yin) come closest together and are thus regarded as ideal locations for religious activity. A human being who goes into the mountains may experience deepened practice, divine communications, and mystical experiences. This connection is so much the case that the Chinese character *xian* 仙, translated as "ascendant," "immortal," or "transcendent," consists of *ren* 人 ("human") and *shan* 山 ("mountain"), and the phrase "to enter the mountains" (*rushan*) may refer not only to actual mountain seclusion, but also more broadly to engaging in Daoist meditation or to ascending the altar during ritual. To cultivate such a connection, of course, requires a particular orientation and intention. Paralleling certain contemporary forms of mountaineering, Daoist "cloud-wandering" (*yunyou*) and pilgrimage (*chaosheng*; lit., "revering the sacred") often have been attempts to participate more completely in the Dao. We might think of this commitment as "mountain contemplation" (*shanguan*).

Specific places have occupied a central position in Daoism, both as sources of revelation and particular communities and as later sacred sites and pilgrimage (and tourist) destinations. There is a strong "sense of place" among Daoists and Daoist communities. In some cases, this came from a perceived aesthetic, energetic, or divine quality of the place. In other cases, it originated in a particular set of experiences that occurred in the associated locale. Various Daoist revelations, mystical experiences, as well as important events and personages are associated with specific places. For example, Chapter 1 of the *Book of Master Zhuang* tells of a "spirit being" (*shenren*) who lives on Gushe mountain: "He doesn't eat the five grains, but sucks the wind, drinks the dew, climbs up on the clouds and mist, rides a flying dragon, and wanders beyond the four seas. By concentrating his spirit, he can protect creatures from sickness and plague and make the harvest plentiful." Such characteristics became seminal in later Daoist ascetic, eremitic, and alchemical ideals.

Tradition also holds that Laozi (Master Lao; pseudo-historical) transmitted the *Scripture on the Dao and Inner Power* to Yin Xi (pseudo-historical), the so-called "Guardian of the Pass," at a specific place.

Hangu Pass

Laozi cultivated the Dao and inner power. He taught that one should efface oneself and be without fame in the world. After he had lived in Zhou for a long time, he saw that the Zhou was in decline. Then he departed. When he reached the pass [Hangu Pass], the keeper of the pass, Yin Xi, said, "We will see no more of you. I request that you write a book for us." Laozi then wrote a book in two parts, discussing the Dao and inner power in 5,000 words. Thereupon, he departed. No one knows where he ended his life. (*Shiji*, Chapter 63)

Although modern scholarship has demonstrated the pseudo-historical nature of "Laozi," the account in the *Shiji* (Records of the Historian), an influential Early Han dynasty historiography, is noteworthy for its emphasis on place-specific transmission. The pass in question was early on identified as Hangu Pass near Lingbao city, Henan province. During the fifth century, Daoists shifted the location of transmission to the Zhongnan (Southern Terminus) mountains in Shaanxi province (see, Kohn 2003a, 2004b). Located in Tayu village in Zhouzhi county, Louguan (Lookout Tower Monastery; a.k.a., Louguan tai) rose to become a major Daoist center in northern China and, in the early sixth century, also served as a refuge for southern Daoists who were persecuted under Emperor Wu (r. 464–549) of the Liang dynasty (502–87). Located in the foothills of the Zhongnan mountains and still a flourishing Complete Perfection Daoist monastery today, Louguan was identified by Daoists as the place where Laozi transmitted the *Scripture on the Dao and Inner Power* to Yin Xi. This version of the transmission legend arose in the mid-fifth century through Yin Tong (398–499?), a self-identified descendent of Yin Xi and owner of the Louguan estate. During the late fifth or early sixth century, a group of Daoists, primarily members of the Northern Celestial Masters, apparently lived within a monastic framework, specifically according to ethical guidelines, communal celibate living, and standardized daily schedule. Both of the famous Daoists Wang Daoyi (fl. 470s) and Wei Jie (496–569) also lived there. In that context, and especially during the Tang dynasty, Louguan, known primarily as Zongsheng gong (Palace of the Ancestral Sage) and Shuojing tai (Terrace of the Revealed Scripture) at the time, received a high degree of imperial patronage, partially because of the Tang ruling family's imagined ancestral connection to Laozi ("Li Er") and various miraculous events that occurred there. In combination with Bozhou, Laozi's supposed birthplace, Louguan's close connection with Laozi, and with Lord Lao by extension, effectively elevated the site to the terrestrial location most proximal to the god. This is documented in texts such as the *Xisheng jing* (Scripture on the Western Ascension; DZ 666), wherein Laozi ascends to the heavens, reappears as the god Lord Lao, and bestows additional, secret Daoist instructions to Yin Xi. Louguan became a Complete Perfection monastery during the early fourteenth century.

As touched upon in other chapters of the present book, various places are centrally important in Daoist history, especially with respect to specific teachers, communities, and experiences, including revelations and intensive training. Some of the most important include the following: Zhang Daoling (fl. 140s), early Celestial Masters, and Heming shan (Crane Cry Mountain; Dayi, Sichuan); Kou Qianzhi (365–448), Northern Celestial Masters, and Songshan (Mount Song; Zhenfang, Henan); Lu Xiujing (406–77), Southern Celestial Masters and Numinous Treasure, and Lushan (Mount Lu; Jiujiang, Jiangxi); the Xu family and Tao Hongjing (456–536), early Highest Clarity, and Maoshan (Mount Mao; Jurong, Jiangsu); Wang Zhe (1113–70), early Complete Perfection, and Liujiang (Huxian, Shaanxi) and the Kunyu mountains (near Weihai and Yantai, Shandong); as well as Qiu Chuji (1148–227), early Complete Perfection and the Dragon Gate lineage, and Panxi (Shaanxi) and Longmen dong (Dragon Gate Grotto; near Longxian, Shaanxi); and so forth (Figure 8.1).

Another key dimension of Daoist views of place centers on standardized geographical schema. Throughout Chinese history, various systems for identifying and elevating sacred sites have been put forward. Some of these were adopted by Daoists, while others were uniquely Daoist expressions. Three systems in particular stand out: the Five Marchmounts (*wuyue*), the grotto-heavens (*dongtian*), and the auspicious sites (*fudi*).

The Five Marchmounts system began under imperial auspices and seems to have been standardized by the Han dynasty. As time went on, these sacred peaks also became the residences of

FIGURE 8.1 *Longmen dong (Dragon Gate Grotto; near Longxian, Shaanxi).*

Source: Louis Komjathy and Kate Townsend.

recluses with diverse religious and cultural commitments as well as the location of Buddhist and Daoist temples and monasteries. There were complex patterns of competition, negotiation, and cooperation on these and other Chinese mountains. In this context, it appears that Daoists first began to adopt and claim jurisdiction over the Five Marchmounts during the Period of Disunion (Robson 2009: 46–52). This move was, at least partially, an attempt to increase Daoists' cultural capital and political power, and drew on a uniquely Daoist understanding of these sites in which each of the Five Marchmounts has an esoteric and talismanic dimension. This is perhaps most clearly expressed in the *Wuyue zhenxing tu* (Diagram of the Perfect Forms of the Five Marchmounts), which Ge Hong discusses.

Diagram of the Perfect Forms of the Five Marchmounts

Lord Zheng [Yin] told me that no Daoist book surpasses the *Sanhuang wen* (Writings of the Three Sovereigns) and *Diagram of the Perfect Forms of the Five Marchmounts* in importance. These books are the honored secrets of ancient immortals and can only be obtained by those with the title of "immortal." They are only transmitted every forty years. When they are transmitted, an oath must be taken and sealed by smearing the blood of a sacrificial victim on the lips [a blood oath]. Presents are also exchanged. All of the famous mountains and the Five Marchmounts have these texts, but they are stored in the darkened recesses of stone caves. If those destined to attain the Dao enter mountains and sincerely keep them in mind, then the mountain deity will respond and open the mountain, allowing them to see the texts. (*Baopuzi neipian*, DZ 1185, 19.8ab)

For those who are worthy to receive the transmission and who maintain their integrity in subsequent transmissions, the *Diagram of the Perfect Forms of the Five Marchmounts* provides protection from potential harmful influences. Its magical nature also provides access into the hidden recesses of mountains.

There are, in turn, a variety of extant versions of the *Diagram of the Perfect Forms of the Five Marchmounts*. As expressed in the fifteenth-century *Wuyue guben zhenxing tu* (Ancient Version of Diagram of the Perfect Forms of the Five Marchmounts; DZ 441), the "true" or "perfect forms" are represented in five fairly abstract topographic charts. They consist of a black shape, located in a square box, which represents the mountain's actual structure and central terrain. There are also inner lines and small inner points, intended to be red in color, which indicate the sources and courses of the waterways. Finally, there are larger points, intended to be yellow in color, which are grottos. In their more well-known expression, the "perfect forms" are preserved in a variety of steles and texts dating from the fourteenth century and later. An early seventeenth-century version preserved at Songshan (Mount Song) and reproduced at the other marchmounts identifies the "perfect forms" as follows: eastern 𝌆, southern 🗡, central 𝌆, northen 🗡, and western 𝌆. These representations are more talismanic and are perhaps even derived from earlier cosmic diagrams. In this way, they parallel the Five Numinous Treasure Talismans. In both cases, the five magical diagrams correspond to the five directions and provide magical protection. While the Five Numinous Treasure Talismans correspond to primordial ethers that maintain the cosmic structure, the Five Perfect Forms are "energetic shapes" of the corresponding landforms. Interestingly, there are also associated practices. In addition to using the talismans for their invocatory and apotropaic power, both when entering mountains and when protecting a specific site, medieval Daoists also visualized their body's five yin-organs as the Five Marchmounts and the Five Planets. One cannot but then wonder if the talismans were utilized as visual aids in Daoist visualization practices.

In their standardized expression, which again seems to have become established to some degree and with occasional variations during the Han dynasty, the Five Marchmounts are as follows:

1 The Northern Marchmount of Hengshan[1] (Mount Heng; Datong, Shanxi). Meaning "stable mountain," Hengshan[1] has an elevation of 2,017 meters or 6,617 feet. This mountain is the highest of the five sacred peaks.

2 The Southern Marchmount of Hengshan[2] (Mount Heng; Hengshan, Hunan). Meaning "balanced mountain," Hengshan[2] has an elevation of 1,290 meters or 4,232 feet.

3 The Western Marchmount of Huashan (Mount Hua; Huayin, Shaanxi). Meaning "splendid" or "flower mountain," Huashan has an elevation of 1,997 meters or 6,551 feet.

4 The Eastern Marchmount of Taishan (Mount Tai; Tai'an, Shandong). Meaning "great," "eminent," or "tranquil mountain," Taishan has an elevation of 1,545 meters or 5,068 feet.

5 The Central Marchmount of Songshan (Mount Song, Zhenfeng, Henan). Meaning "lofty mountain," Songshan has an elevation of 1,494 meters or 4,901 feet.

Recalling our earlier discussion of Chinese correlative cosmology, these mountains correspond to the Five Phases and the associated five cardinal directions: Wood/east; Fire/south; Earth/center; Metal/west; and Water/north. In the Daoist imagination, they often have other associations, including the Five Thearchs, Five Planets, Five Numinous Treasure Talismans, five yin-organs, and so forth. In the contemporary Daoist landscape, Mount Hua has the largest Daoist population. It is characterized by a vast network of cave-hermitages and is significant as the source-location for the Huashan lineage of Complete Perfection Daoism, associated with Chen Tuan and Hao Taigu. Hengshan[2], associated Wei Huacun (251–334; a.k.a. Nanyue furen), is also noteworthy for the recent establishment of a Kundao college to provide seminary training for Daoist nuns.

Unlike the Five Marchmounts system, the second major geographical schema is uniquely Daoist. This is the Daoist notion of *dongtian*, meaning "grotto-heaven" or "cavern-haven." *Dong* specifically denotes caves or caverns, and here we should pause to recognize the importance of caves in the Daoist imagination. Many Daoist hermits lived in such mountain environs, both temporarily and permanently. Some of the best examples of actual Daoist cave-hermitages may be found on Mount Hua. "Grotto-heavens" are a Daoist technical designation. It appears that the earliest *dongtian* system consisted of 36 places (Verellen 1995: 275), which would parallel the early medieval Daoist cosmological and theological system of 36 heavens. However, in its most mature and influential expression, the system is a Tang dynasty development and includes 10 major grottos and 36 minor grottos. This early standardization may be found in the work of Sima Chengzhen (647–735), the twelfth Highest Clarity Patriarch, and of Du Guangting (850–933), the important Tang scholastic and liturgist (Verellen 1995: 275). Developing the cosmogonic account from Chapter 3 of the second century BCE *Book of the Huainan Masters*, Du Guangting writes a description of the cavern-heavens.

The cosmogonic formation of the grotto-heavens

When the heavens and earth divided, and the clear separated from the turbid, they produced the great rivers by melting and the lofty mountains by congealing. Above they arrayed the stellar mansions; below they stored the grotto-heavens. With their affairs administered by great sages and superior Perfected, they contain numinous palaces and divine residences, jade halls and gold terraces. Consisting of coalesced qi, these are soaring structures of accumulated clouds. (*Dongtian fudi yuedu mingshan ji*, DZ 599, preface)

From a Daoist perspective, the grotto-heavens are secret worlds hidden within famous mountains and beautiful places. They are basically terrestrial paradises where one gains greater access to sacred and divine transmissions. They are portals into the numinous presence of the Dao. The 10 major grotto-heavens with their associated mountains are as follows:

1 Xiaoyao qingxu. Located on Mount Wangwu (Jiyuan, Henan)

2 Dayou kongming. Located on Mount Weiyu (Huangyan, Zhejiang)

3 Taixuan zongzhen. Located on Mount Xicheng (Ankang, Shaanxi)

4 Sanyuan jizhen. Located on Mount Xixuan (Huashan; Huayin, Shaanxi)

5 Baoxian jiushi. Located on Mount Qingcheng (Guanxian, Sichuan)

6 Shangqing yuping. Located on Mount Chicheng (Tiantai, Zhejiang)

7 Zhuming huizhen. Located on Mount Luofu (Boluo, Guangdong)

8 Jintan huayang. Located on Mount Gouqu (Jurong, Jiangsu)

9 Youshen youxu. Located on Mount Linwu (Lake Taihu, Jiangsu)

10 Chengde yinxuan. Located on Mount Guacang (Xianju, Zhejiang)

(*Tiandi gongfu tu*, DZ 1032, 27; *Dongtian fudi yuedu mingshan ji*, DZ 599, 3b–4b)

In addition to the cosmological, mythical, and mystical dimensions, the wide-ranging geographical distribution of these sacred sites provides a glimpse into the degree to which Tang dynasty Daoism was a diverse and integrated religious tradition with national distribution and vast temple networks.

The 10 major grotto-heavens are complemented by the 36 minor grotto-heavens and the 72 auspicious sites (*fudi*), with the latter being the last of the three major Daoist geographical schema. Like the grotto-heavens, the auspicious sites, also translated as "blessed lands" or "divine realms," are a system for identifying important energetic and religious sites. Taken together, the three standardized geographical schema of the Five Marchmounts, grotto-heavens, and auspicious lands reveals an esoteric, hidden, and mystical landscape within the visible one. Together they form an interconnected, subterranean network of subtle spatial channels circulating the numinous presence of the Dao, which recalls the ways in which rivers (terrestrial waterways) and meridians (corporeal waterways) overlap in Daoism. The Daoist geo-theological schema reveals the interpenetration of the "spiritual" and the "physical" in a Daoist view: landscapes are manifestations of the Dao and contain portals into the divine. The terrestrial (yin) thus is an entryway into the celestial (yang), and the celestial permeates the terrestrial. Here we may recall the Daoist panenhenic and panentheistic theological views discussed earlier.

Dwelling

Daoists have lived in a various types of abodes and related architectural structures. These include caves, houses, monasteries, temples, and so forth. Such Daoist dwelling-places usually relate to specific Daoist lifeways and types of community, including ascetic, eremitic, householder, monastic, and so forth. In terms of religiously and historically significant places, the designation of major Daoist sacred sites follows a discernable pattern. This involves the identification of the place, its transformation into a "sacred site," and the eventual formation of a residential community and perhaps the construction of a more permanent temple or monastery. If the temple was important enough, such as in the case of Louguan, there were frequent restoration projects as well as accumulated honors, with imperial recognition and redesignation being the most prestigious. For example, the mountain in Sichuan named Heming shan (Crane Cry Mountain) became associated with a revelation from Laojun to Zhang Daoling. At this point the mountain became a Celestial Masters sacred site, and eventually a site sacred to Daoism as a whole. A Daoist temple was eventually built there, and in contemporary China it is inhabited by and under the control of the Complete Perfection monastic order.

The earliest markers of Daoist sacred sites, however, were not temples and monasteries, but rather platforms or open-air altars (*tan*; *daotan*). They usually consisted of several layers of tamped earth or bricks, one slightly narrower than the next, which allowed devotees and petitioners to ascend higher toward the sky and the gods. In the case of Daoism, such altars usually consisted of three levels, symbolizing cosmological forces and representing control of a vast and important mythological heritage (Hahn 2000: 685). While it is unclear when distinctively "sacred sites" with corresponding buildings first emerged in Daoism, the *Book of Master Zhuang* does mention particular hermitages and mountain abodes. As Daoism moved from diffuse and loosely affiliated religious communities of master-disciple lineages to an organized religious tradition during the Later Han dynasty, Daoists began to establish shrines and temples. Within the context of the early Celestial Masters movement, it appears that the community tended to shrines and maintained communal hostels associated with the 24 parishes (*zhi*). When the Celestial Master and libationers conducted purification rites and offered petitions, it appears that they did so in open-air, temporary altars, in a way that parallels much of contemporary Orthodox Unity ritual.

As we move into the Period of Disunion, there is a clear process of distribution and institutionalization, which included the establishment and occupation of temples. It was also during this period that Buddhism began to take a deeper root in the larger Chinese society, with increasing numbers of Han converts and the gradual emergence of Sinified forms of Buddhism. During this process of cultural interaction and cross-pollination, Daoists began to adopt a monastic model from Buddhism. During the late fifth and early sixth century, Daoists established the first Daoist monastery in the Zhongnan mountains. This was the above-mentioned Louguan monastery.

By the Tang dynasty, there was a national network of Daoist temples and monasteries, and a Daoist community consisting of hermits, ordained married priests, celibate monastics, and laity. This network remained relatively intact from the Tang dynasty into the late imperial period, and it continues to exist in our own time. Most of these temples were either on mountains or in close proximity to imperial capitals. The latter fact reveals a close connection between Daoism and the court, including high levels of prestige and patronage.

There are, in turn, a variety of technical terms used to designate Daoist sacred sites. Some of the most important technical designations are as follows: *an*, *ci*, *dong*, *gong*, *guan*[1], *guan*[2], *miao*, *tai*, and *yuan*. Of these, *guan*[2] and *gong* are the most common. With the exception of *ci*, *miao*, and *yuan*, which may also be used for Buddhist sites, each of the terms, as religious designations, indicates a Daoist place. *An* (lit., "hut") refers to hermitages. It is also occasionally used to designate small temples, as in the case of Erxian an (Temple of the Two Immortals), the earlier name of Qingyang gong (Azure Ram Palace). *An* parallels other Daoist technical terms and their associated practices of seclusion and solitary praxis. For example, early medieval Daoist communities used "pure chambers" (*jingshi*; *jingshe*), also translated as "chambers of quiescence"; late medieval Daoists engaged in retreats in "meditation enclosures" (*huandu*; lit., "enclosed and sealed off"), which were eventually integrated into temple architecture. *Ci* ("shrine") and *miao* ("temple") are more generic names for temples, usually with one primary altar and key deity and with a small number of residents. As we saw above, *dong* (lit., "cave) refers to mountain caverns, but more commonly appears as the technical designation of *dongtian* ("grotto-heavens"). *Dong* is occasionally used to denote a hermitage. *Gong* (lit., "palace") is an imperial designation, usually bestowed by the emperor himself. Technically a term for a royal residence, it indicates a higher level of recognition and status. *Gong* may be temples or monasteries, and they usually have a larger footprint, more altars, and larger community. Technically speaking, after the end of the Qing dynasty and thus the dynastic system (1911), there can be no new *gong. Guan*[1] (lit., "hostel" or "hall") is an early Daoist name for a community center; it was widely used before the emergence of Daoist monasticism. In that context, it was used for Daoist mountain communities, such as early medieval Mount Mao, that were not celibate and did not function according to standardized rules (Hahn 2000: 687). The term was eventually replaced by *guan*[2] (lit., "watchtower" or "observatory"). Originally designating an astronomical observatory, and also referring to a specific type of Daoist meditation, *guan*[2] are Daoist monasteries, also referred to as "abbeys", "belvederes", or "cloisters" in order to distinguish them from their Buddhist counterparts referred to as *si* ("temple"). Daoist *guan*[2] tend to be large-scale sites inhabited by monastics, as in the case of Baiyun guan (White Cloud Monastery) in Beijing. Daoist temples and monasteries usually consist of *dian* ("altars") and *tang* ("halls") dedicated to specific deities. Finally, *tai* (lit., "terrace" or "tower") and *yuan* (lit., "courtyard") may designate Daoist temples, although they refer to specific architectural features as well (Steinhardt 2000: 58–9). Thus, in the case of Louguan tai, the name indicates both the monastery's architecture ("tower") and a place to observe the constellations ("observatory").

With these details in mind, we may now consider a few important and representative contemporary sites. All of the key Daoist sacred sites and pilgrimage destinations are located in mainland China. This is also true of major Daoist temples, although there are some in Hong Kong, Taiwan, and the larger Chinese cultural sphere. As discussed briefly in the next chapter, the mainland Chinese sites are usually under the jurisdiction of the Bureau of Tourism, Bureau of Religious Affairs, and of national, regional, and local Daoist associations. Although contemporary Daoism in mainland China technically consists of Orthodox Unity priests, Complete Perfection monastics, and their communities, most of the major sacred sites and temples are overseen by the Complete Perfection monastic order, especially by administrative monastics (monks and nuns) associated with its Dragon Gate lineage. The number and geographical distribution of these Daoist places are nearly limitless (most recently estimated at more than 1,500). Some of the most important and prominent contemporary mainland Chinese Daoist temples with active communities are as follows:

- Baxian gong (Eight Immortals Palace; Xi'an, Shaanxi), named after the famous Eight Immortals, who became central objects of popular devotion from the Yuan dynasty forward, and associated with Wang Zhe's mystical experiences.

- Baiyun guan (White Cloud Monastery; Beijing), the headquarters of Complete Perfection and its Dragon Gate lineage as well as of the Chinese Daoist Association.

- Heming shan (Crane Cry Mountain; Dayi, Sichuan), associated with the original Celestial Masters revelation, but today inhabited by a Complete Perfection monastic community.

- Louguan tai (Lookout Tower Monastery; Zhouzhi, Shaanxi), associated with the supposed transmission of the *Scripture on the Dao and Inner Power* from Laozi to Yin Xi.

- Jianfu gong (Palace for Establishing Happiness; base), Tianshi dong (Celestial Master Grotto; mid-level), and Shangqing gong (Palace of Highest Clarity; summit) at Qingcheng shan (Azure Wall Mountain; Guanxian, Sichuan), associated with the early Celestial Masters community and the fifth major grotto-heaven.

- Qingyang gong (Azure Ram Palace; mistranslated as Black Sheep Temple), associated with a vision of Yin Xi wherein he saw the divinized Laozi as a boy leading a green ram.

- Taiqing gong (Place of Great Clarity) and Shangqing gong (Palace of Highest Clarity) at Laoshan (Mount Lao; near Qingdao, Shandong).

- Tianshi fu (Celestial Masters Mansion) at Longhu shan (Dragon-Tiger Mountain; near Yingtan, Jiangxi), the headquarters of the Celestial Master from at least the Tang dynasty into the early modern period.

- Wanfu gong (Palace of Myriad Blessings) at Maoshan (Mount Mao; Jurong, Jiangsu), associated with early Highest Clarity and with the three Mao brothers and Tao Hongjing in particular.

- Yuquan yuan (Temple of the Jade Spring) at Huashan (Mount Hua; near Huayin, Shaanxi), associated with the Huashan lineage of Complete Perfection and with the immortal Chen Tuan, famous practitioner of Daoyin and sleep exercises, and Hao Taigu in particular.

- Zixiao gong (Palace of the Purple Empyrean) at Wudang shan (Mount Wudang; near Shiyan, Hubei), associated with the god Zhenwu (Perfect Warrior; a.k.a. Xuanwu [Mysterious Warrior]), Zhang Sanfeng (fourteenth c.?), and the mythical origin of Chinese internal martial arts such as Taiji quan (T'ai-chi ch'üan; Great Ultimate Boxing).

While most of these places are located in rural and mountain locales, Eight Immortals Palace, White Cloud Monastery, and Azure Ram Palace are urban sites. As mentioned, most of the sites are inhabited by Complete Perfection monastics, but Dragon-Tiger Mountain and Mount Mao are specifically Orthodox Unity communities. At present, most of their dates of establishment and historical development are currently unknown.

Spatiality

Spatiality refers to the Daoist engagement with and organization of space, especially with respect to dwelling-places. It also relates to Daoist aesthetics and spatial awareness. In terms of uniquely Daoist places, spatiality specifically pertains to temple architecture and layout. Daoist temple architecture is largely based on the traditional Chinese architecture. The earliest temple-like structures appear to have been built by the early Celestial Masters community, and the first Daoist monastery, Louguan (Lookout Tower Monastery; Zhouzhi, Shaanxi), appeared in the fifth century. The earliest extant Daoist buildings date from the Song and Yuan dynasties, specifically from the twelfth and thirteenth centuries. One of the most important examples is Yongle gong (Palace of Eternal Joy; Ruicheng, Shanxi), which includes major temple murals related to early Complete Perfection Daoism (Katz 1999).

Daoist temple architecture has utilized and continues to utilize the primary materials, construction methods, and styles of traditional Chinese architecture (Qiao 2001; Steinhardt 2000). Most surviving Daoist temples utilize brick and timber construction. They include large wood columns and sloping tile roofs with over-arching eaves. They also have various stone elements, including stone steps, railings, and arches.

Following traditional Chinese architecture, one of the most interesting architectural features of Daoist temples is the door-sill (*menkan*; *hukun*). Usually part of the larger doorframe, door-sills are located at the entrance of temples and altars and measure about one foot to two feet in height. They have practical, mythological, and spiritual dimensions. On the most basic level, they prevent rain and mud from entering. In terms of mythology, I have heard a variety of explanations. One of the most interesting is that there are short, one-legged demons whose only form of mobility is hopping; the door-sill is too high for them to jump over. On a deeper spiritual level, door-sills demarcate sacred space; they are physical and spiritual boundaries. For residents and pilgrims, to cross this threshold is to enter a Daoist sacred place. This involves stepping over the raised, wooden ledge with the left foot first. It involves awareness and attentiveness. One can enter the sacred space consciously or not. Like Daoist bowing, stepping over door-sills can be a Daoist contemplative practice, and that experience may influence one's daily life more generally. In application, one remains attentive to boundaries, crossing thresholds, and abiding in sacred space. One also becomes more sensitive to the qualities and functions of space.

The layout of Daoist temples varies depending on size and location. Specifically, the uniformity and conformity to the standard layout is greater for lowland and urban temples, and less for mountain sites. Moreover, there is often a deeper mythological and soteriological dimension of the layout. Again paralleling traditional Chinese architecture, and specifically imperial temples, the standard Daoist temple layout is along a north-south axis (Figure 8.2). Ideally speaking, this is actually and symbolically the case, that is, it is sited facing south. However, from a Fengshui perspective, the temple is always discussed along these lines, with the entrance being "ritual south." Facing south, the back of the temple is north (Mysterious Warrior/snake-turtle), the front is south (vermilion bird), the right is west (white tiger), and the

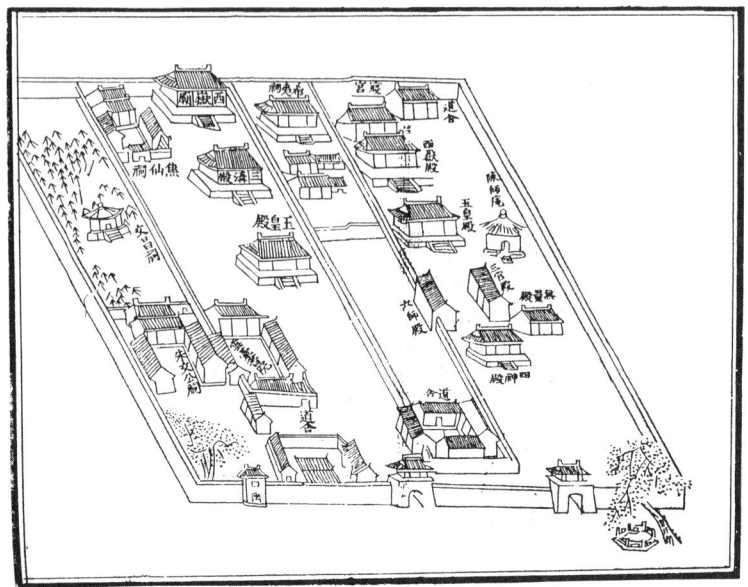

FIGURE 8.2 *Traditional Daoist Temple Architecture and Layout.*
Source: *Huayin xianzhi.*

left is east (azure dragon). Here we should note that, although utilized in Daoist architecture and by some Daoists, Fengshui (lit., "wind and water"), also known as Chinese geomancy, is not Daoist; like some other elements of the Daoist tradition, such as correlative cosmology (yin-yang/Five Phases), calendrics, and the incorporation of popular gods into the Daoist pantheon and altars, it is best understood as part of "traditional Chinese culture."

In terms of Daoist architectural layout, a paradigmatic example is White Cloud Monastery in Beijing (Komjathy 2013a; Qiao 2001; Yoshioka 1979). This sacred site consists of the main altars along the central, vertical axis as well as side altars along horizontal axes. If one were moving through the actual temple, one would notice open courtyards, sheltering trees, places to sit, as well as other architectural features and dimensions of Daoist material culture. One would note the spaciousness and peacefulness characteristic of traditional Daoist temples and spaces. Returning to the layout, the altars are usually arranged hierarchically. Moving along the north-south axis, with north in back and representing Mystery, the front altars contain "lower" deities, while the back altars contain "higher" deities, those that are more primordial and closer to the Dao as Source. The deepest altar, or the most elevated altar in the case of Daoist mountain temples, is the highest in terms of the pantheon. In contemporary Daoist temples, the central altar is usually dedicated to the Sanqing (Three Purities), the earliest, primordial emanations of the Dao. Thus Daoist temples are often structural expressions of Daoist theology, and Daoist theology becomes expressed in the materiality of Daoist temples. These dimensions of Daoist architecture and temple layout also bring our attention to altars, whether personal or communal, as one of the key centers of the Daoist universe. These are the sites where incense is offered, petitions are made, and relationships are maintained. They are simultaneously body, temple, and landscape.

All of the examples so far derive from traditional Daoist temples and sacred sites. However, as I have suggested in sections of the present book, and as discussed more fully in the next chapter, Daoism is now a global religious tradition. Like modern "Daoist art" and Daoism more generally, there is the possibility and perhaps necessity of cultural adaptation. With respect to Daoist architecture and uses of space, one can identify particular principles and characteristics. Daoist temples frequently contain large open spaces, covered walkways, various partitions and corridors, as well as many natural features such as trees and stones. There is a guiding aesthetics, energetic attentiveness, and refined spatiality that could be applied to other forms of architecture. Although yet to appear, one can imagine new Daoist sacred sites and religious spaces, which combine traditional Chinese Daoist aesthetics with new architectural designs and more local materials. Here we should note that there are few, if any, actual Daoist temples and sacred sites outside of China and the Chinese cultural sphere. While there are some Daoist spaces, such as altars in commercial buildings, there are few actual Daoist places in the West. One is most likely to find self-identified Daoist organizations located in private homes, commercial spaces, or former Christian churches. This is largely a matter of the expense of purchasing land and undertaking new construction projects as well as the lack of support for tradition-based Daoist communities in the West. The main exception with which I am familiar is a Daoist temple utilizing traditional Chinese architecture near Toronto. Completed in 2007 and located in Orangeville, Ontario, this temple was constructed by the Taoist Tai Chi Society/Fung Loy Kok, which has some connection to the Yuen Yuen Institute (Yuanxuan xueyuan) of Hong Kong. As one might expect, this temple received major funding from overseas, immigrant, and ethnic Chinese members, and it is no coincidence that it has connections to Hong Kong Daoism.

These points notwithstanding, the Daoist view of the Dao-as-world, including as manifested in specific locations, and the Daoist sense of place inspire one to be attentive to habitation. Where one dwells influences one's life. One may also bring awareness to one's residence. Aesthetics and spatiality may be modified to be more beneficial and transformative. Moreover, just as place influences inhabitants, individuals and communities influence place. Place includes a complex and mutually influential relationship among individuals, communities, abodes, and sites. The Daoist energetic understanding of space recognizes the way in which each contributes to the other. This may inspire one to embrace a conservationist ethic and a commitment to stewardship. Deeper Daoist self-cultivation may enhance the Daoist presence and characteristic of a place, and that place in turn supports deeper practice and experience. In this respect, we may recall the Daoist view of mountain as simultaneously physical mountain, altar, and stillness. Each is a portal into the Dao.

Further reading

Hahn, Thomas. 2000, "Daoist Sacred Sites." In *Daoism Handbook*, ed. Livia Kohn, 683–708. Leiden: Brill.

Qiao Yun. 2001, *Taoist Buildings*. Trans. Zhou Wenzheng. New York: Springer-Verlag, Wien New York.

Verellen, Franciscus, 1995, "The Beyond Within: Grotto-Heavens. (*dongtian*) in Taoist Ritual and Cosmology." *Cahiers d'Extrême-Asie* 8: 265–90.

Yin Zhihua. 2005, *Chinese Tourism: Taoism*. Beijing: Foreign Languages Press.

CHAPTER NINE

Modernity

Daoism is now a global religious tradition characterized by cultural, ethnic, linguistic, and national diversity. Daoism is now a "world religion" with global distribution and international adherence. Although "global Daoism" remains rooted in "Chinese Daoism" as source-tradition, it is being transmitted within and adapted to new historical influences and cultural contexts. The center of global Daoism remains mainland China, followed closely by Hong Kong, Taiwan, and the larger Chinese cultural sphere. At the same time, "non-Chinese" people are becoming increasingly interested in Daoism, with some even going so far as to convert or to seek out training and ordination. Our engagement with global Daoism thus recalls our earlier consideration of adherence, affiliation, and identity. It also brings the issue of conversion into high relief. Strictly speaking, Daoists are adherents of Daoism, and the designation of "Daoist" indicates connection to the religious tradition. We may, in turn, make a distinction between Daoist adherents and Daoist sympathizers, with the latter referring to individuals who find some aspect of Daoism interesting. It is also important to consider the way in which someone or something relates to Daoism, not simply intellectually or rhetorically, but actually. This draws our attention to "family resemblances" and "recognizability," or the extent to which phenomena are actually Daoist. Here we are particularly concerned with individuals and communities on the "close relations" side of the spectrum, especially ordained and lineage-based Daoists.

The modern history of Daoism is a turbulent one. It is closely linked with the tumultuous events of early modern China, especially the end of dynastic rule, the emergence of a secular nationstate rooted in Western socio-political ideologies, and the Chinese Communist takeover in 1949. Daoism has entered the modern world not only in the form of physical presence and immigration, but also through intellectual engagement and popular appropriation. In this respect, the history of "Daoism" is as much an intellectual history as a social history. Daoism exists as both a lived and living religion as well as a series of intellectual constructs and popular fabrications. We may, in turn, map the modern history and globalization of Daoism along as spectrum: from transmission/traditionalism through adaptation/innovation to appropriation/fabrication. Here I will primarily concentrate on the first, while briefly touching on the second and third. The modern history of Daoism may, in turn, be approached through the framework of diminishment, revitalization, and globalization.

Diminishment

Diminishment refers to the devaluation, damage, and impoverishment inflicted on the Daoist tradition during the early modern period. Here it is important to remember that "Daoism" is a placeholder for Daoist adherents, communities, and their religious expressions. People and place-specific communities are involved. Although many would assign the primary responsibility for the diminishment of Daoism to the Chinese Communists, the process actually began in the late nineteenth and early twentieth century. To fully understand this occurrence, one must acknowledge the influence and legacy of indigenous Confucian prejudices, European and Japanese colonialism, Protestant Christian missionization, and Orientalism. For example, following the Opium Wars (1839–42;

1856–60), so named because of European attempts to trade Chinese addiction to opium for material wealth, there were Germans in Shandong, French and British in Shanghai, British in Guangdong and Hong Kong, Portuguese in Macao, and a number of other smaller protectorates along the coast. It is no coincidence that the origins of modern Daoist Studies began in two of the principal imperialistic countries, namely, France and Japan. Along similar lines, this period also saw the increasing influence of Orientalism, or the Western engagement with the "Orient." For present purposes, Orientalism specifically refers to the privileging of Western constructions and representations of Daoism over Chinese Daoist ones. In terms of the early modern decline of Daoism, it is no coincidence that much of traditional Daoist material culture has been "preserved" in personal and museum collections in Europe, Japan, and the United States. Thus a diverse group of protagonists, both Chinese and "non-Chinese," is implicated in the modern diminishment of Daoism.

As previously mentioned, in the present book, early modern Daoism refers to developments from 1912 to 1978, while late modern Daoism corresponds to the years of 1978 to the present. For simplicity's sake, the former period primarily corresponds to diminishment, while the latter period relates to revitalization. 1912 was the year when the Republic of China (ROC), the first modern, secular Chinese nationstate, was established. The ROC modernization of China involved strong anti-traditionalism and Chinese nationalism paradoxically mixed with Western political ideologies, value-systems, and social structures. The early Republican engagement with the past is clearly expressed in the May Fourth Movement (1919), which identified traditional Chinese culture, Confucianism in particular, as primarily responsible for the loss of Chinese power and supremacy. This movement was partially in response to the Treaty of Versailles (1919), which ceded Shandong province from the Germans to the Japanese, and indirectly prepared the way for the Japanese "rape of Nanjing" (1937). The Republicans replaced the pre-modern and traditional Chinese "logic of precedence" with the Western "logic of subsequence." The fight for a modern China eventually resulted in a civil war between the Republicans and the Communists (1927–50). This led to the establishment of the People's Republic of China (1949), the current Chinese Communist nationstate, and the flight of the Guomindang (Kuo-min-tang; KMT) and establishment of the Republic of China in Taiwan. The early modern period culminated in the so-called Cultural Revolution (1966–76), which involved systematic destruction of traditional Chinese culture, anti-intellectualism, and "reeducation programs."

As Daoism is first and foremost an indigenous Chinese religion, these details are important for understanding the turbulent modern history of the tradition. The end of the Qing dynasty and establishment of the Republic of China corresponded to the end of the Chinese dynastic system. For Daoism, this involved a loss of imperial patronage, cultural capital, and actual social power. The modern history of Daoism is one of upheaval, disruption, and almost complete devastation. It is largely a history of loss: the loss of community, cultural capital, patronage, place, tradition, and actual material culture. Prior to the 1980s, the modern history of Daoism was primarily one of geographical contraction, cultural diminishment, and spiritual dissolution. In the early Communist period, monastic life was attacked as a form of escape from a country in need of workers and soldiers, while religious worldviews and lifeways were condemned as superstitious and wasteful. Such critiques were partially rooted in Marxist and Stalinist political ideologies, including the famous view that "religion is the opiate of the masses." Although the Marxist leadership of the PRC did not believe in the validity of religion (atheism is required for CCP membership), they did include "freedom of religious belief" in their new constitution. However, "religion" (*zongjiao*) was very different from "feudal superstition" (*mixin*). Daoism often fell into the latter, especially as it had no diplomatic significance. Traditional myths and stories were rejected, gods denounced, and organizations disbanded. Simultaneously, smaller-scale and more regional forms of "religious" practice were more difficult to control; spirit-writing cults as well as longevity and martial arts societies flourished. The latter was also employed as a form of nationalistic up-building: the atrophied bodies of older Chinese imperial courts, perhaps most clearly represented by eunuch culture and the practice of foot-binding, would become replaced by a nation of soldiers with high-level martial arts prowess. Such changes manifested in two important ways for the Daoist tradition. First, Daoism was effectively banned in mainland China as feudal superstition, with its monks sent out to work, marry, or be "reeducated;" its monasteries destroyed, closed, or used for military installations; and its priests forbidden to conduct rituals. Second, such persecution and suppression initiated an exodus from the "Central Kingdom" (Zhongguo). More and more Daoists fled to other East Asian countries such as Hong Kong (then an independent British territory; 1841–1997), Korea, Malaysia, Singapore, Taiwan, and Thailand. Simultaneously, Chinese Daoists began a slow immigration to European and North American countries. That is, the Chinese Communist revolution had the unintended consequence of disseminating Chinese religious culture throughout the world and helping to make Daoism a "world religion."

Although the establishment of the People's Republic of China was nearly catastrophic for mainland Chinese Daoism, other developments problematize an overly simplistic narrative based on "diminishment." In the early years of the Republic, Daoists attempted to establish Daoist organizations (see, Goossaert 2007; Wang 2006). In 1912, a Central Association of Daoism was founded, but it was principally a local (Beijing) and sectarian (Dragon Gate) organization. During the same year, Orthodox Unity Daoists created their own General Daoist Assembly of the Republic of China. Then, in 1932, another group came to the fore: the Chinese Daoist Association (Zhongguo daojiao xiehui). After World War II, Daoists in Shanghai planned the revival of Daoism. In 1947, they set up the Shanghai Municipal Daoist Association, with Zhang Enpu (1904–69), the 63rd Celestial Master, and Chen Yingning (1880–1969), a lay Daoist, as leaders. After the establishment of the PRC, Zhang Enpu fled to Taiwan and established Taiwan as the *de facto* headquarters of the Orthodox Unity tradition, although Dragon-Tiger Mountain would later return to prominence. It was also during the early years of the PRC (1957) that the national Daoist Association was founded. In 1961, they defined their objectives as follows: to study the history of Daoism, publish journals, and set up training programs for young candidates. However, the so-called Cultural Revolution (1966–76), also referred to as the "Ten Years of Chaos," with its socially engineered and fanatical youth brigade known as the Red Guards, stopped all efforts. All religious organizations suffered immensely, with monasteries and temples destroyed or closed and Daoist monks and priests forced into dominant ideological patterns. This resulted in a "lost generation" of mainland Chinese Daoists (ages 50–80) and a massive disruption in the continuity of the tradition. The degree of destruction is still evident in contemporary temples. Only since 1978 has there been a comeback. These details reveal that there has always been Daoist struggle within a context of apparent diminishment. As one modern Complete Perfection Daoist monastic recently reflected on modern challenges to the tradition: "Daoism may die, but the Dao will not."

Another, and perhaps more insidious factor in the diminishment of Daoism involves Western intellectualism and spiritual colonialism. The former most often involves the construction of Daoism as "philosophy" (read: disembodied ideas) and "thought." The latter often involves the appropriation of aspects of Daoism as "resources" for some "personal spirituality." Both modern patterns of engagement undermine Daoism as a lived and living religious tradition. They are rooted in colonialist, missionary, and Orientalist legacies. Just as the modern construction of Confucianism is largely a seventeenth and eighteenth century Catholic missionary representation, the modern construction of Daoism is largely a nineteenth century Protestant one. Daoism is the only major religious tradition not represented by formal members of the tradition. The dominant construction of Daoism makes a distinction between so-called "philosophical Daoism," defined as "pure," "true," and "original Daoism," and so-called "religious Daoism," a supposedly degenerate "institutional" adjunct to the former that has lost the "original teachings." Moreover, according to this modern fiction, true Daoists follow Laozi (Jesus) and study the *Daode jing* (Bible/Gospels). They work to have a personal relationship with the Dao (God/Jesus). In addition, "original Daoism" (Jesus' teachings) has been lost by the "Daoist religion" (Catholicism). Thus, real Daoists (Protestants) reject clergy, church, and ritual (Catholicism). Just as much of traditional Daoist material culture is contained in personal and museum collections, so too "Daoism" primarily exists in the minds of Orientalist connoisseurs. It is primarily fabrication, fiction, and fantasy. Here we might understand Daoism as a living and lived religion, as old growth forest, sacred site, and intact culture. In contrast, the Daoism of the popular imagination may be compared to a strip-mine, taxidermy trophy, and tourist souvenir.

At the far end of appropriation and fabrication is a new religious movement (NRM) that may be labeled "Popular Western Taoism" (PWT), with Taoism pronounced with a hard "t" sound. As discussed below, PWT and its cognates should be distinguished from actual global Daoism, which is characterized by a connection to Chinese Daoism as source-tradition and by cultural, ethnic, linguistic, and national diversity. We must avoid two types of Orientialism: one that unquestioningly accepts Western representations, and the other that only views Chinese Daoism as "true Daoism." In any case, PWT and its expression in so-called Tao Groups and so-called Tao-ists have exerted a ubiquitous influence on popular Western culture. As the bumper-sticker has it: "That was Zen; this is Tao." While the earlier Orientalist gaze was directed at Zen, it has now shifted toward Daoism, or more specifically toward appropriated fragments of the tradition. However, unlike the Western engagement with Zen Buddhism, which has become informed by actual practicing Zen Buddhists, the "Daoism" of the popular Western imagination remains immune to the voices of actual Daoists and scholars of Daoism. The influence of dominant Western constructions has occurred through various popular publications, "virtual communities," and its all-pervasive presence on the internet. That is, on some level, PWT has become institutionalized, with a cognitive and virtual infrastructure, as the primary form of "Daoism" in the West. Following the above-mentioned defining characteristics of the Protestant Christian missionary construction of Daoism, PWT adherents also view the Dao (Tao) as a trans-cultural and trans-religious concept. In such contexts, the Dao, a Chinese character and Daoist cosmological and theological category, becomes appropriated as a universal designation for the sacred. Here one may note that Mystery, One, or Reality might be more appropriate. PWT adherents also deny most of the defining characteristics of Daoism. They are most likely to claim that Daoism is about "going with the flow" (read: following one's own desires and egoistic motivations), including practicing so-called "Taoist sexual yoga." Such accounts of "Daoism" are characterized by ahistorical, acultural, and anti-religious views. Here the *Scripture on the Dao and Inner Power* is read, most often in inaccurate popular translations, as the "Daoist Bible," as source of "universal wisdom," and as a guidebook for alternative spirituality. When people read such "translations," they are not reading a Daoist scripture (sacred text written in classical Chinese), but rather a contemporary American cultural production.

To analyze PWT along the Daoist concern for lineage, we may say that its intellectual genealogy largely derives from "non-Daoist sources." While its roots extend back to the first moments of the "Western encounter with the Orient," including received legacies of colonialism, missionization, and Orientalism, PWT as an emerging form of alternative hybrid spirituality first emerged in the mid to late 1970s. Major early players in the formation of Popular Western Taoism included James Legge (1815–1987), John Blofeld (1913–87), Alan Watts (1915–73), Gia-fu Feng (1919–85; Stillpoint Foundation), Al Chung-liang Huang (b. ca. 1930; Living Tao Foundation), Stephen Chang (b. ca. 1940; Foundation of Tao), Bruce Lee (1940–73), and Kwai Chang Caine (David Carradine; 1972–75). While PWT appropriates certain elements from Daoism (e.g. the Dao [Way] and *Daode jing*), its primary informing worldview derives from modern cultural influences. In the case of the United States, these include Protestant Christianity, American Transcendentalism, 1960s counter-culture, the human potential movement, New Age spirituality, Perennial Philosophy, alternative healthcare, health and fitness movements, self-help and popular psychology, and so forth. Contemporary PWT adherents are most likely to conflate Daoism with other Chinese cultural traditions, including Chinese correlative cosmology (yin-yang, Five Phases), Traditional Chinese Medicine (TCM), Fengshui, Chinese martial arts (e.g. Taiji quan), and Qigong, which have only tenuous connections with the Daoist tradition. Almost everything found on the internet is one form or another of PWT. It, along its representatives' ubiquitous influence on the popular understanding of "Daoism", has now become institutionalized in such groups, physically existing and virtual, as the Reform Taoist Congregation, Tao Bums, Wandering Daoists, and various other "Tao Groups." The PWT construction of "Daoism" is found in the whole gamut of "new age capitalism" and "alternative spirituality," from Fengshui consultations and *Yijing* divination to "Yin Yoga," "Taoist sexual yoga," and the "Tao of" genre of literature. There are also various popular appropriations of the *Daode jing* (Tao-te-ching) by such individuals as Wayne Dyer, Benjamin Hoff, Ursula LeGuin, and Stephen Mitchell, none of whom knows Chinese. In such cultural productions, the "*Daode jing*" is no longer Daoist; it has become part of Perennial Philosophy, hybrid spirituality, and "wisdom literature." It is part of a different "tradition." It is a *simulacra* (Jean Baudrillard), a copy without an original. We may contrast such cultural productions with actual translations and draw insights upon translation as a helpful metaphor. Just as translation attempts to carry-over meaning from a source language to a target language, Daoist transmission involves a connection with Chinese Daoism as source-tradition. Here we may recall the Daoist practice of "returning to the Source" (*guigen*). Of course, while perhaps disturbing or uncomfortable for some, these points are not meant to deny the search for personal meaning, purpose, and affinity ("spirituality"), but anyone who has reflected on the modern construction of "Daoism," and its deviation from Daoism as such, must admit that invincible ignorance seems to be the norm. PWT is a contributing factor in Western perplexity concerning Daoism.

From my perspective, PWT and similar cultural phenomena relate, first and foremost, to diminishment. They involve the suppression of Daoists and Daoism by so-called "Tao-ists" and their supporters. Few self-identified Tao-ists (followers of Tao), to follow their own self-representations, have met, let alone studied with actual tradition-based Daoists. If they have, they are most likely to construct them as sage-monks who have transmitted secret wisdom or as corrupt representatives of a degenerate "institutional religion." There is a recurring loop of uninformed views and insular discourse. As I believe that there are ethical and political dimensions involved in the Western construction and appropriation of Daoism, including among those who choose to be "neutral" or "objective," here I apparently depart from academic conventions and take an ethico-political stance: anyone who claims to be Daoist while simultaneously denying the defining characteristics of Daoism and disempowering actual Daoists and Daoist communities has negated his or her claim of religious identity and affiliation. I choose not to provide tacit legitimation by accepting self-promoting identity narratives. Developing this social critique further, if one were more daring and willing to take Daoist views seriously, one might recognize that something important is actually at stake, and such a recognition may require that one take a stand. It is not mere "fundamentalism," "factionalism," "sectarianism," and "exclusivism." From a Daoist perspective, Daoism itself is the path to the Dao. This includes a radically different understanding of being, embodiment, materiality, sacrality, and so forth. For Daoists, Daoism has a specific soteriology and theology. This includes distinctive aesthetics, forms of community, places, practices, types of experience, and so forth. Here we must recognize that Daoist practice is not reducible to techniques. There is a complex interplay among views, practice, and experience. It is possible to practice a "Daoist method" in a "non-Daoist way;" this point recalls informing Daoist views and fundamental Daoist principles. In addition, Daoists have distinctive commitments, concerns, values, and so forth. In terms of "family resemblances" and "recognizability," Daoist views of religious adherence, community, connection, embodiment, and identity transcend conventional academic and popular categories rooted in secular materialism and hyper-relativism. There is a numinous presence that pervades the being of realized Daoists.

Thus, advocating an informed understanding of the Daoist tradition, one that includes actual Daoist views, I choose to privilege the voices and perspectives of tradition-based Daoists, specifically ordained and lineage-based Daoists as well as their formal religious communities. Here "real Daoism" exists in specific lives, communities, and places, rather than in the "minds" and desires of digital identities and "virtual communities." This approach of course is challenged by a certain degree of corruption in modern Daoism, including the absence of personal integrity, sale of ordination certificates, lack of deep understanding, practice, and experience, and misuse of ordination and lineage as sources of legitimation and marketing. This includes an increasing conflation of ordination with certification, partially under the influence of TCM schools and Qigong practitioners. That is, in the modern world, ordination and lineage, including the rhetoric of tradition and mastery, are as likely to inhibit as to assist the identification of authentic teachers and communities. From a critical perspective, many self-proclaimed "Daoist masters" lack deep practice, understanding, and experience, let alone "mastery." Many Daoists are themselves contributing to the diminishment of Daoism. This is another potential source of perplexity with respect to Daoism.

Nonetheless, there are dedicated Daoists and actual Daoist communities in the modern world. Although diminishment, including in the ongoing process of spiritual colonialism, is one part of the modern story of Daoism, the other includes revitalization and globalization.

Revitalization

Beyond the diminishment of Daoism, whether historical or cognitive, there is preservation, transmission, and revitalization. In terms of our historical periodization, revitalization basically corresponds to the late modern period, including contemporary developments. With respect to mainland Chinese Daoism, it specifically relates to the socio-economic reforms of Deng Xiaoping beginning in 1978. These developments opened the way for increased religious freedom and revitalization. However, unlike in the United States where there is legal separation of church and state, religious activity is monitored and managed by the state in the modern PRC. The Chinese Communist government recognizes five official religions, including Buddhism (*fojiao*), Catholicism (*tianzhu jiao*), Daoism (*daojiao*), Islam (*yiselan jiao*), and Protestant Christianity (*jidu jiao*). All of these occur within institutional structures that are overseen by the Bureau of Religious Affairs, and the corresponding religious association. In the case of historically and culturally significant sacred sites, the Bureau of Religious Affairs oversees the clergy and their activities, while the Bureau of Culture controls important artifacts and the Bureau of Tourism oversees tourist activity, including entrance fees. Thus, mainland Chinese Daoist sites are not primarily under the control of Daoists.

Nonetheless, mainland Chinese Daoists are contributing to the contemporary resurgence of Daoism, specifically by restoring Daoist temples, training novices and apprentices, preserving cultural materials, publishing articles and books, and so forth. Even with its turbulent modern history, mainland Chinese Daoism remains the center of modern Daoism, followed closely behind by Taiwanese and Hong Kong Daoism. That is, Daoism as such remains predominantly an indigenous Chinese religion practiced by people of Han ethnicity in China and the larger Chinese cultural sphere. It is largely a Chinese religion rooted in traditional Chinese culture. The latter includes Chinese aesthetics, cultural values, food, language, worldviews, and so forth.

Contemporary Daoism in mainland China is dominated by two primary movements: Orthodox Unity and Complete Perfection, especially the latter's Dragon Gate lineage. While this is undoubtedly the case, such statements should also be qualified.

Daoism has also been popularized through various Daoist and "non-Daoist" Yangsheng (Qigong) and internal alchemy practices, continuing the process of simplification, popularization, and laicization that began during the late imperial period. That is, there are non-clerical and non-institutional expressions of Daoism in contemporary China. This engagement with "Daoism" also appears as interest in so-called "Daoist philosophy" (*zhexue*) and "Daoist thought" (*sixiang*). A number of modern Chinese intellectuals, such as Hu Fuchen (Chinese Academy of Social Studies) and Liu Xiaogan (Chinese University of Hong Kong), have attempted to establish so-called "New Daojia" (*xin daojia*), in a manner perhaps paralleling "New Confucianism" in the twentieth century.

These points notwithstanding, Orthodox Unity and Complete Perfection remain the primary forms of Daoism in contemporary China, especially when one considers Daoism as a religious tradition, an intact culture, and an integrated soteriology. As we have seen in previous chapters, Orthodox Unity is an alternate name for the Celestial Masters movement. The former name refers to the revelation and covenant, while the latter name refers to the highest clerical position, the Celestial Master. In the modern world, the Celestial Master is less important, but we should at least know something about the complex modern history of the position. The most recent Celestial Masters are as follows: Zhang Yuanxu (1862–1924; 62nd), Zhang Enpu (1904–69; 63rd), Zhang Yuanxian (1930–2008; 64th) (Kleeman 2008), and possibly Zhang Jiyu (b. 1962; 65th). The eldest son of the 62nd Celestial Master, Zhang Enpu fled to Taiwan with the Nationalists, where he established Taipei, Taiwan as the *de facto* headquarters of Celestial Masters Daoism. Zhang Enpu was instrumental in establishing the Taiwan Daoist Association (Taiwan sheng daojiao hui) in 1950, later renamed the Daoist Association of the Republic of China (Zhonghua minguo daojiao hui), and in securing the reprinting of the Ming-dynasty Daoist Canon in 1962. Following Zhang Enpu's death, the position of the Celestial Master passed to his nephew, Zhang Yuanxian and then possibly to Zhang Jiyu following the former's death in 2008. The circumstances of the most recent transfer are unclear, but it is significant because the Celestial Master now appears to be in mainland China, rather than in Taiwan. Zhang Jiyu is currently one of the vice-presidents of the Chinese Daoist Association.

Perhaps more important than the Celestial Master himself are the various family lineages and local Orthodox Unity communities, which are especially prominent in southeastern China and Taiwan. These groups have received a relatively high degree of scholarly consideration, especially through ethnographic fieldwork, and have in turn exerted strong influence on Western academic accounts of Daoism. Particularly noteworthy are the Taiwanese priests Zhuang-Chen Dengyun (1911–76), who was studied by Michael Saso, and Chen Rongsheng (b. 1927), studied first by Kristofer Schipper, then by John Lagerwey and Poul Andersen, among others. In terms of the history of modern Daoism, we should also note that both Saso (b. 1930) and Schipper (b. 1934) were among the first known Westerners ordained as Daoist priests. They are both ordained members of Orthodox Unity, and they have also helped to establish a model of Daoist scholar-practitioners inside of Daoist Studies. In contemporary mainland China, the two principal sacred sites associated with Orthodox Unity are Dragon-Tiger Mountain (near Yingtan, Jiangxi) and Mount Mao (Jurong, Jiangsu). It also appears that the recent reinstitution of large-scale ordination ceremonies at Dragon-Tiger Mountain has included a number of Westerners. As discussed in previous chapters, Orthodox Unity priests are householders who follow traditional Chinese cultural practices such as alcohol consumption and meat-eating. They are supported by their associated community, usually through sponsorship of commissioned ritual services.

Although there are Orthodox Unity priests and communities throughout contemporary mainland China, most of the major temples and sacred sites are under the jurisdiction of Complete Perfection, and specifically its Dragon Gate lineage. At the same time, contemporary mainland Chinese Complete Perfection is deeply bound to the Bureau of Religious Affairs and the Chinese Daoist (Taoist) Association (CDA/CTA; Zhongguo daojiao xiehui). The CDA was established in 1957, with its headquarters at White Cloud Monastery in Beijing. The first assembly was attended by 91 representatives including Daoist scholars and priests from Daoist lineages, mountains, and temples located throughout China. 61 members were elected, and Yue Chongdai (1888–1958), the abbot of Taiqing gong (Palace of Great Clarity; Shenyang, Liaoning), was chosen as president (Wang 2006: 137–72). The activities of the CDA were suspended during the Cultural

Revolution, but recommenced in 1980. The CDA functions under the direction of the Bureau of Religious Affairs, which is the primary bureaucratic organization governing contemporary mainland Chinese Daoism. Its national presidents (*huizhang*) have included the following individuals: (1) Yue Chongdai (1888–1958), (2) Chen Yingning (1880–1969), (3 and 4) Li Yuhang (1916–2002), (5) Fu Yuantian (1925–97; Dragon Gate), (6) Min Zhiting (Yuxi [Jade Stream]; 1924–2004; Mount Hua), and (7) Ren Farong (Miaohua [Wondrous Transformation]; b. 1936; Dragon Gate). The CDA is based at White Cloud Monastery, which also serves as a major research center for Chinese Daoist Studies and as one of the principal training centers and ordination sites for Dragon Gate novices. In terms of training, the Chinese Daoist Seminary (Daojiao xueyuan) is there. As discussed in previous chapters, mainland Complete Perfection Daoists are monastics, although there are lay initiates. These Daoists technically adhere to three foundational commitments: celibacy (no sex), sobriety (no intoxicants), and vegetarianism (no meat). While Complete Perfection Daoists practice ritual, especially daily recitation of the Complete Perfection liturgy, their primary practice is solitary meditation, especially lineage-based internal alchemy.

The revitalization of Daoism has also been strengthened through Taiwanese and Hong Kong Daoists. Contemporary Taiwanese Daoism has received a relatively high degree of attention in modern Western scholarship. This was largely a response to contemporary Chinese history, with mainland China being relatively inaccessible prior to the 1980s. During the Cultural Revolution in mainland China, Taiwanese Daoists played a major role in preserving traditional Daoist culture, including material culture of historical significance such as Daoist liturgical art, manuscripts, and ritual traditions. Contemporary Taiwanese Daoism is dominated by the Orthodox Unity movement, with hereditary priests and Daoist families who perform rituals for local communities. Generally speaking, these are full-time ritual experts whose services are commissioned by members of the local community. Like Hong Kong Daoism, Taiwanese Daoism is highly syncretic, often combining elements from Confucianism, Buddhism, Chinese popular religion, and even Christianity. In addition, due to Taiwanese laws concerning legal status, many newer religious movements such as Yiguan dao (I-kuan tao; All-pervading Truth; Unity Sect), with only tenuous connections to Daoism, have been categorized as Daoist.

Outside of Hong Kong itself, contemporary Hong Kong Daoism is less well known than its Taiwanese counterpart. To date, it has only received one Western-language study (see, Tsui 1991). Much of Hong Kong Daoism is dominated by powerful and wealthy Daoist families. There are also a number of large and prominent temples, with Ching Chung Koon (Qingsong guan; Azure Pine Monastery; New Territories), Fung Ying Seen Koon (Peng-Ying xianguan; Immortal Community of Peng and Ying; New Territories), Wong Tai Sin (Huang daxian; Great Immortal Wong; Kowloon), Yuen Yuen Institute (Yuanxuan xueyue; Complete Mystery Institute; New Territories), and Yuk Hui Temple (Yuxu gong; Palace of Jade Emptiness; Cheung Chau Island) being among the most influential. In particular, Wong Tai Sin is probably the most famous and popular temple as well as a major tourist destination. In addition, it appears that Moy Lin-shin (1931–98) and Mui Ming-to (d.u.), the co-founders of Fung Loy Kok (Penglai ge; Penglai Pavilion) in North America, had some connections with the Yuen Yuen Institute. As many of the Hong Kong temples are highly syncretic and incorporate a variety of elements of popular Chinese religiosity, their categorization as "Daoist" deserves additional research and reflection.

Due to the somewhat factional nature of Hong Kong Daoism, there are also a number of competing Hong Kong Taoist Associations. Hong Kong Daoism in turn consists of Orthodox Unity, Dragon Gate, as well as various family lineages with less clear histories. With respect to Orthodox Unity, Orthodox Unity priests are the main ritual experts for festivals and for the *jiao*-offering rituals in the villages of the New Territories and outlying islands; they also dominate the market for "non-Christian" funeral services (David Palmer, per. comm.). In terms of Dragon Gate, as in Taiwan, the lineage differs from its mainland Chinese counterpart; generally speaking, it is not monastic and does not adhere to foundational Complete Perfection religious commitments. In fact, research suggests that the establishment of Daoist communities and institutions in Hong Kong was largely an extension of popular spirit-writing cults and charitable societies in southern China during the late Qing dynasty. Many of the former specifically focused on mediumistic activity related to Lü Dongbin ("Ancestor Lü"), a famous Tang dynasty immortal and wonder-worker identified as the patriarch of certain internal alchemy lineages. For some reason, these groups often identified themselves as Dragon

Gate. If one believes the internal histories of certain southern families, it seems that there were also formal Dragon Gate temples in southern China, whose affiliates eventually migrated to Hong Kong. According to the *Luofu zhinan* (Guide to Luofu), ordained Dragon Gate priests first established temples in Guangdong in the late seventeenth century (Tsui 1991: 66–70), but the actual relationship between these temples and the Daoist temples in Hong Kong remains unclear. In any case, major Daoist temples and organizations began to be established in Hong Kong from the late nineteenth through the middle of the twentieth century.

The Hong Kong organizations consist of both ordained, married clergy as well as a much larger lay community. Hong Kong Daoism has developed its own unique characteristics and forms of ritual activities, including newer forms of Daoist liturgical practice. It seems that the dissemination and growth of Daoism among southern Chinese groups who eventually migrated to Hong Kong was largely due to two major factors. First, in the case of Ancestor Lü cultic activity and temples, individuals were given insights into an unpredictable future through spirit-writing sessions. In addition, many people reported supernatural and healing experiences. Such events no doubt proved appealing to potential converts. Second, in the case of charitable societies, people were given assistance in times of need. Combined together, one finds a context where popular devotionalism and social solidarity flourished. Such patterns of community involvement continue in the contemporary Hong Kong Daoist emphasis on services for departed ancestors. Here we should also mention that, given their relatively high degree of cultural capital and material resources, Taiwanese and Hong Kong Daoist organizations have played a major role in the revitalization of contemporary mainland Chinese Daoism, especially in terms of funding mainland Chinese Daoist restoration projects and research on Chinese Daoism. Many temple construction and renovation projects are the result of their funding. In the case of Hong Kong Daoism, this is partially due to the status of Hong Kong as one of the so-called Four Tigers, major East Asian socio-economic sectors, and to the status of Hong Kong as a Special Administration Region (SAR) of the PRC, under the latter's "one country, two systems" system. Here we may recall that the British transferred Hong Kong to the PRC in 1997. These dimensions of modern Chinese Daoism also draw our attention to its global dimensions.

Globalization

Daoism is now a global religious tradition characterized by cultural, ethnic, linguistic, and national diversity. Here "global Daoism" refers to individuals, communities, and organizations with a connection to "Chinese Daoism" as source-tradition. Global Daoism consists of the diverse adherents and communities with international distribution. In addition to mainland China, Hong Kong, and Taiwan, there are now tradition-based Daoist communities in Australia, Brazil, Canada, England, France, Italy, Mexico, Singapore, Spain, Switzerland, the United States, and so forth. In this respect, it is important to remember the above-mentioned spectrum of global Daoism, with tradition-based adherents and communities being the focus here. In terms of a viable approach, I would advocate self-identification as an initial methodology, followed by critical evaluation. That is, one begins with a comprehensive and inclusive mapping of "Daoism" in the relevant society or country. This includes the entire spectrum of actual adherence and conversion, intellectual engagement and popular appropriation. Anyone who self-identifies and any phenomenon identified as "Daoist" is included in one's inventory. This exercise is, of course, complicated because of certain foundational Daoist values (e.g. deference, hiddenness, modesty) and because many tradition-based Daoist communities are local. Specifically, tradition-based immigrant and ethnic Daoist communities tend to be "hidden" in international districts ("Chinatowns"), without websites or other forms of self-promotion or marketing. In any case, an inventory based on self-identification should be followed by critical evaluation, especially with respect to questions concerning actual affiliation and recognizability. As touched upon above, much of what goes by the name of "Daoism" in the modern world is fabrication, fiction, and fantasy. There is little if any actual connection to the religious tradition which is Daoism. Nonetheless, the interpreter of "global Daoism" is left to determine, based on religious literacy and critical reflection, which criteria to use for "authentication." Ethical and political issues, as well as lives and communities, are involved.

In terms of modern Daoism, globalization begins following the Chinese Communist takeover of mainland China in 1949, but really emerges in the 1970s and 1980s, and becomes more prominent in the 1990s and 2000s. Thus, it is a very recent phenomenon when compared to other global "Asian religions." However, although Daoism is not a missionary religion, and Daoists have very little interest in conversion beyond personal affinities, the globalization of Daoism, especially when viewed in terms of conversion and distribution, has a variety of historical precedents. For example, during the Period of Disunion, members of the Ba ethnic minority converted to Daoism (see, Kleeman 1998). During the Tang dynasty, Daoism as an organized religion was transmitted to Korea, and there was some Korean conversion (see, Jung 2000; Miura 2008). Concurrently, Daoist views and practices were introduced to Japan (see, Masuo 2000; Sakade 2008a). In addition, members of the Yao ethnic minority began converting to Daoism during the Song dynasty (see, Alberts 2006; Lemoine 1982; Pourret 2002; Strickmann 1982). These patterns complexify our interpretation of global Daoism for a variety of reasons. First, the Ba and Yao conversion to Daoism involved Sinification ("becoming Chinese"); they adopted classical Chinese as the language of ordination, scripture and ritual. Second, in terms of pre-modern Korea and Japan, China was the cultural center, and Daoism was recognized as an important component of traditional Chinese culture. In the modern world, global Daoism often departs from these earlier patterns.

These examples notwithstanding, global Daoism, or Daoism as a "world religion" with global distribution and international adherence, is a late twentieth century development. As mentioned, this involves the emergence of a global religious tradition rooted in "Chinese Daoism" as source-tradition, but characterized by cultural, ethnic, linguistic, and national diversity. Our understanding of global Daoism is complicated by a number of factors. These include a scarcity of scholarship; few academics, especially specialists on Daoism, have yet to take the phenomenon seriously. Such inquiry also is challenged because one needs to have a deep understanding of not only Chinese Daoism, but also cultural studies, intellectual history, and the religious history of distinct societies and countries. The latter must address specific immigration patterns, including relevant immigration legislation. Here I will provide a few insights concerning patterns within global Daoism. This will be followed by some representative examples of tradition-based communities.

On the most basic level, we may consider global Daoist adherence and identity in terms of birthright or convert adherents. Outside of the Chinese cultural sphere, birthright Daoists tend to be Chinese immigrants or ethnic Chinese ("Han"). Daoist convert adherents have diverse cultural and ethnic identities, which are society- and country-specific. In the case of the United States, converts tend to be Euro-Americans ("whites"), or people of Western European ancestry. There are few "non-Chinese" birthright adherents, that is, descendants of individuals who converted to Daoism. Western expressions of global Daoism are largely a convert phenomenon, although these tend to be influenced by immigrant and ethnic Chinese teachers along a diverse spectrum of religious location. Here we must recognize various motivations for conversion to Daoism, including personal affinity, meaning and purpose as well as communal belonging. Also challenging for dominant secular materialist views, some convert Daoists claim "pre-destined affinities" (*yuanfen*) and mystical experiences. The former encompasses belief in reincarnation, while the latter involves encounters with Daoist immortals or deities. Reincarnation is especially challenging to notions of "conversion," as it suggests the possibility that one's so-called "birth-tradition" is only apparently so. Along similar lines, it is also important to consider Daoist views of conversion. Daoism is not a missionary religion, and Daoists have tended to have little interest in conversion. This is partially because Chinese Daoists have traditionally viewed Daoism as solely a Chinese religion practiced by Chinese people. As will be discussed momentarily, there is a close connection between being a Daoist and being Chinese, both ethnically and culturally. This means that most tradition-based Daoists have assumed Sinification on the part of "non-Chinese" people, especially with respect to culture and language. In addition, conversion has been generally viewed as a matter of personal affinity. Whether others adhere or convert to Daoism is largely irrelevant from a Daoist perspective. The opposite is also true. Different people have different affinities and needs, which result in adherence to different beliefs and practices. Daoists thus tend to be more inclusive and pluralistic with respect to other religious traditions.

In terms of patterns within the global Daoist community, birthright Chinese members of Daoism tend to see a fundamental interconnection among cultural, ethnic, and religious identity. To be Daoist is to be culturally Chinese and ethnically Han. These members of the global Daoist community tend to have a higher level of respect for converts who not only understand Daoism, but also speak and read Chinese language as well as understand traditional Chinese culture. The latter includes framing values and social systems. Outside of mainland China, birthright Chinese Daoists also tend to observe popular morality and favor "other-power" types of practices, especially theistic devotionalism and ritual intervention. They tend to be part of communities overseen by Chinese teachers and rarely recognize "non-Chinese" teachers. These communities are largely comprised of immigrant and ethnic Chinese people, although there are some multi-ethnic communities. However, there tends to be a clear hierarchy, especially in terms of leadership and power relationships. While diverse, convert Daoists, especially in the West, tend to see culture, ethnicity, and religion as distinct and separable. One need not be Chinese, either ethnically or culturally, to be Daoist, although some tradition-based "non-Chinese" Daoists view Daoism as deeply rooted in traditional Chinese culture, and in turn become Sinified on some level. Convert Daoists tend to favor "self-power" practices, especially meditation and Yangsheng. In the case of the United States, they tend to be part of largely Euro-American communities. Many of these are overseen by Chinese teachers or teachers who studied with Chinese teachers. There often is a complex mixture of Sincentrism and Orientalism in such communities. That is, many convert adherents tend to view Chinese teachers as more "authentic" simply based on their ethnicity, and regardless of their level of training or actual affiliation.

Nonetheless, global Daoism consists of adherents from diverse cultural and ethnic backgrounds (Figure 9.1). The global Daoist community includes ordained Daoist priests and monastics of "non-Chinese" ancestry. These individuals have either trained under Chinese Daoist priests in China or in their corresponding countries. Even by the most conservative definitions of Daoist identity, that is, ones that privilege Chineseness, lineage, and ordination, there are now tradition-based Daoists and their associated communities throughout the modern world. These individuals and communities are comprised of a wide spectrum

FIGURE 9.1 *Founding Members of the British Taoist Association.*
Source: British Taoist Association.

of ethnicities and cultural backgrounds. That is, "real Daoists" may no longer be equated with "Chinese Daoists." Although complex, post-modernist and post-colonial religious adherence makes space for both the voices of birthright Chinese adherents, especially ordained Chinese Daoists, and of convert adherents, especially ordained and lineage-based Daoists. However, this cannot be an unrecognized Orientalism, in which Chinese voices are privileged simply because they are Chinese. The search for the "Oriental Monk" (Jane Iwamura) and the "Daoist Master" has led many astray. Here I would also caution us not to focus only on prominent and charismatic teachers, although many of these individuals would delight in such tendencies. Rather, I would suggest that we focus more on communities, including the diverse lives that comprise such communities. From an anthropological and sociological perspective, we may also map such communities in terms of demographics, including age, birth-tradition, educational level, ethnicity, gender, geographical distribution, nationality, socio-economic status, and so forth.

As mentioned, global Daoism first and foremost consists of tradition-based Daoists and Daoist communities. The latter tend to be under the direction of one or more ordained Daoist priests, who are usually located within specific lineages. Some prominent global Daoist organizations include the following:

- Associación de Taoísmo de España (Spanish Taoist Association [STA]; Xibanya daojiao xiehui; est. 2001). Located in Barcelona, Spain. Spanish convert and sympathizer community established by and under the direction of Tian Chengyang (b. ca. 1965), a Chinese immigrant and ordained Dragon Gate priest.

- Association Française Daoïste (French Daoist Association [FDA]; Faguo daojiao xiehui; est. 2003). Located in Fontainebleau, France. French convert and sympathizer community established by Karine Martin (Jingxiu; b. ca. 1970) and Igor Scerbo (Xinming; b. ca. 1970), French converts and ordained Dragon Gate priests, and now under the direction of Bernard Doublet (Zhitong; b. 1942), a lay French convert Daoist.

- Associazione Taoista d'Italia (Italian Taoist Association [ITA]; Yidali daojiao xiehui; est. 1993). Located in Caserta, Italy. Italian convert and sympathizer community established by and under the direction of Vincenzo di Ieso (Li Xuanzong; b. 1956), an Italian convert and ordained Wudang priest.

- British Taoist Association (BTA; Yingguo daojiao xiehui; est. 1996). Based in Buckhurst Hill, just outside of London, England. British convert and sympathizer community established by four British converts and under the direction of Shijing (Alan Redman; b. ca. 1950), an ordained Dragon Gate priest.

- Daoist Foundation (DF; Daojiao jijin hui; est. 2007). Based in San Diego, California. Euro-American convert and sympathizer community established by and under the direction of Louis Komjathy (Kang Xiujing; b. 1971) and Kate Townsend (Tang Baojing; b. 1962), Euro-American converts and ordained Huashan priests.

- Singapore Taoist Mission (STM; Xinjiapo daojiao xiehui; est. 1996). Singapore birthright and convert community largely composed of individuals of Chinese ancestry. Established and under the direction of Lee Zhiwang (b. ca. 1945), a Singapore citizen of Chinese ancestry and ordained Dragon Gate priest.

- Sociedade Taoísta do Brasil (Brazilian Taoist Association; Baxi daojiao hui; est. 1991). Brazilian convert and sympathizer community established by Wu Jyh Cherng (Wu Zhicheng; 1958–2004), a Taiwanese immigrant and ordained Orthodox Unity priest, and now under the direction of Hamilton Fonseca Filho (Fang Erhe/Sancheng; b. ca. 1970) and Wagner Canalonga (Ka Nangu/Sanxin; b. ca. 1965), Brazilian converts and ordained Orthodox Unity priests.

From this list, attentive readers will note the frequent appearance of *xiehui* in the Chinese names of the organizations. Although this term is technically a modern Chinese Communist political designation, it indicates the strong influence of the Chinese Daoist Association (CDA; Zhongguo daojiao xiehui) on certain tradition-based organizations. Outside of China and the Chinese cultural sphere, tradition-based Daoists and Daoist communities face a variety of challenges, including systematic misunderstanding of the tradition and a lack of support. They often lack the necessary financial support to acquire property and to establish infrastructure. For example, there are few if any formal Daoist temples and retreat centers in the United States, although some groups are working on such projects.

Here we should recognize that there are other tradition-based Daoist organizations in various countries. In the case of the United States, there are immigrant and ethnic communities such as the American Taoist and Buddhist Association (ATBA; New York City, New York), Ching Chung Taoist Association (CCTA; San Francisco, California), and Fung Loy Kok/Taoist Tai Chi Society (FLK/TTCS; headquartered in Toronto, Canada, but with US branches). CCTA and FLK are connected to source-organizations in Hong Kong. There also are organizations such as Healing Tao/Universal Tao (HT; Mantak Chia) and Universal

Society of the Integral Way (USIW; Ni Hua-ching), although these groups have only tenuous connections to Daoism as such, and are better understood as forms of hybrid spirituality. Recalling our spectrum, under a generous reading they fall into the categories of "adaptation" and "innovation;" under a more critical reading, they involve "appropriation" and "fabrication." On one level, they contribute to the revitalization and globalization of Daoism; on another, they are involved in its diminishment.

By way of conclusion, we may recall two of our guiding metaphors, namely, translation and sacred site. Like the translation of classical Chinese Daoist scriptures into Western languages, Daoism is now being translated from an indigenous Chinese religion into a global one comprised of adherents from diverse cultural, ethnic, and national backgrounds. It remains to be seen to what extent the resultant expressions will remain connected to the source-tradition of Chinese Daoism. While creativity and inspiration are necessarily involved, the question of fidelity and recognizability remains. Along similar lines, one may view Daoism as a sacred site. Just as actual Daoist sacred sites are comprised of specific places, cultures, communities, and individuals, this is also the case for Daoism as a living and lived religion. Different individuals have different relationships and social locations with respect to it. One may approach it as inhabitant, pilgrim, or tourist. As is the case with so many landscapes and places, some may also view Daoism as mining site or future strip mall. However, if one follows the advice the "Inward Training" chapter of the *Book of Master Guan*, perhaps one will be "inwardly still and outwardly reverent." Then one may find unexpected openings, hidden courtyards, and inner altars. One may find entrance into the Daoist tradition.

Further reading

Lai Chi-tim. 2003, "Daoism in China Today, 1980–2002." In *Religion in China Today*, ed. Daniel Overmyer. 107–21. Cambridge and New York: Cambridge University Press.

Kirkland, Russell. 1997, "The Taoism of the Western Imagination and the Taoism of China: De-colonizing the Exotic Teachings of the East." <http://kirkland.myweb.uga.edu/rk/pdf/pubs/pres/TENN97.pdf>. Accessed June 1, 2013.

Komjathy, Louis. 2004, "Tracing the Contours of Daoism in North America." *Nova Religio* 8.2 (November 2004): 5–27.

Siegler, Elijah. 2003, *The Dao of America: The History and Practice of American Daoism*. Ph.D. diss., University of California, Santa Barbara.

BIBLIOGRAPHY

Adler, Joseph. 2002, *Chinese Religious Traditions*. Upper Saddle River, NJ: Prentice Hall.

Alberts, Eli. 2006, *A History of Daoism and the Yao People of South China*. Youngstown, NY: Cambria Press.

Berkowitz, Alan. 2000, *Patterns of Disengagement: The Practice and Portrayal of Reclusion in Early Medieval China*. Stanford: Stanford University Press.

Berling, Judith. 1993, "Death and Afterlife in Chinese Religions." In *Death and Afterlife: Perspectives of World Religions*, ed. Hiroshi Obayashi, 181–92. New York: Praeger.

Bokenkamp, Stephen. 1983, "Sources of the Ling-pao Scriptures." In *Tantric and Taoist Studies*, ed. Michel Strickmann, 2.434–86. Bruxelles: Institut Belge des Hautes Études Chinoises.

—1997, *Early Daoist Scriptures*. Berkeley, CA: University of California Press.

—2005, "Daoism: An Overview." In *Encyclopedia of Religion*, ed. Lindsay Jones, vol. 14, 2176–92. New York and London: MacMillan.

Boltz, Judith M. 1987, *A Survey of Taoist Literature: Tenth to Seventeenth Centuries*. Berkeley, CA: University of California, Institute of East Asian Studies.

Bradbury, Steve. 1992, "The American Conquest of Philosophical Taoism." In *Translation East and West*, ed. Cornelia Moore and Lucy Lower, 29–41. Honolulu, HI: University of Hawaii, College of Language, Linguistics and Literature and the East-West Center.

Cahill, Suzanne. 1993, *Transcendence and Divine Passion: The Queen Mother of the West in Medieval China*. Stanford: Stanford University Press.

—2006, *Divine Traces of the Daoist Sisterhood: Records of the Assembled Transcendents of the Fortified Walled City*. Cambridge, MA: Three Pines Press.

Campany, Robert. 2001, "Ingesting the Marvelous: The Practitioner's Relationship to Nature According to Ge Hong." In *Daoism and Ecology*, ed. Norman Girardot et al., 125–46. Cambridge, MA: Center for the Study of World Religions, Harvard University Press.

—2002, *To Live as Long as Heaven and Earth: A Translation and Study of Ge Hong's Traditions of Divine Transcendents*. Berkeley, CA: University of California Press.

—2003, "On the Very Idea of Religions (In the Modern West and in Early Medieval China)." *History of Religions* 42: 287–319.

— 2005, "Eating Better than Gods and Ancestors." In *Of Tripod and Palate*, ed. Roel Sterckx, 96–122. New York: Palgrave Macmillan.

Carrette, Jeremy, and Richard King. 2004, *Selling Spirituality: The Silent Takeover of Religion*. London and New York: Routledge.

Cassell, Susie Lan, ed. 2002, *The Chinese in America: A History from Gold Mountain to the New Millenium*. Walnut Creek, CA: Altamira Press.

Cedzich, Ursula-Angelika. 2001, "Corpse Deliverance, Substitute Bodies, Name Change, and Feigned Death: Aspects of Metamorphosis and Immortality in Early Medieval China." *Journal of Chinese Religions* 29: 1–68.

Center for Daoist Studies (CDS). n.d. "Daoist Sacred Sites." <www.daoistcenter.org/basic.html>. Accessed on June 1, 2013.

—n.d. "Popular Western Taoism (PWT)." <www.daoistcenter.org/pwt. html>. Accessed June 1, 2013.

— n.d. "Taoist Yoga." <www.daoistcenter.org/taoistyoga.html>. Accessed on June 1, 2013.

Chan, Alan K.L. 1991a, *Two Visions of the Way: A Study of the Wang Pi and the Ho-shang Kung Commentaries on the Lao-Tzu*. Albany: State University of New York Press.

—1991b, "The Formation of the Heshang Gong Legend." In *Sages and Filial Sons*, eds Julia Ching and Robert Guisso, 101–34. Hong Kong: Chinese University Press.

—2000, "The *Daode jing* and Its Tradition." In *Daoism Handbook*, ed. Livia Kohn, 1–29. Leiden: Brill.

Chao, Shin-yi. 2008, "Good Career Moves: Life Stories of Daoist Nuns of the Twelfth and Thirteenth Centuries." *Nan Nu: Men, Women and Gender in Early and Imperial China* 10.1: 121–51.

Chen Yaoting. 2008, "Taoism in the People's Republic of China." In *The Encyclopedia of Taoism*, ed. Fabrizio Pregadio, 174–5. London and New York: Routledge.

Chinese Daoist Association (CDA). 1995, *Daojiao shenxian huaji/Album for Taoist Deities and Divine Immortals*. Beijing: Huaxia chuban she.

—2002, *Taoism*. Beijing: Chinese Taoist Association.

—2003, "Faith Statement on Ecology: Daoism." In *Faith in Conservation: New Approaches to Religions and the Environment*, ed. Martin Palmer and Victoria Finlay, 87–90. Washington, DC: World Bank.

Clarke, J. J. 2000, *The Tao of the West: Western Transformations of Taoist Thought*. London and New York: Routledge.

Csikszentmihalyi, Mark. 2000, "Han Cosmology and Mantic Practice." In *Daoism Handbook*, ed. Livia Kohn, 53–73. Leiden: Brill.

—2002, "Traditional Taxonomies and Revealed Texts in the Han." In *Daoist Identity*, eds Livia Kohn and Harold Roth, 81–101. Honolulu: University of Hawaii Press.

Csikszentmihalyi, Mark and Philip J. Ivanhoe, eds. 1999, *Religious and Philosophical Aspects of the Laozi*. Albany, NY: State University of New York Press.

Csikszentmihalyi, Mark, and Michael Nylan. 2003, "Constructing Lineages and Inventing Traditions through Exemplary Figures in Early China." *T'oung Pao* 89: 59–99.

Daoist Foundation. 2008a. "Morning Liturgy of Complete Perfection." Olympia, WA: Wandering Cloud Press.

—2008b, "Evening Liturgy of Complete Perfection." Olympia, WA: Wandering Cloud Press.

—n.d. "Lineage." <www.daoistfoundation.org/lineage.html>. Accessed June 1, 2013.

De Bruyn, Pierre-Henry. 2000, "Daoism in the Ming (1368–1644)." In *Daoism Handbook*, ed. Livia Kohn, 594–622. Leiden: Brill.

De Michelis, Elizabeth. 2005, *A History of Modern Yoga: Patanjali and Western Esotericism*. London and New York: Continuum.

Dean, Kenneth. 1993, *Taoist Ritual and Popular Cults in Southeast China*. Princeton, NJ: Princeton University Press.

—2000, "Daoist Ritual Today." In *Daoism Handbook*, ed. Livia Kohn, 659–82. Leiden: Brill.

Despeux, Catherine. 1989, "Gymnastics: The Ancient Tradition." In *Taoist Meditation and Longevity Techniques*, ed. Livia Kohn, 225–61. Ann Arbor, MI: Center for Chinese Studies, University of Michigan.

—2000a, "Women in Daoism." In *Daoism Handbook*, ed. Livia Kohn, 384–412. Leiden: Brill.

—2000b, "Talismans and Sacred Diagrams." In *Daoism Handbook*, ed. Livia Kohn, 498–540. Leiden: Brill.

Despeux, Catherine, and Livia Kohn. 2003, *Women in Daoism*. Cambridge, MA: Three Pines Press.

DeWit, Han F. 1991, *Contemplative Psychology*. Trans. Marie Louise Baird. Pittsburgh: Duquesne University Press.

DeWoskin, Kenneth. 1983, *Doctors, Diviners, and Magicians in Ancient China*. New York: Columbia University Press.

Dippmann, Jeffrey. 2001, "The Tao of Textbooks: Taoism in Introductory World Religion Texts." *Teaching Theology & Religion* 4.1: 40–54.

Englehardt, Ute. 1989, "Qi for Life: Longevity in the Tang." In *Taoist Meditation and Longevity Techniques*, ed. Livia Kohn, 263–96. Ann Arbor, MI: Center for Chinese Studies, University of Michigan.

—2000, "Longevity Techniques and Chinese Medicine." In *Daoism Handbook*, ed. Livia Kohn, 74–108. Leiden: Brill.

Eskildsen, Stephen. 1998, *Asceticism in Early Taoist Religion*. Albany, NY: State University of New York Press.

—2001, "Seeking Signs of Proof: Visions and Other Trance Phenomena in Early Quanzhen Taoism." *Journal of Chinese Religions* 29: 139–60.

—2004, *The Teachings and Practices of the Early Quanzhen Taoist Masters*. Albany, NY: State University of New York Press.

Esposito, Monica. 2000, "Daoism in the Qing (1644–1911)." In *Daoism Handbook*, ed. Livia Kohn, 623–58. Leiden: Brill.

—2001, "Longmen Taoism in Qing China: Doctrinal Ideal and Local Reality." *Journal of Chinese Religions* 29: 191–231.

— 2004, "The Longmen School and Its Controversial History during the Qing Dynasty." In *Religion and Chinese Society*, ed. John Lagerwey, vol. 2, 621–98. Hong Kong: Chinese University of Hong Kong.

Fairbank, John, and Merle Goldman. 2006, *China: A New History*, 2nd rev. edn. Cambridge, MA: Harvard University Press.

Foucault, Michel. 1982 (1969), *The Archaeology of Knowledge*. Trans A. M. Sheridan Smith. New York: Vintage Books.

Gamer, Robert E., ed. 2008, *Understanding Contemporary China*. 3rd edn. Boulder, CO: Lynne Rienner Publishers.

Geertz, Clifford. 1977, *The Interpretation of Cultures*. New York: Basic Books.

Girardot, Norman. 2002, *The Victorian Translation of China: James Legge's Oriental Pilgrimage*. Berkeley, CA: University of California Press.

—2008, "My Way: Teaching the *Daode Jing* at the Beginning of a New Millenium." In *Teaching the Daode jing*, ed. Gary DeAngelis and Warren Frisina, 105–29. Oxford and New York: Oxford University Press.

Girardot, Norman, James Miller, and Liu Xiaogan, eds. 2001, *Daoism and Ecology: Ways within a Cosmic Landscape*. Cambridge, MA: Center for the Study of World Religions, Harvard University Press.

Goossaert, Vincent. 2007, *The Taoists of Peking, 1800–1949: A Social History of Urban Clerics*. Cambridge, MA: Harvard University Asia Center/Harvard University Press.

Goossaert, Vincent, and David Palmer. 2011, *The Religious Question in Modern China*. Chicago, IL: University of Chicago Press.

Graham, A.C. 1989, *Disputers of the Tao: Philosophical Argumentation in Ancient China*. La Salle, IL: Open Court.

—1998 (1986), "The Origins of the Legend of Lao Tan." In *Lao-tzu and the Tao-te-ching*, eds Livia Kohn and Michael LaFargue, 23–40. Albany, NY: State University of New York Press.

Hahn, Thomas. 1988a, "New Developments concerning Daoist and Buddhist Monasteries." In *The Turning of the Tide*, ed. Julian Pas, 79–101. Hong Kong: Royal Asiatic Society.

—1988b, "The Standard Taoist Mountain." *Cahiers d'Extrême-Asie* 4: 145–56.

—2000, "Daoist Sacred Sites." In *Daoism Handbook*, ed. Livia Kohn, 683–708. Leiden: Brill.

—2001, "An Introductory Study on Daoist Notions of Wilderness." In *Daoism and Ecology: Ways within a Cosmic Landscape*, ed. Norman Girardot et al., 201–18. Cambridge, MA: Center for the Study of World Religions, Harvard University Press.

Hammerstrom, Erik. 2003, "The Mysterious Gate: Daoist Monastic Liturgy in Late Imperial China." Master's thesis, University of Hawaii.

Hardy, Julia. 1998, "Influential Western Interpretations of the *Tao-te-ching*." In *Lao-tzu and the Tao-te-ching*, eds Livia Kohn and Michael LaFargue, 165–88. Albany, NY: State University of New York Press.

Harper, Donald. 1998, *Early Chinese Medical Literature: The Mawangdui Medical Manuscripts*. London and New York: Kegan Paul International.

Hendrischke (Kandel), Barbara. 2000, "Early Daoist Movements." In *Daoism Handbook*, ed. Livia Kohn, 134–64. Leiden: Brill.

—2007, *The Scripture on Great Peace: The Taiping jing and the Beginnings of Daoism*. Berkeley, CA: University of California Press.

Hendrischke, Barbara, and Benjamin Penny. 1996, "The 180 Precepts Spoken by Lord Lao: A Translation and Textual Study." *Taoist Resources* 6.2: 17–29.

Henricks, Robert. 1989, *Lao-tzu Te-Tao Ching: A New Translation Based on the Recently Discovered Ma-wang-tui Texts*. New York: Ballantine.

—2000, *Lao Tzu's Tao Te Ching: A Translation of the Startling New Documents Found at Guodian*. New York: Columbia University Press.

Herrou, Adeline. 2013, *A World of Their Own: Daoist Monks and Their Community in Contemporary China*. St. Petersburg, FL: Three Pines Press.

Ho, Wan-li. 2009, "Daoist Nuns in Taiwan." *Journal of Daoist Studies* 2: 137–64.

Hobsbawm, Eric, and Terence Ranger. 1983, *The Invention of Tradition*. Cambridge and New York: Cambridge University Press.

Hsien Yuen. 1988, *The Taoism of Sage Religion: Tan Ting Sitting Meditation*. New York: North Pole Gold Temple & Temple of Transcendental Wisdom.

Huang, Shih-shan Susan. 2012, *Picturing the True Form: Daoist Visual Culture in Traditional China*. Cambridge, MA: Harvard University Asia Center.

Iwamura, Jane. 2000, "The Oriental Monk in American Popular Culture." In *Religion and Popular Culture in America*, ed. Bruce David Forbes and Jeffrey H. Mahan, 25–43. Berkeley, CA: University of California Press.

Jordan, David. 1972, *Gods, Ghosts and Ancestors: Folk Religion in a Taiwanese Village*. Berkeley, CA: University of California Press.

Jung Jae-seo. 2000, "Daoism in Korea." In *Daoism Handbook*, ed. Livia Kohn, 792–820. Leiden: Brill.

Kaptchuk, Ted. 2000 (1983), *The Web That Has No Weaver: Understanding Chinese Medicine*. Chicago, IL: Contemporary Books.

Karlgren, Bernhard. 1964, *Grammata Serica Recensa*. Goteborg: Elanders Boktryckeri Aktiebolag.

Katz, Paul. 1999, *Images of the Immortal: The Cult of Lü Dongbin at the Palace of Eternal Joy*. Honolulu, HI: University of Hawaii Press.

Kim, Sung-Hae. 2006, "Daoist Monasticism in Contemporary China." In *Chinese Religions in Contemporary Societies*, ed. James Miller, 101–22. Santa Barbara, CA: ABC-CLIO.

King, Richard. 1999, *Orientalism and Religion: Postcolonial Theory, India, and 'The Mystic East'*. London and New York: Routledge.

Kirkland, Russell. 1997a, "The Historical Contours of Taoism in China: Thoughts on Issues of Classification and Terminology." *Journal of Chinese Religions* 25: 57–82.

—1997b, "The Taoism of the Western Imagination and the Taoism of China: De-colonizing the Exotic Teachings of the East." <http://kirkland.myweb.uga.edu/rk/pdf/pubs/pres/TENN97.pdf>. Accessed June 1, 2013.

—1998, "Teaching Taoism in the 1990s." *Teaching Theology and Religion* 1.2: 121–9.

—2002, "The History of Taoism: A New Outline." *Journal of Chinese Religions* 30: 177–93.

—2004, *Taoism: The Enduring Tradition*. London and New York: Routledge.

Kleeman, Terry. 1991, "Taoist Ethics." In *A Bibliographic Guide to Comparative Ethics*, ed. John Carman and Mark Juergensmeyer, 162–94. Cambridge: Cambridge University Press.

—1994a, "Licentious Cults and Bloody Victuals: Sacrifice, Reciprocity, and Violence in Traditional China." *Asia Major* 3.7: 185–211.

—1994b, "Mountain Deities in China: The Domestication of the Mountain God and the Subjugation of the Margins." *Journal of the American Oriental Society* 114.2: 226–38.

—1998, *Great Perfection: Religion and Ethnicity in a Chinese Millennial Kingdom.* Honolulu, HI: University of Hawaii Press.

—2002, "Ethnic Identity and Daoist Identity in Traditional China." In *Daoist Identity*, ed. Livia Kohn and Harold Roth, 23–38. Honolulu, HI: University of Hawaii Press.

—2005, "Feasting Without the Victuals: The Evolution of the Daoist Communal Kitchen." In *Of Tripod and Palate*, ed. Roel Sterckx, 140–62. New York: Palgrave Macmillan.

—2008, "Tianshi dao." In *The Encyclopedia of Taoism*, ed. Fabrizio Pregadio, 981–6. London and New York: Routledge.

—2012, "'Take Charge of Households and Convert the Citizenry': The Parish Priest in Celestial Master Transmission." In *Affiliation and Transmission in Daoism*, ed. Florian Reiter, 19–39. Wiesban, Germany: Harrassowitz Verlag.

Kobayashi Masayoshi. 1995, "The Establishment of the Taoist Religion (*Tao-chiao*) and Its Structure." *Acta Asiatica: Bulletin of the Institute of Eastern Culture* 68: 19–36.

Kohn (Knaul), Livia. 1987, *Seven Steps to the Tao: Sima Chengzhen's Zuowang lun.* St. Augustin: Steyler Verlag.

—ed. 1989, *Taoist Meditation and Longevity Techniques.* Ann Arbor, MI: University of Michigan, Center for Chinese Studies.

—1991a, *Early Chinese Mysticism: Philosophy and Soteriology in the Taoist Tradition.* Princeton, NJ: Princeton University Press.

—1991b, "Taoist Visions of the Body." *Journal of Chinese Philosophy* 18: 227–52.

—1993, *The Taoist Experience: An Anthology.* Albany, NY: State University of New York Press.

—1998a, *God of the Dao: Lord Lao in History and Myth.* Ann Arbor, MI: Center for Chinese Studies, University of Michigan.

—1998b, "The *Tao-te-ching* in Ritual." In *Lao-tzu and the Tao-te-ching*, ed. Livia Kohn and Michael LaFargue, 143–61. Albany, NY: State University of New York Press.

—ed. 2000a, *Daoism Handbook.* Leiden: Brill.

—2000b, "The Northern Celestial Masters." In *Daoism Handbook*, ed. Livia Kohn, 283–308. Leiden: Brill.

—2002, *Living with the Dao: Conceptual Issues in Daoist Practice.* E-dao (electronic) publication. Cambridge, MA: Three Pines Press.

—2003, *Monastic Life in Medieval Daoism.* Honolulu, HI: University of Hawaii Press.

—2004a (2001), *Daoism and Chinese Culture*, 2nd rev. edn. Cambridge, MA: Three Pines Press.

—2004b, *The Daoist Monastic Manual: A Translation of the Fengdao kejie*. Oxford and New York: Oxford University Press.

—2004c, *Cosmos and Community: The Ethical Dimension of Daoism*. Cambridge, MA: Three Pines Press.

—ed. 2006, *Daoist Body Cultivation: Traditional Models and Contemporary Practices*. Cambridge, MA: Three Pines Press.

—2008a, *Chinese Healing Exercises: The Tradition of Daoyin*. Honolulu, HI: University of Hawaii Press.

—2009, *Introducing Daoism*. London and New York: Routledge.

—2010, *Daoist Dietetics: Food for Immortality*. Dunedin, FL: Three Pines Press.

Kohn, Livia and Russell Kirkland. 2000, "Daoism in the Tang." In *Daoism Handbook*, ed. Livia Kohn, 339–83. Leiden: Brill.

Kohn, Livia and Michael LaFargue, eds. 1998, *Lao-tzu and the Tao-te-ching*. Albany, NY: State University of New York Press.

Kohn, Livia and Harold Roth, eds. 2002, *Daoist Identity: History, Lineage, and Ritual*. Honolulu, HI: University of Hawaii Press.

Komjathy, Louis. 2002, *Title Index to Daoist Collections*. Cambridge, MA: Three Pines Press.

—2003a, "Daoist Texts in Translation." <www.daoistcenter.org/articles.html>. Posted on September 15, 2003. Accessed June 1, 2013.

—2003b, "Daoist Teachers in North America." Center for Daoist Studies. <www.daoistcenter.org/advanced>. Accessed on June 1, 2013.

—2003c, "Daoist Organizations in North America." Center for Daoist Studies. <www.daoistcenter.org/advanced>. Accessed on June 1, 2013.

—2004, "Tracing the Contours of Daoism in North America." *Nova Religio* 8.2 (November 2004): 5–27.

—2006, "Qigong in America." In *Daoist Body Cultivation*, ed. Livia Kohn, 203–35. Cambridge, MA: Three Pines Press.

—2007a, *Cultivating Perfection: Mysticism and Self-transformation in Early Quanzhen Daoism*. Leiden: Brill.

—2007b, "Clothed in the Dao: The Styles, Functions, and Symbolism of Daoist Dress." Unpublished paper.

—2008a (2003), *Handbooks for Daoist Practice*. 10 vols. Hong Kong: Yuen Yuen Institute.

—2008b, "Models of Daoist Practice and Attainment." Center for Daoist Studies. <www.daoistcenter.org/basic>. Accessed on June 1, 2013.

—2008c, "Mapping the Daoist Body: Part I: The *Neijing tu* in History." *Journal of Daoist Studies* 1: 67–92.

—2009, "Mapping the Daoist Body: Part II: The Text of the *Neijing tu*." *Journal of Daoist Studies* 2: 64–108.

—2011a, "Basic Information Sheet on Daoism." Center for Daoist Studies. <www.daoistcenter.org/basic>. Accessed on June 1, 2013.

—2011b, "Common Misconceptions concerning Daoism." Center for Daoist Studies. <www.daoistcenter.org/basic>. Accessed on June 1, 2013.

—2011c, "Daoism: From Meat Avoidance to Compassion-based Vegetarianism." In *Call to Compassion: Religious Reflections on Animal Advocacy from the World's Religions*, ed. Lisa Kemmerer and Anthony J. Nocella II, 83–103. New York: Lantern Books.

—2011d, "The Daoist Mystical Body." In *Perceiving the Divine through the Human Body: Mystical Sensuality*, ed. Thomas Cottai and June McDaniel, 67–103. New York: Palgrave MacMillan.

—2011e, "Sun Buer: Early Quanzhen Matriarch and the Beginnings of Female Alchemy (*Nüdan*)." Paper presented at the Seventh International Conference on Daoist Studies, June 24–27, 2011, Changsha, Hunan.

—2011f, "Animals and Daoism." Encyclopedia Britannica Advocacy for Animals. <advocacy.britannica.com/blog/advocacy/2011/09/daoism-and-animals>. Assessed on June 1, 2013.

—2012a, "Daoism." In *Encyclopedia of Global Religion*, eds Mark Juergensmeyer and Wade Clark Roof, 281–6. Thousand Oaks, CA: Sage Publications.

—2012b, "The Daoist Tradition in China." In *The Wiley-Blackwell Companion to Chinese Religions*, ed. Randall Nadeau, 171–96. Malden, MA: Wiley-Blackwell.

—2013a, *The Way of Complete Perfection: A Quanzhen Daoist Anthology*. Albany, NY: State University of New York Press.

—2013b, *The Daoist Tradition: An Introduction*. London and New York: Bloomsbury Academic.

Komjathy, Louis and Kate Townsend. 2010a, *Daoist Precept Manual*. San Diego, CA: Wandering Cloud Press.

—2010b, *Daoist Quiet Sitting*. San Diego, CA: Wandering Cloud Press.

Kroll, Paul. 1996, "Body Gods and Inner Vision: The Scripture of the Yellow Court." In *Religions of China in Practice*, ed. Donald S. Lopez, Jr., 149–55. Princeton, NJ: Princeton University Press.

Kwong, Peter and Dusanka Miscevic. 2007, *Chinese America: The Untold Story of America's Oldest New Community*. New York: New Press.

LaFargue, Michael. 1992, *The Tao of the Tao Te Ching*. Albany, NY: State University of New York Press.

—1994, *Tao and Method: A Reasoned Approach to the Tao Te Ching.* Albany, NY: State University of New York Press.

—1998, "Recovering the *Tao-te-ching*'s Original Meaning: Some Remarks on Historical Hermeneutics." In *Lao-tzu and the Tao-te-ching*, eds Livia Kohn and Michael LaFargue, 255–75. Albany, NY: State University of New York Press.

LaFargue, Michael and Julian Pas. 1998, "On Translating the *Tao-te-ching*." In *Lao-tzu and the Tao-te-ching*, ed. Livia Kohn and Michael LaFargue, 277–301. Albany, NY: State University of New York Press.

Lagerwey, John. 1987, *Taoist Ritual in Chinese Society and History.* New York: MacMillan.

—1992, "The Pilgrimage to Wu-tang Shan." In *Pilgrims and Sacred Sites in China*, eds Susan Naquin and Chun-fang Yü, 293–332. Berkeley, CA: University of California Press.

—ed. 2004, *Religion and Chinese Society.* 2 vols. Hong Kong: Chinese University Press.

— 2010, *China: A Religious State.* Seattle, WA: University of Washington Press.

Lai Chi-tim. 1998, "Ko Hung's Discourse of *Hsien*-Immortality: A Taoist Configuration of an Alternate Ideal of Self-identity." *Numen* 45.2: 183–220.

—2003, "Daoism in China Today, 1980–2002." In *Religion in China Today*, ed. Daniel Overmyer, 107–21. Cambridge and New York: Cambridge University Press.

Lakoff, George and Mark Johnson. 1980, *Metaphors We Life By.* Chicago, IL: University of Chicago Press.

Lang, Graeme. 1993, *The Rise of a Refugee God: Hong Kong's Wong Tai Sin.* Oxford and New York: Oxford University Press.

Lau, D.C. 1963, *Lao Tzu Tao Te Ching.* New York: Penguin.

Lau, D.C. and Roger Ames. 1998, *Yuan Dao: Tracing Dao to Its Source.* New York: Ballantine Books.

Lau, Kimberly. 2000, *New Age Capitalism: Making Money East of Eden.* Philadelphia, PA: University of Pennsylvania Press.

Lee, Jonathan H. X. 2010, "Daoist Temples in California." In *Asian American History and Culture: An Encyclopedia*, eds Huping Ling and Allan W. Austin, 169–70. Armonk, NY: M.E. Sharpe.

Lemoine, Jacques. 1982, *Yao Ceremonial Paintings.* Bangkok: White Lotus.

Lévi, Jean. 1989, "The Body: The Daoists' Coat of Arms." Trans. Lydia Davis. In *Fragments for a History of the Human Body*, ed. Michel Feher, Part One, 104–26. New York: Zone.

Little, Stephen. 2000a, *Taoism and the Arts of China.* Berkeley, CA: University of California Press.

—2000b, "Daoist Art." In *Daoism Handbook*, ed. Livia Kohn, 709–46. Leiden: Brill.

Liu Ming (Charles Belyea). 1998, *The Blue Book: A Text Concerning Orthodox Daoist Conduct*, 3rd edn. Santa Cruz, CA: Orthodox Daoism in America.

Liu Xun. 2009, *Daoist Modern: Innovation, Lay Practice, and the Community of Inner Alchemy in Republican Shanghai*. Cambridge, MA: Harvard University Asia Center.

Lo, Vivienne. 2005, *Medieval Chinese Medicine: The Dunhuang Medical Manuscripts*. London and New York: Routledge.

—(Forthcoming), *Healing Arts in Early China*. Leiden: Brill.

MacInnis, Donald. 1989, *Religion in China Today: Policy and Practice*. New York: Orbis Books.

Maciocia, Giovanni. 1989, *The Foundations of Chinese Medicine*. New York: Churchill Livingstone.

Mair, Victor. 1998 (1994), *Wandering on the Way: Early Taoist Tales and Parables of Chuang Tzu*. Honolulu, HI: University of Hawaii Press.

—2000, "The *Zhuangzi* and Its Impact." In *Daoism Handbook*, ed. Livia Kohn, 30–52. Leiden: Brill.

Major, John S. 1993, *Heaven and Earth in Early Han Thought: Chapters Three, Four, and Five of the Huainanzi*. Albany, NY: State University of New York Press.

Major, John, Sarah Queen, Andrew Seth Meyer, and Harold Roth. 2010, *The Huainanzi: A Guide to the Theory and Practice of Government in Early Han China*. New York: Columbia University Press.

Maruyama Hiroshi. 2002, "Documents Used in Rituals of Merit in Taiwanese Daoism." In *Daoist Identity*, ed. Livia Kohn and Harold Roth, 256–73. Honolulu, HI: University of Hawaii Press.

Maspero, Henri. 1981, *Taoism and Chinese Religion*. Trans. Frank Kierman. Amherst, MA: University of Massachusetts Press.

Masuo Shin'ichiro. 2000, "Daoism in Japan." In *Daoism Handbook*, ed. Livia Kohn, 821–42. Leiden: Brill.

Mather, Richard. 1979, "K'ou Ch'ien-chih and the Taoist Theocracy." In *Facets of Taoism*, ed. Holmes Welch and Anna Seidel, 103–22. New Haven, CT: Yale University Press.

Matthews, R. H. 1943 (1931), *Mathews' Chinese-English Dictionary*. Cambridge, MA: Harvard University Press.

McDannell, Colleen. 1995, *Material Christianity: Religion and Popular Culture in America*. New Haven, CT: Yale University Press.

McMahan, David. 2008, *The Making of Buddhist Modernism*. Oxford and New York: Oxford University Press.

Miller, James. 2000, "The Economy of Cosmic Power: A Theory of
  Religious Transaction and a Comparative Study of Shangqing."
  Ph.D. diss., Boston University.
—2003, *Daoism: A Short Introduction*. Oxford: Oneworld.
— ed. 2006, *Chinese Religions in Contemporary Societies*, 101–22.
  Santa Barbara, CA: ABC-CLIO.
—2008, *The Way of Highest Clarity: Nature, Vision and Revelation in
  Medieval China*. Magdalena, NM: Three Pines Press.
Miller, James and Elijah Siegler. 2007, "Of Alchemy and Authenticity:
  Teaching about Daoism Today." *Teaching Theology and Religion*
  10.2: 101–8.
Min Zhiting et al. 2000, *Xuanmen risong zaowan gongke jingzhu*.
  Beijing: Zongjiao wenhua chubanshe.
Miura, Kunio. 1989, "The Revival of *Qi*: Qigong in Contemporary
  China." In *Taoist Meditation and Longevity Techniques*, ed. Livia
  Kohn, 329–58. Ann Arbor, MI: Center for Chinese Studies, University
  of Michigan.
—2008, "Taoism in the Korean Peninsula." In *The Encyclopedia of
  Taoism*, ed. Fabrizio Pregadio, 190–2. London and New York:
  Routledge.
Mori Yuria. 2002, "Identity and Lineage: The *Taiyi jinhua zongzhi* and
  the Spirit-writing Cult to Patriarch Lü in Qing China." In *Daoist
  Identity*, eds Livia Kohn and Harold Roth, 165–84. Honolulu, HI:
  University of Hawaii Press.
Mungello, D. E. 1985, *Curious Land: Jesuit Accommodation and the
  Origins of Sinology*. Honolulu, HI: University of Hawaii Press.
Naquin, Susan and Chun-fang Yü, eds. 1992, *Pilgrims and Sacred Sites
  in China*. Berkeley, CA: University of California Press.
Nattier, Jan. 1997, "Buddhism Comes to Main Street." *Wilson
  Quarterly* 21.2: 72–81.
—1998, "Who Is a Buddhist? Charting the Landscape of Buddhist
  America." In *The Faces of Buddhism in America*, eds Charles S.
  Prebish and Kenneth K. Tanaka, 183–95. Berkeley, CA: University of
  California Press.
Needham, Joseph, et al. 1976, *Science and Civilisation*. Vol. V:
  Chemistry and Chemical Technology. Part 3: *Spagyrical Discovery
  and Invention: Historical Survey, from Cinnabar Elixirs to Synthetic
  Insulin*. Cambridge: Cambridge University Press.
—1980, *Science and Civilisation*. Vol. V: *Chemistry and Chemical
  Technology*. Part 4: *Spagyrical Discovery and Invention: Apparatus,
  Theories and Gifts*. Cambridge: Cambridge University Press.
—1983, *Science and Civilisation in China*. Vol. V: *Chemistry and
  Chemical Technology*. Part 5: *Spagyrical Discovery and Invention:
  Physiological Alchemy*. Cambridge: Cambridge University Press.

—2000, *Science and Civilisation in China*. Vol. 6, part VI: *Biological Technology—Medicine*, ed. Nathan Sivin. Cambridge: Cambridge University Press.

Neswald, Sara. 2007, "Rhetorical Voices in the Neidan Tradition: An Interdisciplinary Analysis of the *Nüdan hebian* Compiled by He Longxiang." Ph.D. diss., McGill University.

Nickerson, Peter. 2000, "The Southern Celestial Masters." In *Daoism Handbook*, ed. Livia Kohn, 256–82. Leiden: Brill.

Nietzsche, Friedrich. 1967 (1887), *On the Genealogy of Morals*. Trans. Walter Kaufmann and R. J. Hollingdale. New York: Vintage Books.

—1980 (1874), *On the Advantage and Disadvantage of History for Life*. Trans. Peter Preuss. Indianapolis, IN: Hackett.

Overmyer, Daniel, ed. 2003, *Religion in China Today*. Cambridge: Cambridge University Press.

Ōzaki Masaharu. 1986, "The Taoist Priesthood: From Tsai-chia to Ch'u-chia." In *Religion and Family in East Asia*, ed. George DeVos and T. Sofue, 97–109. Berkeley, CA: University of California Press.

Palmer, David. 2007, *Qigong Fever: Body, Science, and Utopia in China*. New York: Columbia University Press.

Palmer, David and Liu Xun, eds. 2012, *Daoism in the Twentieth Century: Between Eternity and Modernity*. Berkeley, CA: University of California Press.

Pas, Julian, ed. 1989, *The Turning of the Tide: Religion in China Today*. Oxford and New York: Oxford University Press.

Peerenboom, R. P. 1993, *Law and Morality in Ancient China: The Silk Manuscripts of Huang-Lao*. Albany, NY: State University of New York Press.

Penny, Benjamin. 1996, "Buddhism and Daoism in 'The 180 Precepts Spoken by Lord Lao'." *Taoist Resources* 6.2: 1–16.

—2000, "Immortality and Transcendence." In *Daoism Handbook*, ed. Livia Kohn, 109–33. Leiden: Brill.

Pitchford, Paul. 2003 (1993), *Healing with Whole Foods: Asian Traditions and Modern Nutrition*, 3rd rev. edn. San Francisco: North Atlantic Books.

Poceski, Mario. 2009, *Introducing Chinese Religions*. London and New York: Routledge.

Porkert, Manfred. 1974, *The Theoretical Foundations of Chinese Medicine*. Cambridge, MA: MIT Press.

Porter, Bill. 1993, *The Road to Heaven: Encounters with Chinese Hermits*. San Francisco: Mercury House.

Pourret, Jess. 2002, *The Yao: The Mien and Mun Yao in China, Vietnam, Laos and Thailand*. London: Thames and Hudson.

Prebish, Charles and Martin Baumann, eds. 2002, *Westward Dharma: Buddhism beyond Asia*. Berkeley, CA: University of California Press.

Pregadio, Fabrizio. 2006a, *Great Clarity: Daoism and Alchemy in Early Medieval China*. Stanford: Stanford University Press.

—2006b, "Early Daoist Meditation and the Origins of Inner Alchemy." In *Daoism in History*, ed. Benjamin Penny, 121–58. London and New York: Routledge.

—ed. 2008a, *The Encyclopedia of Taoism*. 2 vols. London and New York: Routledge.

Pregadio, Fabrizio and Lowell Skar. 2000, "Inner Alchemy (*Neidan*)." In *Daoism Handbook*, ed. Livia Kohn, 464–97. Leiden: Brill.

Puett, Michael. 2002, *To Become a God: Cosmology, Sacrifice, and Self-Divinization in Early China*. Cambridge, MA: Harvard University Asia Center.

Qiao Yun. 2001, *Taoist Buildings*. Trans. Zhou Wenzheng. New York: Springer-Verlag Wien New York.

Reinders, Eric. 2004, *Borrowed Gods and Foreign Bodies: Christian Missionaries Imagine Chinese Religion*. Berkeley, CA: University of California Press.

Reiter, Florian. 1998, *The Aspirations and Standards of Taoist Priests in the Early T'ang Period*. Wiesbaden: Harrassowitz.

—ed. 2009, *Foundations of Daoist Ritual*. Wiesbaden: Harrassowitz Verlag.

Robinet, Isabelle. 1977, *Les commentaires du Tao to king jusqu'au VIIe siècle*. Paris: Mémoires de l'Institute des Hautes Études Chinoises 5.

—1989a, "Visualization and Ecstatic Flight in Shangqing Taoism." In *Taoist Meditation and Longevity Techniques*, ed. Livia Kohn, 159–91. Ann Arbor, MI: Center for Chinese Studies, University of Michigan.

—1989b, "Original Contributions of *Neidan* to Taoism and Chinese Thought." In *Taoist Meditation and Longevity Techniques*, ed. Livia Kohn, 297–330. Ann Arbor, MI: Center for Chinese Studies, University of Michigan.

—1993, *Taoist Meditation: The Mao-shan Tradition of Great Purity*. Trans. Julian F. Pas and Norman J. Girardot. Albany, NY: State University of New York Press.

—1995, *Introduction à l'alchimie intérieure taoïste: De l'unité et de la multiplicité*. Paris: Editions Cerf.

—1997, *Taoism: Growth of a Religion*. Trans. Phyllis Brooks. Stanford: Stanford University Press.

—1998, "Later Commentaries: Textual Polysemy and Syncretistic Interpretations." In *Lao-tzu and the Tao-te-ching*, ed. Livia Kohn and Michael LaFargue, 119–42. Albany, NY: State University of New York Press.

—1999, "The Diverse Interpretations of the *Laozi*." In *Religious and Philosophical Aspects of the Laozi*, ed. Mark Csikszentmihalyi and

Philip Ivanhoe, 127–59. Albany, NY: State University of New York Press.

—2000, "Shangqing—Highest Clarity." In *Daoism Handbook*, ed. Livia Kohn, 196–224. Leiden: Brill.

—2008, "Shangqing." In *Encyclopedia of Taoism*, ed. Fabrizio Pregadio, 858–66. London and New York: Routledge.

Robson, James. 2009, *Power of Place: The Religious Landscape of the Southern Sacred Peak (Nanyue) in Medieval China*. Cambridge, MA: Harvard University Asia Center.

Roof, Wade Clark. 2001, *Spiritual Marketplace: Baby Boomers and the Remaking of American Religion*. Princeton, NJ: Princeton University Press.

Roth, Harold. 1991, "Psychology and Self-Cultivation in Early Taoistic Thought." *Harvard Journal of Asiatic Studies* 51.2: 599–650.

—1996, "The Inner Cultivation Tradition of Early Daoism." In *Religions of China in Practice*, ed. Donald S. Lopez, Jr., 123–38. Princeton, NJ: Princeton University Press.

—1997, "Evidence for Stages of Meditation in Early Taoism." *Bulletin of the School of Oriental and African Studies* 60.2: 295–314.

—1999a, *Original Tao: Inward Training (Nei-yeh) and the Foundations of Taoist Mysticism*. New York: Columbia University Press.

—1999b, "*Laozi* in the Context of Early Daoist Mystical Praxis." In *Religious and Philosophical Aspects of the Laozi*, ed. Mark Csikszentmihalyi and Philip J. Ivanhoe, 59–96. Albany, NY: State University of New York Press.

—2000, "Bimodal Mystical Experience in the 'Qiwu lun' Chapter of the *Zhuangzi*." *Journal of Chinese Religions* 28: 31–50.

—2008, "Against Cognitive Imperialism: A Call for a Non-Ethnocentric Approach to Cognitive Science and Religious Studies." *Religion East & West* 8 (October 2008): 1–26.

Roth, Harold and Sarah Queen. 1999a, "A Syncretist Perspective on the Six Schools." In *Sources of Chinese Tradition*, ed. Wm. Theodore de Bary and Irene Bloom, vol. 1, 278–82. New York: Columbia University Press.

Said, Edward W. 1979, *Orientalism*. New York: Vintage Books.

Sakade Yoshinobu. 2008a, "Daoism in Japan." In *The Encyclopedia of Taoism*, ed. Fabrizio Pregadio, 192–6. London and New York: Routledge.

—2008b, "Zhongguo daojiao xiehui." In *The Encyclopedia of Taoism*, ed. Fabrizio Pregadio, 1281–2. London and New York: Routledge.

Saso, Michael. 1970, "The Taoist Tradition in Taiwan." *The China Quarterly* 41: 83–103.

1971, "On Ritual Meditation in Orthodox Taoism." *Journal of the China Society* 8: 1–19.

—1972a, *Taoism and the Rite of Cosmic Renewal*. Pullman, WA: Washington State University Press.

—1972b, "Classification of Taoist Orders According to the Documents of the 61st Generation Heavenly Master." *Bulletin of the Institute of Ethnography* 30: 69–79.

—1974a, "Orthodoxy and Heterodoxy in Taoist Ritual." In *Religion and Ritual in Chinese Society*, ed. Arthur Wolf, 325–48. Stanford: Stanford University Press.

—1974b, "On the Meditative Use of the Yellow Court Canon." *Journal of the China Society* 9: 1–20.

—1978, *The Teachings of Taoist Master Chuang*. New Haven, CT: Yale University Press.

—1983, "The *Chuang-tzu nei-p'ien*: A Taoist Meditation." In *Experimental Essays on Chuang-tzu*, ed. Victor Mair, 140–57. Honolulu: University of Hawaii Press.

—1989, "The Structure of Taoist Liturgy in Taiwan." In *Studies of Taoist Rituals and Music of Today*, eds Tsao Pen-yeh and Daniel Law, 36–60. Hong Kong: Society for Ethnomusicological Research.

—1994, *A Taoist Cookbook*. Tuttle. North Clarendon, VT: Tuttle Publishing.

—1997, "The Taoist Body and Cosmic Prayer." In *Religion and the Body*, ed. Sarah Coakley, 231–47. Cambridge: Cambridge University Press.

—2012 (1978), *The Teachings of Daoist Master Zhuang*, 3rd rev. edn. Los Angeles, CA: Oracle Bones Press.

Schafer, Edward. 1980, *Mao Shan in T'ang Times*. Boulder, CO: Society for the Study of Chinese Religions.

—1981, "Wu Yün's 'Cantos on Pacing the Void'." *Harvard Journal of Asiatic Studies* 41: 377–415.

—1983, "Wu Yün's Stanzas on 'Saunters in Sylphdom'." *Monumenta Serica* 35: 1–37.

Schipper, Kristofer. 1975, *Le Fen-teng: Ritual taoïste*. Paris: Publications de l'École française d'Extrême-Orient.

—1978, "The Taoist Body." *History of Religions* 17.3/4: 355–86.

—1985a, "Taoist Ordination Ranks in the Dunhuang Manuscripts." In *Religion und Philosophie in Ostasien*, ed. Gert Naundorf et al., 127–48. Würzburg: Königshausen und Neumann.

—1985b, "Vernacular and Classical Ritual in Taoism." *Journal of Asian Studies* 65: 21–51.

—1993, *The Taoist Body*. Trans. Karen C. Duval. Berkeley, CA: University of California Press.

—2000, "Taoism: The Story of the Way." In *Taoism and the Arts of China*, ed. Stephen Little, 33–55. Chicago/Berkeley, CA: Art Institute of Chicago/University of California Press.

—2001, "Daoist Ecology: The Inner Transformation. A Study of the Precepts of the Early Daoist Ecclesia." In *Daoism and Ecology*, ed. Norman Girardot et al., 79–94. Cambridge, MA: Center for the Study of World Religions, Harvard University.

Schipper, Kristofer and Franciscus Verellen, eds. 2004, *The Taoist Canon: A Historical Guide*. 3 vols. Chicago, IL: University of Chicago Press.

Schirokauer, Conrad and Miranda Brown. 2006, *A Brief History of Chinese Civilization*, 2nd rev. edn. New York: Houghton Mifflin.

Schwartz, Benjamin. 1985, *The World of Thought in Ancient China*. Cambridge, MA: Harvard University Press.

Seager, Richard. 2000, *Buddhism in America*. New York: Columbia University Press.

Seidel, Anna. 1987, "Traces of Han Religion in Funeral Texts Found in Tombs." In *Dōkyō to shūkyō bunka*, ed. Akizuki Kan'ei, 21–57. Tokyo: Hirakawa shuppansha.

—1988, "Early Taoist Ritual." *Cahiers d'Extrême Asie* 5: 199–204.

—1989–90, "Chronicle of Taoist Studies in the West 1950–1990." *Cahiers d'Extrême-Asie* 5: 223–347.

—1997, "Taoism: The Unofficial High Religion of China." *Taoist Resources* 7.2: 39–72.

Shahar, Meir. 2008, *The Shaolin Monastery: History, Religion, and the Chinese Martial Arts*. Honolulu, HI: University of Hawaii Press.

Sharma, Arvind, ed. 1995, *Our Religions: The Seven World Religions Introduced by Preeminent Scholars from Each Tradition*. New York: HarperCollins.

Shiga Ichiko. 2002, "Manifestations of Lüzu in Modern Guangdong and Hong Kong." In *Daoist Identity*, ed. Livia Kohn and Harold Roth, 185–209. Honolulu, HI: University of Hawaii Press.

Siegler, Elijah. 2003, *The Dao of America: The History and Practice of American Daoism*. Ph.D. diss., University of California, Santa Barbara.

—2010, "Back to the Pristine": Identity Formation and Legitimation in Contemporary American Daoism." *Nova Religio* 14.1: 45–66.

Silvers, Brock. 2005, *The Taoist Manual: Applying Taoism to Daily Life*. Nederland, CO: Sacred Mountain Press.

Singleton, Mark. 2010, *Yoga Body: The Origins of Modern Posture Practice*. Oxford and New York: Oxford University Press.

Sivin, Nathan. 1978, "On the Word 'Taoist' as a Source of Perplexity (With Special Reference to the Relation of Science and Religion in Traditional China)." *History of Religions* 17: 303–30.

Skar, Lowell. 2000, "Ritual Movements, Deity Cults and the Transformation of Daoism in Song and Yuan Times." In *Daoism Handbook*, ed. Livia Kohn, 413–63. Leiden: Brill.

Skar, Lowell and Fabrizio Pregadio. 2000, "Inner Alchemy." In *Daoism Handbook*, ed. Livia Kohn, 464–97. Leiden: Brill.

Smart, Ninian. 1999, *Dimensions of the Sacred: An Anatomy of the World's Beliefs*. Berkeley, CA: University of California Press.

Smith, J. Z. 1988, *Imagining Religion: From Babylon to Jonestown*. Chicago, IL: University of Chicago Press.

—1998, "Religions, Religion, Religious." In *Critical Terms for Religious Studies*, ed. Mark C. Taylor, 269–84. Chicago, IL: University of Chicago Press.

—2004, *Relating Religion: Essays in the Study of Religion*. Chicago, IL: University of Chicago Press.

Smith, Kidder. 2003, "Sima Tan and the Invention of 'Daoism,' 'Legalism,' et cetera." *Journal of Asian Studies* 62.1: 129–56.

Smith, Wilfred Cantwell. 1993, *What Is Scripture?: A Comparative Approach*. Minneapolis, MN: Fortress Press.

Stein, Rolf A. 1979, "Religious Taoism and Popular Religion from the Second to the Seventh Century." In *Facets of Taoism*, ed. Holmes Welch and Anna Seidel, 53–81. New Haven, CT: Yale University Press.

Steinhardt, Nancy Shatzman. 2000, "Taoist Architecture." In *Taoism and the Arts of China*, ed. Stephen Little, 57–75. Berkeley, CA: Art Institute of Chicago/University of California Press.

Sterckx, Roel. 2002, *The Animal and the Daemon in Early China*. Albany, NY: State University of New York Press.

—ed. 2005, *Of Tripod and Palate: Food, Politics, and Religion in Traditional China*. New York: Palgrave Macmillan.

Strickmann, Michel. 1977, "The Mao Shan Revelations: Taoism and the Aristocracy." *T'oung Pao* 63.1: 1–64.

—1978, "The Longest Taoist Scripture." *History of Religions* 17.3/4: 331–54.

—1979, "On the Alchemy of T'ao Hung-ching." In *Facets of Taoism*, eds Holmes Welch and Anna Seidel, 123–92. New Haven, CT: Yale University Press.

—1982, "The Tao among the Yao: Taoism and the Sinification of the South." In *Rekishi ni oberu minshū to bunka*, 23–30. Tokyo: Kokusho kankōkai.

—2002 (posthumous), *Chinese Magical Medicine*. Ed. Bernard Faure. Stanford: Stanford University Press.

Takimoto, Yūzō and Liu Hong. 2000, "Daoist Ritual Music." In *Daoism Handbook*, ed. Livia Kohn, 747–64. Ledien: Brill.

Towler, Solala. 1996, *A Gathering of Cranes: Bringing the Tao to the West*. Eugene, OR: Abode of the Eternal Tao.

Tsao Pen-yeh and Daniel Law, eds. 1989, *Studies of Taoist Rituals and Music of Today*. Hong Kong: Society for Ethnomusicological Research.

Tsao Pen-yeh and Shi Xinming. 1992, "Current Research of Taoist Ritual Music in Mainland China and Hong Kong." *Yearbook for Traditional Music* 24: 118–25.

Tsien, Tsuen-Hsuin. 1985, *Science and Civilisation in China*. Vol. 5: Chemistry and Chemical Technology, Part I: Paper and Printing. Edited by Joseph Needham et al. Cambridge: Cambridge University Press.

—2004 (1962), *Written on Bamboo and Silk: The Beginnings of Chinese Books and Inscriptions*, 2nd edn. Chicago, IL: University of Chicago Press.

Tsui, Bartholomew P.M. 1991, *Taoist Tradition and Change: The Story of the Complete Perfection School in Hong Kong*. Hong Kong: Christian Study Centre on Chinese Religion and Culture.

Tweed, Thomas. 1992, *The American Encounter with Buddhism, 1844–1912: Victorian Culture and the Limits of Dissent*. Bloomington, IN: Indiana University Press.

— 2002, "Who Is a Buddhist? Night-Stand Buddhists and Other Creatures." In *Westward Dharma*, eds Charles Prebish and Martin Baumann, 17–33. Berkeley, CA: University of California Press.

Tweed, Thomas and Stephen Prothero, eds. 1998, *Asian Religions in America*. Oxford and New York: Oxford University Press.

Unschuld, Paul. 1985, *Medicine in China: A History of Ideas*. Berkeley, CA: University of California Press.

—1986, *Medicine in China: A History of Pharmaceutics*. Berkeley, CA: University of California Press.

Valussi, Elena. 2002, "Beheading the Red Dragon: A History of Female Inner Alchemy in China." Ph.D. diss., University of London.

Verellen, Franciscus. 1995, "The Beyond Within: Grotto-Heavens (*dongtian*) in Taoist Ritual and Cosmology." *Cahiers d'Extrême-Asie* 8: 265–90.

—2003, "The Twenty-four Dioceses and Zhang Daoling. In *Pilgrims, Patrons, and Place*, eds Phyllis Granoff and Koichi Shinohara, 15–67. Vancouver: University of British Columbia Press.

Vervoorn, Aat. 1990a, *Men of the Cliffs and Caves: The Development of the Chinese Eremitic Tradition to the End of the Han Dynasty*. Hong Kong: Chinese University Press.

—1990b, "Cultural Strata of Hua Shan, the Holy Peak of the West." *Monumenta Serica* 39: 1–30.

Waley, Arthur. 1958, *The Way and Its Power: Lao Tzu's Tao Te Ching and Its Place in Chinese Thought*. New York: Grove Press.

Wallace, B. Allan. 2000, *The Taboo of Subjectivity: Towards a New Science of Consciousness*. Oxford and New York: Oxford University Press.

Wang, Robin. 2008, "Daoists on the Southern Marchmount." *Journal of Daoist Studies* 1: 177–80.

—2009, "Kundao: A Lived Body in Female Daoism." *Journal of Chinese Philosophy* 36.2: 277–92.

Wang Yi'e. 2006 (2004), *Daoism in China: An Introduction*. Warren, CT: Floating World Editions.

Ware, James. 1966, *Alchemy, Medicine and Religion in the China of A.D. 320: The Nei P'ien of Ko Hung*. New York: Dover.

Watson, Burton. 1968, *The Complete Works of Chuang Tzu*. New York: Columbia University Press.

Watson, James and Evelyn Rawski, eds. 1990. *Death Ritual in Late Imperial and Modern China*. Berkeley, CA: University of California Press.

Wikipedia. 2010, *American Taoists*. Memphis, TN: Books LLC.

Wile, Douglas. 1992, *Art of the Bedchamber: The Chinese Sexual Yoga Classics Including Women's Solo Meditation Texts*. Albany, NY: State University of New York Press.

—1999, *T'ai Chi's Ancestors: The Making of an Internal Martial Art*. New City, NY: Sweet Ch'i Press.

—2007, "Taijiquan and Daoism: From Religion to Martial Art and Martial Art to Religion," *Journal of Asian Martial Arts* 16.4: 8–45.

Wilson, Verity. 1995, "Cosmic Raiment: Daoist Traditions of Liturgical Clothing." *Orientations* (May 1995): 42–9.

Wolf, Arthur. 1974, "Gods, Ghosts, and Ancestors." In *Religion and Ritual in Chinese Society*, ed. Arthur Wolf, 131–82. Stanford: Stanford University Press.

Wright, Arthur F. 1959, *Buddhism in Chinese History*. Stanford: Stanford University Press.

Wu Hung. 2000, "Mapping Early Daoist Art: The Visual Culture of Wudoumi dao." In *Taoism and the Arts of China*, ed. Stephen Little, 77–93. Chicago/Berkeley, CA: Art Institute/University of California Press.

Yamada Toshiaki. 1989, "Longevity Techniques and the Compilation of the *Lingbao wufuxu*." In *Taoist Meditation and Longevity Techniques*, ed. Livia Kohn, 99–124. Ann Arbor, MI: Center for Chinese Studies/University of Michigan.

—1995, "The Evolution of Taoist Ritual." *Acta Asiatica* 68: 69–83.

—2000, "The Lingbao School." In *Daoism Handbook*, ed. Livia Kohn, 225–55. Leiden: Brill.

Yao, Xinzhong and Yanxia Zhao. 2010, *Chinese Religion: A Contextual Approach*. London and New York: Continuum.

Yates, Robin D.S. 1997, *Five Lost Classics: Tao, Huang-Lao, and Yin-Yang in Han China*. New York: Ballantine Books.

Yin Zhihua. 2005, *Chinese Tourism: Taoism*. Beijing: Foreign Languages Press.

Yoshioka Yoshitoyo. 1979, "Taoist Monastic Life." In *Facets of Taoism*, ed. Holmes Welch and Anna Seidel, 220–52. New Haven, CT: Yale University Press.

Yü, Ying-shih. 1981, "New Evidence on the Early Chinese Conception of the Afterlife—A Review Article." *Journal of Asian Studies* 41: 81–5.

—1987, "O Soul, Come Back! A Study in the Changing Conceptions of the Soul and Afterlife in Pre-Buddhist China." *Harvard Journal of Asiatic Studies* 47: 363–95.

Zhang Jiyu. 2001, "A Declaration of the Chinese Daoist Association on Global Ecology." In *Daoism and Ecology*, ed. Norman Girardot et al., 361–72. Cambridge, MA: Center for the Study of World Religions, Harvard University Press.

Zürcher, Eric. 1959, *The Buddhist Conquest of China*. Leiden: Brill.

—1980, "Buddhist Influences on Early Taoism." *T'oung Pao* 66: 84–147.

INDEX